The storm breaks

The storm breaks

Job simply explained

Derek Thomas

 EVANGELICAL PRESS

EVANGELICAL PRESS
12 Wooler Street, Darlington, Co. Durham, DL1 1RQ, England

British Library Cataloguing in Publication Data available

ISBN 0 85234 336 1

Printed and bound in Great Britain at the Bath Press, Avon.

to
Mark and Fiona Johnston
in deep gratitude

Vincit qui patitur

Contents

Preface

'What we need is a simple commentary on Job that the average reader can understand.' So said a colleague of mine, hinting that I should take up the challenge. In this, my third contribution to the Welwyn Commentary Series, I feel I have taken on something that is far larger than I ever imagined. My own congregation listened patiently as I took them, somewhat speedily, through the book of Job over the space of four months. I do not now recommend the procedure wholeheartedly, for at least two reasons.

First, there is much in Job that is repetitive. One often feels the pain that Job must have felt when listening to the endless speeches of his friends, for they have little of relevance to say. Sermons which keep on insisting that what is being said in these chapters is not germane to Job's case can become tedious.

Secondly, preachers are tempted to turn to Job in a time of crisis in the local church, perhaps expecting that answers will be given to serious and heart-rending questions that folk ask. Job provides few answers and, unless one is careful, it is far too easy to instil scepticism into God's suffering people.

Though it can be said of any book in the Bible, it must be said of Job in particular that it is crucial, before reading any individual section, to grasp the overall message of the book. Much of what Job's three friends have to say is given in biting sarcasm. Their premise is wrong and their conclusions, however sound they may appear to be, are necessarily suspect. I have tried, therefore, to write in such a manner that the 'average reader' may both grasp the overall message and benefit devotionally in the process. The one ought always to lead to the other.

I am very conscious as I write these lines that some Christians may choose to read this volume because they feel in similar circumstances to Job. I am only too aware that God, so far at least, has kept my life free from the enormity of the pain suffered by Job. His trials I can only imagine. I cannot relate to them personally. That, I know, makes me ill-suited to be the best interpreter of pain, though there are stresses and strains that are common to us all which help us understand a little of what Job was going through. I trust that those whose pains are great will find some help in these pages that will lead them on to live as Job did, trusting in the Lord no matter what. If that is accomplished, even to a small degree, then the purpose of these pages will have been accomplished.

I am grateful to many for their help in the publication of this volume, in particular to the staff of Evangelical Press for their helpful suggestions. Upon completion of this book I have learnt that my colleague and best friend, Mark Johnston, has accepted a call of service that will take him and his family to London. Mark has been a constant source of encouragement to me over the past dozen or so years and his removal to England's capital will benefit that city, but leave Northern Ireland, and myself in particular, the poorer. It is to him and his wife, Fiona, that I dedicate this book.

Derek Thomas
Belfast
August 1995

Introduction

Unlike their counterparts today, Christians of a bygone era prepared themselves for trouble. They expected it. They anticipated the discipline of the cross throughout their earthly lives — until the grave. They understood that pain only dissipates in heaven. The entrance into the kingdom of God is strewn with days of tribulation, some of it intense (cf. Acts 14:22). It is what the apostle Paul longed to know, when he referred to 'the fellowship of sharing in his [Christ's] sufferings' (Phil. 3:10). Union with Christ brings with it a union with his sufferings. This is the interpretive key that unlocks Job, as well as the profound mysteries of providence that affect our lives. God knew, of course, that troubled Christians would need help in times like these. Hence, the book of Job.

Today, new gospels abound which promise Christians 'the earth' if only they follow Jesus. When such sincere folk find themselves floundering despite their evident devotion, they are troubled in mind as well as in body. Promises of health and wealth to pious people are not a new phenomenon, of course. Job's comforters promised the same, only to be labelled by Job as 'miserable' (Job 16:2).

The book of Job is about 'the problem of suffering'. More particularly, it asks the question: 'Why does God allow me to suffer, even when I follow him?' I say, it asks the question, and it does. Time and again Job begs for an explanation to his difficulties. The problem, however, with the book of Job is that answers to this question are not forthcoming. Christians who have turned to Job in a time of crisis looking for immediate solutions to personal questions revolving around the question, 'Why?', have often come away confused and disappointed. Job is a much more complicated book than most Christians initially imagine. Having spent the last year and a half 'in Job', as they say, I have come to realize that the diversity of opinion amongst commentators on Job only serves to confirm that no uniform interpretation of Job exists. (Readers will appreciate in the section on Elihu that few commentators, old or modern, agree on whether his contribution is helpful or not!)

Theodore Beza, whose commentary on Job was first published in English in 1587, spoke of the difficulty of the task: 'I am minded to expound the histories of Job, in which ... there are many dark and hard places, insomuch as I must here of necessity sail, as it were, among the rocks: and yet I hope I shall not make any shipwreck.'[1]

The fear of 'shipwreck' explains why we hear so few sermons on Job. It is interesting, for example, to see that C. H. Spurgeon preached eighty-eight sermons on Job during his lifetime, though it must be admitted that many of them do scant justice to the context of the book of Job. To avoid making shipwreck, it is necessary to obtain keys in order to unlock the mysteries of the book of Job. One key is provided for us in the book of James: 'You have heard of Job's perseverance and have seen what the Lord finally brought about. The Lord is full of compassion and mercy' (James 5:11). The book of Job swivels on two hinges: Job as a man of enduring, persevering godliness under the most acute sufferings; and God as a sovereign, covenantally faithful Father who will not abandon his own children. Another key is to be found in John Calvin's expository sermons on Job translated into English by Arthur Golding and published just over a decade before Beza's commentary, in 1574.[2]

Calvin's contribution to our understanding of Job and his sufferings is crucial. Job was one of the few books of the Bible on which Calvin did not write a commentary. He did, however, preach 159 sermons on Job, delivered every day over a period of just under six months. The sermons were published in 1574, though they were preached some twenty years earlier in 1554, at a crucial moment in Calvin's life. Although the *Institutes* were first published in 1536 and had already been through six editions, two more were to follow and the final definitive edition was still five years away from completion (1559).

Calvin's doctrine of predestination was under severe attack from all quarters. For Calvin, the issue of predestination was a pastoral one. At its core lay a reluctance to enter into controversy over issues to which there were no answers; there are aspects of God's sovereignty which we cannot fathom. Calvin seemed more concerned to reflect the sense of awe and wonder that God's sovereignty was what had saved him. 'Predestination, as Calvin understood it, is neither a church steeple from which to view the human landscape, nor a pillow to sleep on. It is rather a stronghold in times of temptation and trials and a confession of praise to God's grace and to His glory.'[3] This pastoral concern, to submit to God's sovereignty rather than questioning it, or even comprehending it, is evident in Calvin's sermons on Job. That Calvin needed the solace that comes from such submission is evident when we recall that in 1547 a piece of paper was found attached to his pulpit threatening him that if he did not leave, 'No one will save you from destruction... Revenge will be had at last.'[4]

In addition we know of Calvin's physical condition and the constant pain he suffered. His afflictions included painful stomach cramps, intestinal influenza, migraine headaches, fevers, pleurisy, gout, colic, haemorrhoids, arthritis, acute pain in the knees and feet, gallstones and kidney stones. Calvin, like Job, was suffering.[5]

In the opening sermon on Job 1:1, Calvin gives us the key that unlocks the book of Job: 'In all this disputation, Job maintains a good case, and contrariwise his adversaries maintain an evil case. And yet it is more, that Job maintains a good quarrel, did handle it ill, and that the other setting forth a poor case, did convey it well. The understanding of this will be as a key to open unto us all this whole book.'[6]

Suffering: punishment, warning, or what?

So what is the message of the book of Job? The answer of Job's counsellors is easy enough: suffering is God's punishment, inflicted here and now, on sin. The message is as contemporary as would-be counsellors who tell cancer patients that if only they had more faith, they would be healed. In other words, the reason why they are suffering is because of their sinful unbelief. The cure to pain, according to this view, is repentance. Here, at least, all commentators agree that the message of the book of Job is that such theology is bankrupt and soul-destroying. Anyone who has been the victim of such ill-judged advice will immediately concur.

Elihu, on the other hand, seems to point to another solution. Suffering, he thinks, may have nothing at all to do with some sin in the *past;* it may be in order *to prevent a sin in the future.* Creating a sense of dependency, which is what suffering can do (though not invariably), can keep us from sliding into error. This much is true, and Elihu's contribution takes the argument a step closer to a 'final solution' — but only a step, for his contributions are confused and sometimes in error. There are occasions when he, too, falls prey to the premise of the three 'friends', namely, that suffering is punishment.

The book as a whole offers another way of looking at suffering. Suffering comes to Job in order to justify God's claim to Satan that men can serve him without thought of what they gain from it. According to Satan, this is impossible and the book sets out to prove that he is wrong. Satan's aim is to get Job to blaspheme against God: to worship Satan instead of God. 'The essence of idolatry,' A. W. Tozer once said, 'is the entertainment of thoughts about God that are unworthy of him.' We all have unworthy thoughts about God, especially during times of stress and difficulty. Job succumbed to unworthy thoughts himself during his trial. When he did, Satan gained a partial victory. But he did not gain the triumph he ultimately sought after — that Job should curse God. Throughout his ordeal, in that respect at least, Job remained faithful. Job, of course, was totally unaware of Satan's charge (perhaps even of Satan himself) and had to trust God 'in the dark'. This, despite his exaggerated claims to innocence, and his outbursts (understandable though they are), is what Job does. It is one of the highest points of spiritual dependence in the entire depiction of Job's anguish that he is enabled to say, 'Though he slay me, yet will I hope in him' (13:15).

That suffering is not always punishment is something God emphatically corroborates by telling us so pointedly — before and after the trial — that Job was 'blameless' (1:1,8; 42:7-8). The friends were not aware of this section of the book (nor was Job). Hence their overheated, ill-thought speeches. When Job asks, as he does (e.g. 6:30; 9:15), and as we all tend to do, 'What have I done to deserve this?' the answer that the book of Job gives is that suffering is not related to anything particular that we have done; its reason is for some inscrutable divine purpose. There are times, to be sure, when suffering is God's chastisement for sin. Recognizing and admitting the sin is an essential path to growth in holiness. But there are times when there appears to be no connection, and at such times it is our *response* to suffering that is important. For if the book of Job teaches us anything at all, it teaches us how to respond to difficulties in our lives. We are to respond like Job.

Job's acceptance of his loss is a model of piety. Each one of us desires to be able to say in the face of trials of such magnitude: 'The Lord gave and the Lord has taken away; may the name of the Lord be praised' (Job 1:21). Even when Job responds later with questions, and even a measure of bitterness and anger, his frustration is always taken directly to God. Throughout his ordeal Job sought dealings with God. And eventually, in God's own time, he received an answer that satisfied him. It was not the answer he had sought, but he was content to submit to the truth that God knows best. In contrast to Job's three counsellors, Job — according to God — spoke 'what was right' throughout his trial (42:7). That is an amazing testimony, and important if we are to make sense of Job's outbursts. Even in his anger, Job never lost his faith in God. When trouble comes our way, and it will come, we all desire (if we have any spiritual sense at all) to respond like Job. He is a model of cross-bearing.

Turning to Job will teach us to persevere, as Job did. This is what the New Testament remembers about Job most of all: 'As you know, we consider blessed those who have persevered. You have heard of Job's perseverance and have seen what the Lord finally brought about. The Lord is full of compassion and mercy' (James 5:11). If we can learn to persevere, even in the face of the incomprehensible ways of God in our lives, we shall have learnt the supreme lesson of the book of Job. That lesson is to stick close to God through adversity and pain, no matter what. It is the message of Henry F. Lyte's hymn, 'Jesus, I my cross have taken':

Jesus, I my cross have taken,
All to leave and follow thee;
Naked, poor, despised, forsaken,
Thou from hence my all shalt be:

Perish every fond ambition,
All I've sought, and hoped, and known;
Yet how rich is my condition
God and heaven are still my own!

Go, then, earthly fame and treasure!
Come, disaster, scorn and pain!
In thy service, pain is pleasure;
With thy favour, loss is gain.
I have called thee, 'Abba, Father';
I have stayed my heart on thee
Storms may howl, and clouds may gather;
All must work for good to me.

It is time to turn to the book of Job itself and learn afresh the
harrowing story of a man whose life changed so dramatically
in the course of a few short days.

1.
The storm breaks

Please read Job 1:1 - 2:10

According to Ezekiel, Job was one of the most godly men who had ever lived (14:14,20).

Some Christians leave a testimony that continues to shine to future generations long after they themselves have departed this world. Lives like these encourage us to live as they did. Think of how the lives of William Carey, or David Brainerd, or Amy Carmichael still speak to us today. How important it is to live a godly life — for the sake of others as well as ourselves! Job lived that way. Ever since the story of Job was first written down, believers have turned to it for help and encouragement in the midst of life's appalling trials.

Scene 1: Job — the man of God (1:1-5)

After telling us his name, **'Job'** (1:1), and that he hailed from **'Uz'**[1] — a large territory east of the Jordan (cf. **'the East'** 1:3), which included both Edom in the south (Gen. 36:28) and the Aramean lands in the north (Gen. 10:23; 22:21), the opening section mentions several aspects of Job's life, underlining his immense integrity and faith. Chief amongst them is his *wisdom*: Job **'feared God'** — the hallmark of biblical wisdom (Prov. 9:10; cf. 1:7). It is, as we shall see, a wisdom gained from knowing Jesus Christ, 'who has become for us wisdom from God' (1 Cor. 1:30). For Job, Jesus Christ was still only a promise that God had made, a promise that one day a Redeemer would come. Yet he believed that promise, as did many others before and after his day. His faith, together with that of others who similarly believed the promise, was reckoned to him as righteousness (cf. Gen. 15:6; Rom: 4:3).

Job was not an Israelite, but from the 'east'. Nevertheless, true faith transcends national boundaries, for it is immediately evident that Job was a true believer. His trials are all the more painful because of it. Many in Job's day entertained the notion that faith ought to alleviate trouble, not increase it. This is a view that continues to trouble faithful men and women of God. It is one of the abiding lessons of the book of Job that Christians can expect to suffer. Even if the *cause* of suffering remains a mystery, the *fact* of it does not. Some of the wisest and godliest have known lives of the most excruciating tragedy. Reckon on it, the Bible seems to say to us, and you will not go far wrong. Protest, and you will discover that it will only add to your difficulties. In God's ordering of our lives, for reasons best known to him, he allows some features to be bent out of shape. There is, in each one of our lives, to cite a phrase of Thomas Boston, 'a crook in our lot'.[2]

Job's wisdom

In the space of one verse, four ways are found to define Job's wisdom: he was **'blameless'** and **'upright'**, he **'feared God'** and **'shunned evil'** (1:2). The idea that Job was 'blameless' (the Authorized Version renders it 'perfect') may appear to suggest that Job is being credited with perfection! That would be a fatal misunderstanding. Job was not sinless. Later he confesses his sin quite openly (6:24; 7:21, and especially 42:1-6).

Blamelessness is a recurring theme (8:20; 9:20-22 (three times); 12:4; 36:4; 37:16) and means 'personal integrity'.

Uprightness is closely related to the word for 'righteous' and means 'a faithful adherence to God's statutes and an honest, compassionate manner in relating to others'.[3] These two features manifested themselves in two contrasting directions: Job **'feared God and shunned evil'** (1:1).

1. Positively, Job feared God

Fearing God is the very soul of godliness. It is the attribute, above all others, that reflects a right relationship of a sinner to Almighty God. It is the response of a sinner towards the greatness of God. Reverence, awe and submission are its chief components, as is the notion of being afraid when there is just cause for it. A person who fears God puts God first in every area of life. God is not thought of as an equal, still less an inferior, but an all-powerful, all-knowing, everywhere present God who may do with us as he wills.

Fearing God is not the cowering gesture of one who is terrified by God, though unconfessed, unmortified sin in our lives may, and should, elicit such a response. Rather, it is an honest acknowledgement that God is greater than us in every way. We are never on his level and that is why submission becomes a crucially important issue in Job. Above everything else, Job's attitude to God will eventually be seen to be one of acquiescence. Job may not, indeed, does not, understand what is going on in his life, but he resolves to place his trust in God. As Thomas Boston put it, 'The discerning of a Father's hand in the crook will take out much of the bitterness of it, and sugar the pill to you.'[4] As a sinner — and Job is always aware of that fact — God is angry with Job's sin. As a Sovereign, God has every right to use Job in a way that brings him ultimate glory.

Job's attitude, thus far at least, was one of unquestioning submission to God, ever careful to acknowledge the Lord as King in his life. He was careful never to speak *about* God, or *to* God in a flippant, ill-thought manner. He avoided attributing to God motives ill-befitting the sovereign Creator and Redeemer. He sought each day to abide by the rule that God should be glorified in his life. In this way Job feared God. Of course, it is easier to acknowledge God's goodness when life is free from pain. That is the test to which Job is now put: will he continue to fear God when everything around him is giving way?

2. Negatively, Job shunned evil

How important it is to have this negative element to our lives! Nine of the Ten Commandments are couched in negative terms: 'You shall *not...*' (the only one not in that form is the fifth: 'Honour your parents'). Saying 'No' to sin is something we have no capacity to do without the help of the Holy Spirit in our hearts. Christians display evidence of their regeneration in their desire to avoid occasions for sin. Turning *from* sin and *to* God is the simplest, but most comprehensive, understanding of what repentance is all about and repentance is the reverse side of faith. Together, faith and repentance constitute the two vital elements of saving religion. They constitute, according to the Puritan Thomas Watson, the two wings by which we fly to heaven.[5]

Repentance was a daily feature of Job's life. Luther included in his exposition of the true nature of Christianity, which he nailed to the Wittenberg church door in 1517, the following thesis: 'When our Lord and Master Jesus Christ said, "Repent" [Matt. 4:17], he willed that the whole life of believers should be one of repentance.' Luther, like Job, sought every opportunity to shun that which God hated.

Philip Henry, a Puritan who died in 1696, when challenged that he made too much of repentance, said that he hoped to carry his repentance up to the gate of heaven itself. One of the sure signs of holiness is a growing concern for personal righteousness. Job was aware that sin lay at the root of every attempt to dissuade him from honouring God, with his body and soul, and therefore he was on guard against its every temptation, be it from the flesh, the world, or the devil himself. He avoided unnecessary contact with the fallen world; he chose his close companions carefully; he rigorously rooted out known sin in his life, applying the rule that mortification was the only way to deal with sin; and this was the pathway to glory.

In all of this Job displayed consummate *wisdom*. It is a key to Job's life as people knew and witnessed it. It is the key that unlocks the door to what the book of Job is essentially about: 'The fear of the Lord — that is wisdom, and to shun evil is understanding' (28:28). Job feared God and dealt ruthlessly with known sin and this was the secret of his eminent wisdom. As Calvin wrote, 'Nearly all the wisdom we possess, that is to say, true and sound wisdom, consists of two parts: the knowledge of God and of ourselves.'[6] Job emerges as a man who knows God and knows himself. It is a picture of what God wants us to be and, by his grace, what we can become.

Job's wealth

For some, the record of Job's godliness sits ill at ease with his vast wealth. The Scriptures are unashamed about the connection: '**Also, his possessions were seven thousand sheep, three thousand camels, five hundred yoke of oxen, five hundred female donkeys, and a very large household, so that this man was the greatest of all the people of the East**' (1:3). There is no hint that Job's wealth had been acquired in some illicit way, though this charge will be made by some of Job's companions later. On the contrary, Job's attempts to fulfil his rôle as a man of God in the world in which he lived had been blessed by God. He was given a large family, '**seven sons and three daughters**' (1:2) and an enormous fortune

(1:3). According to his own testimony, he 'dwelt as a king among his troops; I was like one who comforts mourners' (Job 29:25). Not only that, but following the trial his fortune was doubled (42:10).

Solomon's great wealth was regarded as a sign of God's favour (1 Kings 3:13), as was that of Job's contemporary, Abraham (Gen. 12:2-3; 13:2); and Isaac's wealth was to become a source of great envy to the Philistines (Gen. 26:14). The attainment of material prosperity is not in itself wrong, of course; it is the *love* of money that is the root of all evil (1 Tim. 6:10). That is why office-bearers in the church, who are to be characterized by a transparent godliness, are warned not be lovers of money (1 Tim. 3:3). Before his conversion, money had meant everything to Zacchaeus, but a Spirit-wrought repentance changed all that (Luke 19:8). It was the love of money that brought down Ananias and Sapphira (Acts 5:2) and principally Judas, whose thirty pieces of silver were more valuable to him than a good conscience towards God. 'You cannot serve God and mammon,' Jesus said (Matt. 6:24).

Wealth brings its own temptations: 'But woe to you who are rich, for you have already received your comfort' (Luke 6:24). 'No servant can serve two masters; for either he will hate the one and love the other, or else he will be loyal to the one and despise the other. You cannot serve God and mammon' (Luke 16:13). 'Do not store up for yourselves treasures on earth, where moth and rust destroy, and where thieves break in and steal' (Matt. 6:19). 'Again I tell you, it is easier for a camel to go through the eye of a needle than for a rich man to enter the kingdom of God' (Matt. 19:24). 'Take heed and beware of covetousness, for one's life does not consist in the abundance of the things he possesses' (Luke 12:15).

Scripture pours scorn on the wrong *use* of wealth, not the mere possession of it. It was John Wesley who said, 'Gain all you can, save all you can, give all you can.'[7] Wealth is not in itself a sign of God's favour: God has reasons why he makes some wealthy and others poor. Had William Carey's early life not been so painfully poor, one doubts whether his tenacity would have survived the hardships of India.

In handling his great wealth, Job was impeccable and unimpeachable. What makes pleasures right, good and valuable, or wrong, bad and sinful is often determined by that which accompanies wealth. The motivation and outcome of our pleasures need to be examined. Do we chase after them as though they were all-important? Wealth, if acquired righteously and used wisely, is a blessing to be enjoyed for God's glory. But dangers are near, including self-indulgence and greed (Luke 8:14; Heb. 11:25; cf. Isa 58:13; 1 Tim. 5:6; 2 Tim. 3:4; Titus 3:3; James 4:3; 5:5; 2 Peter 2:13), and along with these come boredom and disgust (Eccles. 2:1-11). Job, however, was 'blameless' and 'upright' in the management of his personal affairs.

Job's watchfulness

Enduring afflictions and watchfulness go together in Scripture (2 Tim. 4:5). Job's watchfulness extended beyond himself to the needs of his family. Acting as priest, Job offers a **'burnt offering'** (1:5) on behalf of his family (and presumably himself). Having seven sons and three daughters (both numbers and their sum being symbols of completeness) meant that Job's large family needed to atone for their sins, a responsibility that fell upon the father of the household. The picture of domestic bliss portrayed here is enhanced by Job's assumption of the rôle of chief priest within his own family. Domestic bliss is broken when fathers fail in this rôle. Job's sons and daughters have come together for some family celebration, but Job deems it appropriate that spiritual realities are placed first.

The sin Job fears his children may commit is that they may curse God in their hearts. This is the very sin that Satan hopes Job will fall into (1:11; 2:5) and to which his wife will urge him (2:9). He offers a burnt offering (the commonest: performed every morning and evening and on holy days) on their behalf. It was his habit to do so. Whole burnt offerings were for general sins (Lev. 1) rather than for specific sins, for which sin offerings were prescribed (Lev. 4:1 - 5:4). They made atonement for man. The idea lying behind the sacrifice is that of the payment of a ransom. It is a prefiguring of the one who would come 'to give his life as a ransom for many' (Mark 10:45). In contrast to the burnt offerings offered up by the priests each day, Christ offered up *one* sacrifice: he died 'once for all when he offered himself' on our behalf (Heb. 7:27).

All of this provides us with a picture of an idyllic home. The family has always received special emphasis in Scripture. It is a spiritual unit and a place of training for children to grow into patterns of mature adult character. It is a community of teaching and learning about God and godliness, and one can only assume that Job's children were presented with a model of fatherhood that embodied the finest elements of what God intended it to be. Job's children were instructed in godliness by their father, as the Bible directs (Gen. 18:18-19; Deut. 4:9; 6:6-8; 11:18-21; Prov. 22:6; Eph. 6:4). Furthermore, they were encouraged to take what they were taught seriously and use it as a basis for their own lives. Evidently, as the burnt offerings suggest, they were taught from their earliest moments about sin. Job did not spoil his children, nor camouflage the seriousness of their transgressions. He taught them to grow up through their childish folly to mature adults who might display a wisdom that they saw evidenced in their father (Prov. 13:24; 19:18; 22:15; 23:13-14; 29:15,17). Job could say, as did Joshua, 'But as for me and my household, we will serve the Lord' (Josh. 24:15). Building a strong family was one of Job's priorities.

Scene 2: The heavenly council (1:6-12)

'One day the angels came to present themselves before the
Lord, and Satan also came with them' (1:6). The scene is
one of a heavenly council in which the **'angels'**[8] (1:6) are
reporting to God. Apparently, there are occasions when the
angels relate to God their activities. The verb 'to present' (1:6)
means to 'station yourself before someone', to await orders.
'It's like when the colonels meet with the general to discuss
tactics and receive their final directions,' comments Mark
Littleton.[9] Prominent among the angels is Satan.

The Satan

Satan is God's 'prodigal son'. In the Hebrew he is referred to
as 'the Satan' (1:6) meaning 'the Accuser', though by 1 Chronicles 21:1 the definite article is dropped indicating that by this
time 'Satan' has become a proper name. He is one of the angels
who sinned (2 Peter 2:4), who did not keep their own position
but left their proper dwelling (Jude 6). He is the commander of
the spiritual powers of the air (Eph. 2:2), leading the superhuman forces of evil in the heavens (Eph. 6:12). He is what
Scripture refers to as the 'serpent' (Gen. 3:1; Rev. 20:2), a
dragon (Rev. 12; 20:2), a roaring lion (1 Peter 5:8), the tempter
(Matt. 4:3; 1 Thess. 3:5), the evil one (John 17:15), a liar and a
murderer (John 8:44). He sinned 'from the beginning' (1 John
3:8).

Of Satan, Packer has written, 'The mentality of Satan is a
mystery whose depths we can never plumb: not just because
Satan is an angel, while we are men, but also because Satan is
purely evil, and we cannot conceive what pure evil is like…
Scripture clearly means us to believe in a Satan, and a host of
satanic myrmidons, who are of quite unimaginable badness —
more cruel, more malicious, more proud, more scornful, more

perverted, more destructive, more disgusting, more filthy, more despicable, than anything our minds can conceive.'[10]

That Satan should be present among the holy angels of heaven's court presents obvious problems. It is true that the text does not refer to 'heaven', but it does indicate that God is present in this location and it is difficult to imagine where else it might be.

Would not the presence of Satan in heaven defile it? Is heaven really heaven if Satan is allowed to be present there? Satan's powers seem awesome, but are they a threat to God? The fact that Satan alone is asked his business seems to indicate that he has no right to be there.[11]The fact that he is there, as Calvin comments, shows that even he has to give account of himself to God: 'The Holy Spirit meant us to understand, that not only the angels of heaven which obey God willingly, and are wholly inclined, and given that way, do yield account unto Him, but also the devils of hell which are enemies and rebels to him to the uttermost of their power, which labour to subvert his Majesty, and practise to confound all things; so as they be forced (in spite of their teeth) to be subject unto God and to yield Him account of all their doings, and cannot do anything without His permission and leave.'[12] Satan was obliged to present himself before God. He has no ultimate authority in himself. It was the Lord who initiated the battle by a claim which essentially drew attention to God's own glory: **'Have you considered my servant Job? There is no one on earth like him; he is blameless and upright, a man who fears God and shuns evil'** (1:8). In effect God was drawing attention to the fact that he was already displaying his victory over Satan. Eden's challenge to Adam had brought calamity on mankind, but God had now revealed a plan whereby he would save a people for himself. Job was one of them and his life was a demonstration of his godliness — a God-wrought holiness indicative of his faith in God's promised Saviour.

There in Uz was the proof that God's word, and not Satan's, was supreme. Satan must look on Job as a trophy of redemptive grace. He must admit after all that the enmity of the woman's seed against him had already proved effective. Adam and Eve's covenant with death had been annulled. Their covenant with God had been renewed, and Job was living proof of it.

Four features of Satan's personality and purpose are forthcoming from the passage.

1. Satan is 'the accuser'

It is Satan's nature to think, speak and act in constant malicious opposition to God the Creator, and therefore to God's people also. Satan is Job's accuser. 'He sees in the piety of Job nothing but a refined form of selfishness. He serves God because it is in his interest to do so.'[13] In the courtroom of heaven he is the counsel for the prosecution. He is constantly engaged in levelling charges against God's children, charges which are both hurtful and intent on causing the maximum damage. There is not an ounce of goodness in Satan's character. His every action is bent on one thing: our total demise.

In Zechariah we catch a glimpse of Satan's activity against the church. Joshua, the high priest representing Israel before God, prays on behalf of the people of God. He symbolically bears the nation's guilt and, on their behalf, he enters the 'holy place'. Satan appears as Joshua's adversary and accuser (Zech. 3). He is the one who accuses God's children 'day and night' (Rev. 12:10).

Satan never stops accusing us. That is why we are called upon to resist him (literally 'to be his adversary', James 4:7, since he is ours!). 'As David Livingstone's motto was "Anywhere, provided it be forward", so Satan's is, in effect, "Anything, provided it be against God".'[14]

2. Satan is 'the wanderer'

In reply to the question as to where he had been and what he
had been doing, Satan said, **'From roaming through the
earth and going to and fro in it'** (1:7). It is the 'confession
of a vagabond spirit, pacing the earth with the frustration of a
caged lion and preying upon unsuspecting victims', comments David McKenna, adding: 'Satan epitomizes the ultimate of evil, when alienation, aimlessness, and anxiety — the
essence of hell — obsess the soul.'[15]

3. Satan is 'the cynic'

'Does Job fear God for nothing?', he asks (1:9). To the
jaundiced eye everything appears yellow, and for Satan —
who is incapable of appreciating righteousness in Job — every
act of human goodness must have a sinister, self-serving, or
squalid explanation. Take away Job's prosperity, he contends,
and Job will curse God; his righteousness will crumble to dust
before God's eyes (1:11). The point is true in general: many
trust God only in so far as they get something out of it. As our
Saviour warned, worldly cares and all kinds of glamour cloud
our perspective soon enough (Mark 4:19). The test is established: will Job serve God even though he gets nothing from
it?

There is no respect for God in Satan's words. Unlike Job,
Satan does not fear God. He is at once proud, arrogant, insolent
and rebellious. Satan believes the lie, for he is a lie! Satan has
always wanted to be God (cf. Isa. 14:12-14; Ezek. 28:11-19).

4. Satan as 'the tormentor'

Satan is not omnipotent, but he is powerful. His power is
evident in these verses in his ability to smite Job with disease

(2:7), bring lightning against Job's flocks and servants (1:16), together with a howling gale which destroys Job's sons and daughters (1:19). 'The coming of the lawless one will be in accordance with the work of Satan displayed in all kinds of counterfeit miracles, signs and wonders,' Paul warns the Thessalonian church (2 Thess. 2:9).

Satan's power is derivative. Job was entirely safe until such time as God permitted Satan to touch him. Until God lowers the hedge which he erects to protect his people, Satan is impotent. 'The Lord who holdeth the wind in His fists gave Satan power, and he brought a terrible wind,' comments one of Job's finest expositors.[16]

Satan and the demons are imprisoned and since the Fall have been 'kept in eternal bonds under darkness unto the judgement of the great day' (Jude 6, NASB). They are in chains (Rev. 20:1-6). The chain may appear to be long; but it is a chain. Two distinct limits are set to Satan's authority: first, Satan is allowed to touch all that Job has, but not Job personally (1:12); and secondly, he is allowed to strike Job's body, but not kill him (2:6).

Does Satan hold the power of death? An important passage in comprehending this power is Hebrews 2:14-15: 'Since the children have flesh and blood, he too shared in their humanity so that by his death he might destroy him who holds the power of death — that is, the devil — and free those who all their lives were held in slavery by their fear of death.' Satan uses the fear of death to tyrannize; but he is *not* the 'executioner-in-chief'.[17] As H. L. Ellison points out, 'Satan cannot even mention Job until God invites him to do so' (1:8; 2:3), and adds, 'Equally he has no power over Job or his possessions until God gives it to him... He is not sovereign in a rival kingdom, but a rebel to whom God gives as much rope as will glorify his name.'[18] F. Leahy adds: 'Satan fills a subservient role in the story of Job. Having stripped Job of earthly wealth and comfort, he is cast aside as of no further interest, and is not mentioned at the end of the story. One lesson that we learn from Job, among many more, is that all power and authority belong to God. There is no dualism here.'[19]

God

It is vitally important to grasp the rôle Satan plays in Job's trial. Job confesses to knowing nothing about it. But it is equally a mistake to focus our attention completely upon Satan. That would be his desire, but it would prove a fatal mistake on our part. The one in control of all things is not Satan, but God. Satan's powers are curtailed, as we have seen. Satan holds no power independently of God. Satan is 'God's tool' — though he never has admitted it, nor will he. In his malevolence, Satan is irrational; he has lost his grip on reality. Like Hitler in the bunker, he cannot believe that the war is over, though at this point in redemptive history the decisive battle had yet to be fought. In allowing him some rope, God uses him to execute judgement on a fallen world. 'Just as a man can make use of a savage dog which hates him to drive unwelcome visitors off his estate, so God makes use of Satan to punish those who have sinned.'[20] Job, of course, is not being punished, but tested. God uses Satan to do it.

God places a hedge around Satan's powers. John tells us that Christ, 'who was born of God keeps him safe and the evil one cannot harm him' (1 John 5:18). There came a point in the temptation of Christ when Satan was told to go — and he did (Matt. 4:10-11). Repeatedly, Jesus cast out demons, who were powerless to remain when he gave a command.

Ultimately, God is responsible for Job's suffering, not Satan. Commentators sometimes go to great lengths to deny this in an attempt to prevent God being accused of causing

Job's downfall. Job was clearly of this mind: talking to his wife, he said, **'You are talking like a foolish woman. Shall we accept good from God, and not trouble?'** (2:10).

One commentator argues that Job was confused and mistaken when he uttered the words:

**'Naked I came from my mother's womb,
and naked I shall depart.
The Lord gave and the Lord has taken away;
may the name of the Lord be praised'**

(1:21).

'The Lord gave and the Lord has taken away,' he adds, 'is not a true statement. God didn't do that to Job. Satan did it. But Job thought that God did it... Job didn't rashly accuse God, but he didn't know anybody else to *put it on*, so he said the Lord did it.'[21] According to this view, not only is Job confused: God is too! For God says quite expressly to Satan: **'You incited me against him [Job] to ruin him without any reason'**! (2:3). 'Health and sickness ... yea, all things, come not by chance but by His fatherly hand,' says the Heidelberg Catechism,[22] and it is misguided to attempt to alleviate the problem of Job's suffering by insisting that God is not responsible.

It is, however, vital for us to stress that at no point is God responsible for sin. He permits sin, but he is not the author of sin. This may sound a little clever, but it is absolutely crucial to emphasize. **'The Lord said to Satan, "Very well, then, everything he has is in *your* hands"'** (1:12, emphasis added) thereby implying that the responsibility for what happened is Satan's, not God's. God does not entice us to sin, but he does test us. The difference between the two is crucial. 'Let no one say when he is tempted *[peiradzo]*, "I am tempted by God"; for God cannot be tempted by evil, nor does he himself tempt anyone' (James 1:13). Temptation, here, means that process whereby we are enticed to sin. It forms one of the most common experiences of the Christian life. We are constantly induced to sin. But we are not allowed to infer that God is doing the enticing. God never puts pressure on us to break his law. We are never to say, 'God made me do it.' If we sin, we do so wilfully. We are responsible. But 'temptation' can also mean something else: a process whereby something, or someone, is *tested*. God will place his children in situations where it will not be easy to believe, where great reserves of faith will be needed to survive, where the most basic convictions will be called into question. There will be times when it will be difficult to believe that God is gracious, when faith will be stretched to the limits of endurance and the love of God is veiled and obscured. These are moments that God has brought about. He may use Satan in the process, but ultimately it comes from him. Our suffering is at the hands of one who loves us, not one who despises us. God, and not Satan, has the key to our recovery. 'When we consider the power and policy of Satan,' comments Joseph Caryl, 'let us bless God that he cannot stir to do us that mischief which his nature at once inclines and enables him to do, until God permits him.'[23]

At issue here already is something of the mystery of God's dealings with his children. There are things which happen to us which are just too high for us to comprehend. It is Job's greatest contribution that he teaches us to fall down in obedience to God's ways. Calvin comments: 'We must so cherish moderation that we do not try to make God render account to us, but so reverence his secret judgements as to consider his will the truly just cause of all things. When dense clouds darken the sky, and a violent tempest arises, because a gloomy mist is cast over our eyes, thunder strikes our ears and all our senses are benumbed with fright, everything seems to us to be confused and mixed up; but all the while a constant quiet and serenity ever remain in heaven. So we must infer that, while the disturbances in the world deprive us of judgement [i.e. understanding], God out of the pure light of his justice and wisdom tempers and directs these very movements in the best-conceived order to a right end.'[24]

'What does it profit us to know that God has created, and by His providence still upholds, all things?' asks the *Heidelberg Catechism* (Question 28). The answer? 'That we may be patient in adversity, thankful in prosperity, and with a view to the future may have good confidence in our faithful God and Father that no creature shall separate us from His love, since all creatures are so in His hand that without His will they cannot so much as move.'

Scenes 3-5: Job's wisdom tested (1:13-2:10)

Scene 3 is in direct contrast to what has preceded it. Tranquillity is broken by a storm. Peace is shattered by pain. It provides for us a devastating picture of how trouble comes into Christian lives. It comes unannounced and unsolicited. It shows no respect for persons. And behind it lies the activity of Satan.

The second scene, the gathering of the heavenly council before God, is of course, not known to Job at the time of his suffering. It is crucial for us to understand this point. Job has to face his trials 'in the dark', not knowing the cosmic struggle that lies behind it. The struggle of his faith is not relieved by divine revelations of their significance. Indeed, it is one of the agonies of his trial that God is silent through much of his ordeal. God says nothing. And the question occurs to Job more than once: does God really care? The silence of the Almighty is one of the agonizing questions with which he wrestles.

The trial is staggering in its proportions: in the course of **'one day'** (1:13), Job lost his ten children, his huge stock of animals and thereby his entire source of wealth, including his servants (1:13-21). On **'another day'** (2:1, the fourth scene) the heavenly council meets a second time to hear that Job still **'maintains his integrity'** (2:3). Job has refused to yield to the trial in a sinful way. Consequently, Satan is given leave to try him again — the fifth scene. This time, Job's health is taken away (2:7-8). He is left only with a bitter wife and three unhelpful friends. Surely, Solomon was right. We 'do not know what a day may bring forth' (Prov. 27:1).

Several lessons are immediately apparent.

1. Suffering is part of what we may expect in the Christian life

Job received what he did not want and wished for that which he did not get. That is what suffering essentially is. What happened to Job can, and does, happen to every Christian in some form or another, for to some degree we all experience loss, hurt, pain, grief, weakness, rejection, injustice, disappointment, discouragement, frustration, ridicule, cruelty, anger and ill-treatment. There are moments in our lives when we are exposed to things that have the effect of making us want to run away.

Some of the most awful things that ever occur happen to those who love God the most, and serve him most obediently. If we keep one eye upon Jesus Christ, this fact will not come as too great a surprise. In the strategy of things, we grow to expect that Jesus' followers are called upon to endure similar, but of course, far less painful trials than those which he endured.

Learn it from the outset: do not be surprised by pain (cf. 1 Peter 4:12). Eliphaz got this much, at least, right: 'Man is born to trouble as surely as sparks fly upward' (5:7). He was expressing what Paul came to regard as axiomatic: 'Yes, and

all who desire to live godly in Christ Jesus will suffer persecution' (2 Tim. 3:12). It is part of our lot, the 'losses and
crosses' of the life lived in the footsteps of Jesus, as the
Puritans would have said. Since the world, fallen and cursed
as it is, is opposed to Christ, it is opposed to those who belong
to Christ, too (John 15:18-19; 1 Peter 4:4; 1 John 3:13). Sin has
twisted the world in which we live out of shape and will try its
hardest to do the same to those who follow Christ. It is a law
of physics that every force will face an equal and opposite
reaction. In the spiritual realm, every attempt to live for Christ
will be met with opposition every step of the way that leads to
the gates of heaven.

We throw up our hands in horror when we suffer and ask,
'Why?' But our response ought not to be one of surprise but a
resigned expectation. The time to ask 'Why?' is when all is at
peace! Ease is for heaven, not earth. Life on earth is fundamen-
tally out of shape and out of order by reason of sin. And Satan
makes the most he can with it. God has, so it appears, allowed
this way of things to go on for the time being. So pressures,
pains, disappointments and frustrations of all sorts await us in
the future, if they have not been to the fore in the past. We must
expect suffering, and prepare for it. It is the Bible's clearest
message (though many have missed it), that every Christian
life can anticipate good moments to be interrupted by bad
ones, the joys punctuated with sorrows — and that, to the very
end.

Certain sufferings in the Christian life can only be explained by what J. I. Packer calls 'the law of Harvest'.[25] Taking
as his starting-point John 12:24-26, 'Unless a kernel of wheat
fall to the ground and die, it remains a single seed. But if it dies
it produces a great harvest...', Packer says, 'Every experience
of pain, grief, frustration, disappointment, and being hurt by
others is a little death. When we serve the Saviour in our world,
there are many such deaths to be died. But the call to us is to

endure, since God sanctifies our endurance for fruitfulness in the lives of others.'[26] Thus Paul could say of his own ministry: 'I fill up in my flesh what is still lacking in regard to Christ's afflictions, for the sake of his body, which is the church' (Col. 1:24). These afflictions are edificatory and not propitiatory. Paul is affirming a link between his troubles and Christ's work in building his church. Similar sentiments are to be found in the following remarks of the apostle: 'I, Paul, the prisoner of Christ Jesus for the sake of you Gentiles' (Eph. 3:1); 'Death is at work in us, but life is at work in you' (2 Cor. 4:12); 'I endure everything for the sake of the elect, that they too may obtain the salvation that is in Christ Jesus, with eternal glory' (2 Tim. 2:10). God is pleased at times to break us up into little bits that each bit in turn may become food from which others may draw nourishment and flourish.

Job can help us here. We can learn from the way Job copes (or does not cope) with his own suffering. Calvin comments: 'Wherefore it is good for us to have such examples, as show unto us how there have been other men as frail as we, who nevertheless have resisted temptations, and continued steadfastly in obedience unto God, although he have scourged them even with extremity. Thus have we here an excellent mirror.'[27]

2. No kind of suffering, and no kind of Christian, is exempt

It is the ferocity and suddenness of Job's trial that shocks us. There are some things which we feel it unworthy for a Christian to suffer. It seems intrinsically unfair, for example, that a child of God should suffer AIDS, through no fault of his own (a blood transfusion, say, rather than by sexual misconduct or drug abuse). But a moment's thought will reveal the error of this view. No specific suffering is ruled out by God.

In Job's case three specific trials are mentioned: bereavement, poverty and ill-health. Each one is calculated to underline the enormity of his pain. The road ahead will be punctuated by bad experiences; as a Christian, you can count on it.

If no kind of suffering is exempt, it is equally true that no kind of Christian is exempt either. It is not just backslidden Christians who suffer. Godly ones do too. The purpose of the prologue is to paint a picture of near perfection: as perfect as you are likely to get on earth. And yet, into this picture of bliss comes the most appalling devastation. In the New Testament, Timothy, Trophimus and Epaphroditus were all ill and Paul was helpless to do anything about any of them (1 Tim. 5:23; 2 Tim. 4:20; Phil. 2:25-27). Paul himself lived constantly with a 'thorn' in his side, though he had sought the Lord to remove it on three specific occasions (2 Cor. 12:7-9). He lived with pain, and many of the Lord's people since have done the same. The sweet and sanguine Joni Eareckson Tada has taught us that pain and godliness often go together. It is a reflection of Job's ordeal. And in turn, it is but a pale reflection of what Jesus himself knew. Of the Son of God himself, it was said that 'He learned obedience from what he suffered' (Heb. 5:8).

3. Suffering is not necessarily a chastening from God because we have sinned

Few have grasped Job's message better than John Calvin. As we saw in the introduction he was himself under severe pressure from all quarters. Like Job, Calvin felt under pressure to question God's sovereignty. But like Job, too, Calvin resisted the temptation, seeing it as the way of wisdom to yield to whatever God had in store for him. In addition we know that Calvin suffered constant ill-health and severe pain at the time he was preaching on Job.

In the opening sermon on Job 1:1, Calvin gives us the key that unlocks the book of Job: 'In all this disputation, Job maintains a good case, and contrariwise his adversaries maintain an evil case. And yet it is more, that Job maintains a good quarrel, did handle it ill, and that the other setting forth a poor case, did convey it well. The understanding of this, will be as a key to open unto us all this whole book.'[28] As Harold Decker summarizes, 'Job's "good case" is that affliction is not always divine punishment, and that therefore it is not necessarily a measure of sin. Job pleads it poorly by rash self-defence, excessive self-assertion, seething resistance to God, and unrestrained passion. The poor case of his friends is that affliction is divine punishment, meted out according to the measure of men's sins. They plead it well by making statements about God and man which are altogether true and valid, and which must be accepted as being in themselves the pure teaching of the Holy Spirit. The key thought about a good case poorly presented and a poor case well presented recurs several times...'[29]

It is the recurring theme of Job's friends that Job must have sinned in some specific way to incur his pain. Suffering is God's chastisement on sin — always, and without exception, they insisted. Thus, when Frederick K. Price (one of the leading faith healers and charismatic authors in the USA), comments on Job 1:10, 'As long as Job walked in faith, the wall — the hedge — was up. But when he started walking in unbelief and doubt the hedge was pulled down. Job pulled it down!'[30] he is saying, in effect, that Job suffered because he sinned! Price lines up behind Job's miserable comforters.

Sometimes this is true. Some of the Corinthians became sick and died, and this happened as a chastisement on their sinful behaviour (1 Cor. 11:30). But this is not the case here in Job. Job suffered for other reasons, which he himself was not privy to. Why am I suffering? It may be nothing to do with chastening; it may be nothing to do with anything at all in the past. It may have to do with what God wants me to be in the future. That is the lesson Jesus taught in John 9, about a man born blind. The question was asked, who had sinned, the man or his parents? The answer was: neither of them! The reason for his malady lay, it seems, in what God intended to show through him when he was eventually healed. To this day we remember this blind man and what God did through him! Job's suffering is of this order, too.

4. In every aspect of suffering there is a bigger battle taking place

Abraham Kuyper, one time Prime Minister of the Netherlands, once wrote the following lines by way of a comment on the passage in Ephesians where Paul exhorts every Christian to put on spiritual armour in order to fight the arch-enemy of our souls (Eph. 6:10-18): 'If once the curtain were pulled back and the spiritual world behind it came to view, it would expose to our spiritual vision a struggle so intense, so convulsive, sweeping everything within its range, that the fiercest battle ever fought on earth would seem by comparison a mere game. Not here, but up there — that is where the real conflict is waged.'[31]

There are two equally devastating errors to be made in regard to Satan's activity in our lives. We can, in the first place, make too much of it. Some Christians have become obsessed by the demonic to the extent that they have almost forgotten their security in Jesus Christ. The church has been guilty of this error in its history, particularly during the Middle Ages, when folk distrusted God's power to keep them safe. The Reformers and Puritans regained right emphases by stressing the sovereignty of God, the surety of his promises and the ultimate defeat of Satan and all his forces by virtue of Christ's finished work on the cross, in which he 'disarmed the powers and authorities, [making] a public spectacle of them, triumphing over them by the cross' (Col. 2:15). The apostle John exhorted his readers to remember that the Holy Spirit's power in our hearts is greater than Satan's power (cf. 1 John 4:4). It is crucial to observe in these opening chapters of Job that any power Satan displays is only such as God has allowed him. Satan is not some kind of rival to God. God's control over the situation is never in any doubt. There is no dualism[32] in these chapters.

If it is an error to make too much of Satan, it is equally a mistake to underestimate his power. Satan invariably overreaches himself at the end of the day, but before that day comes we dare not assume that we shall easily escape his onslaughts. We wrestle not against flesh and blood but against principalities and powers. And the greatest power with whom we wrestle is Satan. Peter, who had experienced Satan's power in his own life, calls for sobriety and vigilance in the face of an 'adversary' who 'prowls around like a roaring lion, looking for someone to devour' (1 Peter 5:8).

It is vital, though, not to get the whole thing out of perspective. The devil is only part of the picture. God is the one in ultimate control, not Satan. This truth was an essential feature in bringing stability to Job in his trial: **'Shall we accept good from God and not trouble?'** (2:10). Learning to trust God in adversity is a slow and difficult process, but one that every Christian has to learn.

> Who can speak and have it happen
>   if the Lord has not decreed it?
> Is it not from the mouth of the Most High
>   that both calamities and good things come?
>   (Lam. 3:37-38).

Jesus affirmed God's power over evil, by responding to Pilate's belief in his own power: 'You would have no power over me if it were not given to you from above' (John 19:10-11). Even the death of Jesus was by 'God's set purpose and foreknowledge' (Acts 2:23). Whatever the explanation, and we shall have to try to unravel what God has revealed to us here, we must cling on to the truth that Jeremiah found so helpful at a time when his own world was falling apart:

Though he brings grief, he will show compassion,
  so great is his unfailing love.
For he does not willingly bring affliction
  or grief to the children of men

(Lam. 3:32-33).

Whatever else, hold on to that!

2.
Responding to pain

Please read Job 1:1 - 2:10

Everything seems to be going fine, when suddenly all of hell's forces are let loose against Job. Satan had revealed his cynicism when he had said, **'Does Job fear God for nothing? ... But stretch out your hand and strike everything he has, and he will surely curse you to your face'** (Job 1:9-11). To prove Job's integrity (ultimately, to prove the power of God's own gracious work in Job's heart), God tests Job by allowing Satan to bring the following devastation into Job's life:

> The Sabeans took Job's herds and killed his servants (1:15)
> Lightning struck Job's sheep and his shepherds (1:16)
> Chaldeans raided Job's camels and killed the servants looking after them (1:17)
> A cyclone struck the house where all Job's children were feasting and killed them all (1:18-19)

Apart from the four 'messengers' (1:14,16,17,18) who survived to tell the tale of each disaster, Job was left with an understandably embittered wife. Job's response stands out in Scripture as supremely dignified:

'Naked I came from my mother's womb,
   and naked I shall depart.
The Lord gave and the Lord has taken away;
   may the name of the Lord be praised'
                                                            (1:20).

As a testimony to Job's faith, Scripture adds: **'In all this, Job did not sin by charging God with wrongdoing'** (1:22). It only further amplifies the integrity attributed to Job in the opening assessment of his character. Job truly was **'blameless and upright'**. He really did fear God and shun evil (cf. 1:1; 2:3). In addition, as a result of the first test, God says of Job that he maintained his **'integrity'** (2:3).

In a *second* test, Satan is given leave to attack Job's person, something which he had not been allowed to do in the first one (1:12). Satan twists the knife and suggests that pain will cause Job to curse God (2:4). We must always keep in mind that Job was tested at a stage in history when many of the comforts at our disposal were wanting: 'Job went into his trial destitute of many of those firm supports and grounds of consolation which are now so plentifully supplied to suffering saints.'¹ Trials are the making of some men and the destruction of others. Satan is now endeavouring to destroy Job.

We shall look in detail at Job's sickness in a moment, but first we must consider his response to it: **'In all this, Job did not sin in what he said'** (2:10).

Job's 'patience'

The Holy Spirit has provided us with a commentary on Job's response to his trial. 'You have heard of Job's perseverance' (AV, 'the patience of Job'), James says (James 5:11). We might have expected James to point out the *impatience* of Job, for patience, in the normal sense of the word, is not one of Job's qualities! According to Calvin, this passage (Job 1:2-22) is 'the most excellent there is in Holy Scripture to show us what the word "patience" means'.[2] The word James uses is *hupomoné* and is best translated as 'perseverance' rather than patience. Together, this word, and another related word *(makrothumia)* occur over seventy times in the New Testament, indicating that it is a major theme. Standing firm under pressure is what we are meant to emulate.

Commenting on the need for patience under afflictions, Calvin says, 'But God will have us patient [Calvin uses the word "patience", but we should understand that he means "perseverance"] ... he will have us ready to endure all things, assuring ourselves that good and evil proceed from the hand of him. He will have us to abide his chastisements, desiring nothing but to be governed by him, and renouncing all our own affections. And though it seem troublesome to us, he will have us fight against our own wicked lusts, and to resist them in such a way, as he alone may continue our master: for it is not possible that we should have that patience so frank and free in us, if we take not occasion to comfort ourselves in God.'[3]

1. The need for perseverance underlines that this world is not our home

'Six feet under we decay and are reduced to nothing,' Calvin remarks, adding that 'When we are reduced to nothing, then we remind ourselves of who we are and where we are going.'[4] Focusing on the word **'depart'** (1:20), we can say that Job gives testimony to the fact that he lived his life in this world in the expectation, the certainty even, of his own departure from it.

We must learn to live as the saints before us have lived — *sub specie aeternitatis* — in the light of eternity. 'Teach us to number our days aright, that we may gain a heart of wisdom'

(Ps. 90:12). Packer tells the tale of a student who visited Thomas Goodwin, the president of Magdalen College, Oxford. In the dark study, Goodwin opened the session by enquiring of his visitor whether he was ready to die. The lad fled.⁵ Whatever we may think of Goodwin's technique, the question was valid enough; we ought to be ready to die. Our attachment to the things and relationships of this world must ✝ ever take into account that one day we shall be separated from them by death. When we approach life, packed up and ready to go, the shocks will not be as shocking.

2. Perseverance is a recognition that everything we possess belongs to God and not to us

The word **'naked'** teaches us that Job lived his life on earth in the knowledge that everything he possessed was the Lord's. It is at once a recognition of God as Creator of all things. Knowing that God created everything, including ourselves, is fundamental to Christianity. Realizing, as did Job, our moment by moment dependence on God as Creator for our very existence calls forth from us devotion, commitment, loyalty • and gratitude. Job acknowledged that everything he had was a gift of God — his family, wealth and good health. To demand these things as a right is out of order. To thank him when we ✝ possess them is right. To complain when they are missing is not.

3. Perseverance is a determination to worship God no matter what happens

The word **'praise'** emphasizes Job's worshipful attitude towards God. Our chief end is to glorify God and enjoy him for ever. God wants to be praised for his praiseworthiness and exalted for his greatness and goodness. He wants to be appreciated for what he is. Praise is our response to his self-disclosure. We can do nothing else but adore. That we should be let into a part of the secret of God's being is worthy of the most profound thanksgiving on our part. To know that despite our sin, he has made it possible for us to be rescued ought to call forth the loudest songs from our hearts. That the road to intimate fellowship with God in heaven is punctuated by trials, some of them extremely sore, nevertheless calls forth our gratitude that at each step of the way he is ensuring that we reach the final destination. Job knew it, and confessed it. Worship is the true and best use of afflictions. But only a true believer will find a cross to be the source of thanksgiving. As the Puritan John Flavel once put it, 'A cross without Christ never did good to any man.'

4. Worship involves submission to one who is sovereign

Job's patience involved a refusal to attribute to God anything unreasonable. James 5:11 says that there are two things which lie behind Job's suffering. The first is Job's perseverance, or endurance. The other is God's pity and tender mercy! It sounds incredible, but that is what James says. 'You have seen the end intended by the Lord', he says, and that end, or purpose, was to reveal to Job that he is 'full of compassion and mercy'. God is glorified in our suffering, for in times of weakness and woe he reveals the glorious riches of his resources in keeping us going and enduring. Despite the overwhelming pressures, Job's faith never capitulated. Nor had God abandoned him completely to Satan. Job's initial response to suffering, in that he did not question God's goodness, is exemplary. God treats the worst of us better than the best of us deserves. This will, of course, change, but for now at least, Job is content to acknowledge that God is working everything for his good.

Paul can ask in the face of disturbing truths, 'Is God unjust?' to which he replies, 'Not at all!' (Rom. 9:14). In this respect at least, both Elihu and Bildad were correct when they said, 'Far be it from God to do evil, from the Almighty to do wrong' (34:10), and 'Does God pervert justice? Does the Almighty pervert what is right?' (8:3). 'The Lord is upright ... and there is no wickedness in him' (Ps. 92:15).

For Job, there is only one way to proceed with his pain; it is the Bible's consistent testimony:

Show me your ways, O Lord,
    teach me your paths

                                                                (Ps. 25:4).

The Lord is the everlasting God,
    the Creator of the ends of the earth.
He will not grow tired or weary,
    and his understanding no one can fathom

                                                              (Isa. 40:28).

[God] lives in unapproachable light

                                                            (1 Tim. 6:16).

'Think for a moment,' writes W. H. Green, 'what it would be to encounter crushing sorrows not only without Calvary and Gethsemane and the sympathy of the incarnate Son of God who is Himself touched with the feeling of our infirmities, for He was in all points tempted like as we are, yet without sin; but to go into trials that offer no bright spot this side of the grave, with no clear views of the eternal blessedness in comparison with which all earthly sorrows, however grievous in themselves and long continuing, are nevertheless light and momentary; without the assurance that present griefs and sufferings shall be overbalanced and outweighed by that far more exceeding and eternal weight of glory... What would it be to encounter frowning providences, without the distinct understanding that these are nevertheless consistent with the abiding, unchanging love of our heavenly Father?'[6] If we are to persevere like Job, then we must follow his example. We must run the race like he did. We are to derive strength from the gallery of the faithful and look to Jesus Christ as we make our way towards heaven (cf. Heb. 12:1-2). Job, of course, had fewer insights of Christ than we have.

There is an advertisement for a certain kind of battery which boasts its durability by saying, 'It still keeps going when all the rest have stopped.' Durability is to be a feature of our Christian lives. God glorified himself by keeping Job going. He promises to do the same for us, too.

Coping with ill-health

Poor health has been with us since the Fall and will, so the Bible leads us to believe, be with us until this world is destroyed altogether. Even amongst New Testament leaders, where neither faith nor miraculous powers were lacking, sickness prevailed. Timothy was advised to 'use a little wine because of your stomach and your frequent illnesses' (1 Tim. 5:23), Trophimus was 'left sick ... in Miletus' (2 Tim. 4:20). And Epaphroditus, that exemplary saint from Philippi, was so sick that he 'almost died for the work of Christ'. Paul was devastated at the thought of losing him (Phil. 2:25-27).

Moreover the great apostle himself, to underline the point, lived with pain all his days despite an extended time of prayer to get rid of it (2 Cor. 12:7-9). He called it 'a messenger of Satan' because it tempted him to think hard thoughts about the God who let him suffer. How could he go on travelling, preaching, working night and day, praying, caring, weeping over people with this pain constantly dragging him down? Such thoughts were 'flaming arrows of the evil one' (Eph. 6:16) with which he had to contend constantly, for the thorn remained unhealed. Paul came to appreciate in his discomfort a clue to the reason that lay behind it. The 'thorn' protected him from a far greater malaise, that of a spiritual sickness.

The worst diseases are not physical but spiritual: pride, conceit, arrogance, bitterness, self-seeking. Pain was God's means of keeping him humble (cf. 2 Cor.12:7). By not relieving the physical discomfort as Paul had wished, God kept Paul low in his own self-esteem. Thus Paul boasted in his weakness (2 Cor. 12:9). Theodore Beza, a contemporary and friend of John Calvin, testified that pain had brought him to embrace Jesus Christ: 'Sickness was for me the beginning of true health.'[7]

Job's disease has been diagnosed variously as boils, leprosy and more likely, elephantiasis. A diagnosis is not really possible. The symptoms given in the book include the following: aching, rotting bones (30:17) — though this may well be just a description of acute deep-seated pain; dark (and peeling) skin (30:28,30); wart-like eruptions (7:5); anorexia (19:20); fever (30:30); depression (7:16; 30:15); weeping (16:16); sleeplessness (7:4); nightmares (7:14); putrid breath (19:17; cf. 17:1); failing vision (16:16); rotting teeth (19:20). He evidently looked awful! **'They could hardly recognize him'** (2:12).

Job is a model of cross-bearing. As Christians we are called to follow in the footsteps of our Master, to take up a cross and follow after him (Luke 9:23). Those who carried their own crosses were outcasts, whose rights had been taken away. For the faithful, suffering is intended to aid in self-denial. It ought to draw us nearer to Christ. We are called upon to share in the sufferings of Christ (Phil. 1:29). 'When you crush lavender,' wrote David Watson, shortly before his death, 'you find it is full of fragrance; when you squeeze an orange, you extract its sweet juice. In the same way it is often through pains and hurts that we develop the fragrance and sweetness of Jesus in our lives.'[8]

Pain shapes us into Christ's image

A facet of Jesus' holiness was his willingness to suffer all
kinds of pain for his Father's glory and others' good. A facet
of holiness in Jesus' disciples is a willingness to be led along
a parallel path. In a lengthy section in his very last sermon on
Job, Calvin draws a comparison between Job's suffering and
that of Christ: 'In all our adversities we be shaped like to the
image of our Lord Jesus Christ, who is the eldest Son in the
house of God. And truly if we look but only on the cross of
Jesus Christ, it is cursed by God's own mouth: we shall see
nothing there but shame and terror: and to be short, it will seem
that the very gulf of hell is open to swallow up Jesus Christ. But
when we join his resurrection to his death, behold wherewith
to comfort us, behold wherewith to assuage all our sorrows, to
the end we be not over sorrowful whenever it shall please God
to afflict us. And this was purposely fulfilled in our Lord Jesus
Christ, to the intent we should know that this was not written
for any one person only: but to the intent that all of us should
understand, that the Son of God will make us partakers of his
life if we die with him, and partakers of his glory, if we bear
all the shames and adversities which it shall please God to lay
upon our shoulders ... we should always have an eye to the end
which God hath promised to his children, according as he hath
showed by effect, as well in Job, as also in David, and others,
but chiefly in our Lord Jesus Christ, who is the true and chief
pattern of all the faithful.'[9]

All of this runs counter to modern versions of Christianity
that expect no suffering, or to look for miracles to eliminate it
as soon as it appears. Such a philosophy makes human happiness the highest object. It is a view which leads us to expect
God to shield us from unhappiness and unpleasantness, and is
thereby false because it loses sight of the rôle of pain in
sanctification. God trains his children to share in his holiness

through pain. When Oral Roberts begins a service by saying, 'Something *good* is going to happen to you today,' it runs counter to the possibility that we may be called upon to suffer chastisement like Job. Good health and certain prosperity are not the will of God for all Christians.

Not every blessing intended for heaven is to be enjoyed now. Colin Urqhart, for example, commenting on Isaiah 53:4-5, 'He took up our infirmities', has this to say: 'When Jesus stood bearing the lashes from the Roman Soldiers, all our physical pain and sicknesses were being heaped upon him... It is as if one lash was for cancer, another for bone disease, another for heart disease...'[10] And Kenneth Hagin adds: 'God made him [Jesus] sick with your diseases that you might be perfectly well in Christ.'[11] Such a view contradicts the illnesses of Timothy, Trophimus, Epahroditus and in particular the apostle Paul himself, none of whom is said to have lacked faith or recourse to miraculous powers of healing. Urqhart and Hagin do not have biblical warrant on their side.

Reading the book of Job can only have a remedial effect upon current confusions that prevail as to the place of suffering in the Christian life, particularly ill-health. All Christians can expect trials of some kind and some will be catastrophic. 'Know this,' says Norwell Hayes, 'all bad things that come to visit you are from the devil — all bad things come from hell — not from heaven.' Clearly, this is not true. Job consistently blamed God for his trials — not some second cause like the Sabeans or Chaldeans (cf.1:21; 2:10). He knew that the Sabeans and Chaldeans had robbed him (1:15,17) but he did not mention them. 'If it is not he [God]' asks Job, 'then who is it?' (Job 9:24).[12] Afflictions are 'God's Archers' Calvin comments,[13] to which the best response is one of submission: 'Let us be content to walk whithersoever he leads and directs us, assuring ourselves that his only will must be to us the infallible rule of right: whereas we see Job so overmastered of his affections, let us understand that it is a right hard thing for us to submit ourselves to the single will of God, without asking a reason of his works, and especially of those works that surmount our wit and capacity.'[14] In dealing with the issue of suffering, the purpose of the book of Job is not to provide explanations for it, but to suggest that submission is the way of wisdom.

Job's wife

Job's suffering was not confined to physical illness. He was also to know the pain of an unfeeling, malcontent wife. **'His wife said to him, "Are you still holding on to your integrity? Curse God and die!"'** (2:9). Augustine refers to Job's wife as *diaboli adjutrix* — the 'devil's advocate'. Calvin refers to her as *organum satani* — a 'tool of Satan'. Thomas Aquinas theorized that Satan had spared her in his opening salvo against Job in order to use her against Job. She is a second Eve, who tempts her husband to sin — though, unlike Adam, Job did not listen to her! Job's assessment of her is blunt: **'You are talking like a foolish woman'** (2:10). Job may be referring to her as one of a class of low-life, whose tongues were notoriously earthy. She would not normally have spoken in this way. Her reply 'brings into sharper relief the wisdom of Job's godly patience'.[15] She has identified with the godless in her reply: 'The fool says in his heart, "There is no God"' (Ps. 14:1).

Did you ever think about Mrs Job? She suffered every bit as much as Job did. As a woman she may have felt the loss of household goods more keenly. We get attached to our possessions, no matter how hard we try to 'sit loose' to the things of this world. Burglaries still cause immense pain. Folk speak of them today as a 'violation', as though someone had trespassed upon something private and personal. Habakkuk teaches us a lesson here:

Though the fig tree may not blossom,
  nor fruit be on the vines;
though the labour of the olive may fail,
  and the fields yield no food;
though the flock may be cut off from the fold,
  and there be no herd in the stalls—
yet I will rejoice in the Lord,
  I will joy in the God of my salvation

(Hab. 3:17-18).

As a mother, Job's wife might have felt the crushing loss of her sons and daughters in a keener, deeper way than did Job himself. The experience of sudden bereavement of one's children can bring special burdens, for we all anticipate dying before our children. There is a guilt associated with the loss of children. Grieving parents often express the wish that they could, in some way, trade places with their dead children. Those who have spent hours in an intensive care unit, or nursed their child through death, can identify with Mrs Job.

Job's wife has no 'patience'.[16] She is angry and bitter — with her husband as well as with God. His godliness had brought nothing except a crushing sense of loss: her children, her social standing and her livelihood. Whether it is out of hatred for God, or a desire that Job's pain be ended quickly, she urges her husband to **'Curse God and die!'** (2:9).

We instinctively feel for Job's wife. Something of a similar reaction wells up within our own hearts. Which one of us can ever be sure how we would respond in similar circumstances? When a young couple, whom I know, discovered the murdered body of their nine-year-old daughter, Jennifer, it might have destroyed them completely. Both have found peace and strength in knowing Jesus Christ. Giving testimony to their faith, Jennifer's father writes, 'I lost a daughter, Jennifer. She was only nine years old at the time. She went out on her bicycle one day and didn't come back. And that was the last we saw of her until her body was found in a dam a week later. I was comforted to know that even at that age she was saved, that she was with the Lord.'[17]

Somerset Maughan, the novelist, kept a cracked cup on the mantelpiece of his beautiful home in London. Explaining why he allowed this to offend by its presence the many exquisite artefacts which surrounded it, he said, 'During the First World War, on a troop ship crossing the ocean, our rations of water were reduced to just one cup a day. I drank my ration of water from that cup and keep it on the mantel as a reminder that I can never take my blessings for granted.'[18]

> Count your blessings,
> Name them one by one,
> And it will surprise you
> What the Lord has done.

Joni Eareckson Tada has the right to speak about trials. A quadriplegic through a diving accident, she has wrestled with her emotions in public about her pain — what she calls her 'intruder'. 'Today — right now,' she has written, 'I want to resolve to know something about the intruder that will invariably knock at my door. Before I get up to answer his knock, I want to remember that this unwelcome visitor, for all his ill manners has come for *my good*, for the good of my character. No matter what my emotions tell me, I want to welcome him in. Why? Because deep down, real character is more important to me than temporary comfort.'[19] Job's 'real character' shines through these passages, partly due to the staggering nature of the contrast between his response and that of his wife.

The refrain, 'Give me joy in my heart, keep me smiling...' may be theologically inadequate as a Christian apologetic, but it nevertheless expresses a profound lack in many of our lives. We simply do not have the joy that the Bible insists we should know. Too large a part of our lives is spent in miserable defeat, yielding to the inner pull of our sins. We grumble too much, complain too much. The lack of joy in our lives is a testimony to the strides in sanctification we have yet to make if we are to conform to the image of biblical Christianity. 'When I think of God', wrote Franz Josef Haydn, 'my heart is so full of joy that the notes leap and dance as they leave my pen,' and he added, 'Since God has given me a cheerful heart, I serve him with a cheerful spirit.'

Job's testimony in these opening chapters is immense. Like California Redwood trees that reach up to the skies, Job stands out as almost superhuman. But he was not superhuman and the story as it unfolds will show that Job had feet of clay. He persevered *by God's strength.* Were we to attempt to follow him in our own strength we would find ourselves sinking within an instant. David testifies that 'None can keep alive his own soul' (Ps. 22:29, AV). Job would have been the first to testify that his response was due to the supernatural power of God.

The same response can be seen in the testimony of Horatio Spafford. Having known financial disaster in the fires of Chicago in 1873, he sent his wife and four children to England aboard the ship SS. *Ville de Havre.* Halfway across the Atlantic, it collided with another ship, the SS. *Lochearn.* Over 200 people drowned, including Spafford's four children. Upon reaching the shores of Britain, Mrs Spafford sent a telegram. There were just two words written on it: 'Saved Alone'. Horatio Spafford caught the next available steamship and was told by the captain of the spot where his daughters had drowned. It is believed that it was then he composed the words of the hymn:

When peace like a river, attendeth my soul,
When sorrows like sea-billows roll;

Whatever my lot, thou hast taught me to say,
It is well, it is well with my soul.

That is the way God wants us to live. We have no right to expect that our lives are going to be free from trouble. But in every circumstance, if we are the Lord's people, we are assured of God's care and providence. He is working out every detail. There are no mistakes with him (Rom. 8:32-39). Every moment of our existence is cause enough for joy: the good and the bad together should integrate to form a Hallelujah symphony to the praise of Almighty God. Job's response teaches us that lesson.

3.
Job curses the day he was born

Please read Job 2:11 - 3:26

Job has been reduced from 'the greatest man among all the people of the East' (1:3) to one who 'sat among the ashes' (2:8). As he sits there, 'painful sores' (2:7) break out over his body. He relieves the itching by scraping himself with broken pieces of pottery (2:8).

Outside every ancient town was a place where the refuse was dumped and burned. The heap of ash produced grew larger with each burning, and it was here that lepers and the like gathered. This is where Job is to be found. It is a symbol of desolation and rejection. David had felt like this, too: 'No one cares for my life' (Ps.142:4). And one cannot ignore a much more painful picture of rejection, when Jesus was systematically rejected, first by a group of soldiers, then by chief priests, scribes and elders of the Sanhedrin council, by Passover worshippers in Jerusalem who passed by the cross, by two criminals on either side of him, by the sun which refused to give him warmth and even by God who forsook him (cf. Matt 27:27-31,39-46).

Enter three 'friends': **'Eliphaz the Temanite, Bildad the Shuhite and Zophar the Naamathite'** (2:11),[1] three wise men from the East. They come from three different cities, having covenanted together to comfort their good friend, Job. We shall see in the course of this commentary that these three friends, together with Elihu the Buzite who appears later (chs 32-37), all believe in God — the true God of creation. Their views often appear inadequate, sometimes utterly wrong; but none of them is inclined to call on Job to believe on another god.[2]

When they first catch sight of their good friend, they can hardly recognize him. Job is disfigured by his illness. He is also in mourning. His robe is rent[3] and his head is shaved[4] (1:20). Evidently, the three friends mimic the first gesture, but not the second. Instead of shaving their heads, they sprinkle dust on them instead (2:12). Dust was symbolic of death and disease, and Job's friends were thereby associating themselves with him. It was a form of empathy, and a needful requirement in counselling those who find themselves in pain.

They also respond by weeping. They say nothing to Job at all, but treat him as though he is already dead. They remain with Job in silence on the ash-heap for seven days, the statutory period for mourning the dead — i.e. Job's sons and daughters, and perhaps his servants, but perhaps also for Job himself! (cf. Gen. 50:10; 1 Sam. 31:13).

Silence is often a good response initially to another's trouble. Joseph Caryl comments: 'When a man is resolved to mourn let him mourn; your advice may anger him, but it will not help him. Let sorrow have its way a while, and that will make way for comfort.'[5] Too often we feel the need to rush in with words of explanation in a crisis, when often no words are suitable. It is not always appropriate to cite Romans 8:28, 'And we know that in all things God works for the good of those who love him...', at the very moment of crisis, comforting and helpful though these words prove to be in their time. Job's friends, initially at least, did the right thing: they wept with him that wept (Eccles. 3:4; Rom. 12:15). But to say nothing for se*ven days* must have strained their relationship no end. Silence, after a while, can become deafening. As we shall see, these 'friends' could not really believe that Job did not, in some degree at least, deserve this torment of his. Even before they came they had adopted the view that all of human suffering is directly attributed to our sinfulness. There is no such thing as an 'innocent' who suffers.

Job's cry of grief: his first speech

Following the period of silence on the ash-heap, Job has had time to brood over his tragedy. However magnanimous his reaction had been initially (1:20-22; 2:10), Job's perception of his difficulties has increased. He discovers that he is not as strong as he thought he was. The battle has begun and has revealed that beneath the surface of Job's eminent piety, there lies a heart which can quickly shame him.[6]

The pain is unbearable now; the pain of bereavement often grows after the immediate shock of it all has passed away. What follows in chapter 3 is a cry from the heart — a mournful lamentation that touches us deeply. In that sense it is like many of the individual psalms of lament (cf. Ps. 3-7; 140-143). C. S. Lewis, recalling the pain of losing his wife, speaks of his prayers as more like a 'yell' than anything else.

In this chapter we find ourselves in the inner, personal experiences of Job. Now that he has had some time to reflect, Job's words are filled with an unbearable anguish and sorrow. He does not succumb to his wife's suggestion to curse God, but he does curse **'the day of his birth'** (3:1; cf. 2:9). Job is not vitriolic towards God; still less is he asking deep questions about the nature of suffering and why the righteous should suffer at all. Instead, Job is overwhelmed by how horrible life can be. It is the cry of a man overcome with depression, not anger. He pronounces a curse upon something which cannot be changed — the past. It were better that life did not exist at all. If only he had not been born, or even conceived! (here viewed as one event).

Two words dominate Job's first speech: **'May'** (thirteen times in vv. 2-10) and **'Why?'** (five times in vv.11-26, 3:4-6). Together they reveal the extent of Job's emotional outburst. We must not imagine that Stoicism is the right response to pain and suffering. Job is telling us how he feels. 'The Lord is not trying to find out if Job can sit unmoved like a piece of wood.'[7]

The lament: an unhappy birthday! (3:1-10)

Job curses the day of his birth, **'because it did not shut up the doors of my mother's womb, nor hide sorrow from my eyes'** (3:10). The announcement of a birth of child, **'A boy is born!'** (3:3) is one of the happiest moments in any parent's life. It must have been so for Job's parents, too. But overtaken by trouble, Job now contemplates the sorrow (even shame) he now must prove to be to his family and those who knew him. Job wants the day of his birth to be removed from the calendar as though it had never existed; then he, too, would not exist (3:6). He calls on soothsayers to pronounce the day of his birth 'unlucky' by pronouncing a curse on it, thus making it impossible for his parents to conceive (3:8,10). In a deliberate counter to God's 'Let there be light' at the creation of the world (Gen. 1:3), Job says of the day of his own creation, **'That day — let it be darkness'** (3:4) and goes on to speak of **'deep shadow'**, **'cloud'**, **'blackness'** and **'thick darkness'** in connection with it (vv. 5-6).

Job even suggests that these soothsayers call up **'Leviathan'** (3:8) to swallow the day-night of his birth. Who, or what, is 'Leviathan'? Two creatures (monsters) are mentioned in Job: one is 'Leviathan' and another is 'Behemoth' (both are mentioned later in chapters 40 and 41). They correspond to no living creature known to us. Leviathan may have been one of the great aquatic animals (now extinct) — reports continue to exist of great sea serpents and plesiosaurus-like animals in oceans and deep lakes around the world (one immediately thinks of the so-called 'Loch Ness Monster'!).

Many commentators insist on calling Leviathan the 'crocodile', but the description in Job 41 does not altogether fit. Some have suggested the 'whale'. Others have suggested that these creatures refer to animals which once existed, but are now extinct.[8] The 'leviathan' is also mentioned in Isaiah, where it is further called 'the monster of the sea', or 'the dragon that is in the sea' (Isa. 27:1; cf. Ps. 104:26). In referring to 'monsters' or 'dragons' it is possible that the Bible is merely making use of man's (erroneous) belief in the existence of such monsters, which were thought to possess supernatural powers. In the minds of ordinary folk they existed as monsters; whether or not they actually were is of no importance. Job then blurts out the wish that these soothsayers in some way might arouse 'leviathan', who will in turn swallow up the day-night of his birth.[9]

Such feelings of anguish about one's existence are not uncommon. A comparison with Jeremiah shows that the prophet had also travelled down this lonely path. Both Job and Jeremiah are in **'trouble'** and **'sorrow'** (3:10,20; cf. Jer. 20:18). Hence Jeremiah's response:

> Cursed be the day I was born!
>   May the day my mother bore me not be blessed!
> Cursed be the man who brought my father the news,
>   who made him very glad, saying,
>   'A child is born to you — a son!'
> May that man be like the towns
>   the Lord overthrew without pity.
> May he hear wailing in the morning,
>   a battle cry at noon.
> For he did not kill me in the womb,
>   with my mother as my grave,
>   her womb enlarged for ever.

Why did I ever come out of the womb
to see trouble and sorrow
and to end my days in shame?

(Jer. 20:14-18).

Jeremiah had obeyed God's call to be a prophet as a young man. Instead of fame and fortune, he received rejection, not only from the people and his friends, but (seemingly) from God also. This was Job's experience, too.

Lamentation has always been part of the expression of faith. Almost a half of Israel's hymn-book consisted of psalms of lament. It is, perhaps, one of the reasons for the demise of psalm-singing in churches of the twentieth century that the church has drifted away from biblical expressions of faith. In our own day, everything must go 'with a swing' if it is to be included in Christian worship. Plaintive songs in minor keys are thought dull and sometimes sub-Christian. But they are part of biblical testimony as to how we sometimes feel, whether we admit it or not. To avoid facing the reality of pain distorts the nature of faith, for faith often reveals its greatest triumphs through anguish.

In these uncensored protests, the innermost soul of Job is being revealed. Those who ache inside because of the loss of a child, memories of abuse, or crippling disease can identify with Job. Something inside us just wants to lash out and respond in irrational gestures. What Job says here makes no sense at all, but it is an honest expression of how he felt.

From cursing to questioning (3:11-26)

Joni Eareckson Tada has written, 'One of the first places I turned after my diving accident was to the book of Job. As I lay immobilized in the hospital, my mind swirled with questions. When I learned that my paralysis was going to be permanent, it raised even more questions. I was desperate to find answers. Job, I reasoned, had suffered terribly and questioned God again and again. Perhaps I could find comfort and insight from following his search for answers.'[10]

Job asks a series of pointed, sharp questions in this book:

Why didn't you let me die at birth? (3:11).

Why didn't you dry up my mother's breasts so that I would starve? (3:12).

Why do you keep wretched people like me alive? (3:20-22).

How do you expect me to have hope and patience? (6:12).

If life is so short, does it have to be miserable, too? (7:1-10).

Why don't you stop hurting me for a while? (7:17,19).

What did I ever do to you that I became the target for your arrows? (7:20).

Why don't you forgive me before I die and it's too late? (7:21).

How can mortal man be righteous before a holy God? (9:2).

Why do you favour the wicked? (9:24).

Since you have already decided I'm guilty, why should I even try? (9:29).

You are the one who created me, so why are you destroying me? (10:8).

Why do you hide your face and consider me your enemy? (13:24).

Why do you not let me meet you somewhere face to face so that I can state my case? (23:3-6).

Why do you not set a time to judge wicked men? (24:1).

These are tough, searching questions! Job's friends perhaps expected a bolt of lightning to fall each time he asked them. But the lightning never fell. This is one of the greatest encouragements in the book of Job. Despite Job's anger and frustration, he is never condemned. God never abandons him. God listens to Job's questions. Job may not have received the answers that he wished for, but he is allowed to ask these terrible questions.

Could Job have handled the answers had they been given to him? Hardly! Nor could we. Can we understand the reason why a cosmic battle of greater proportions than we can ever imagine is taking place, one whose outcome is assured by the death of Christ on the cross? Our finite minds cannot possibly take it all in — one of the reasons why the Bible's revelation of this aspect of things is limited.

God was not threatened in any way by Job's questions. But did Job find any answers? Just this one: that God will be glorified, no matter what, and the sooner we knuckle under and submit to it, the better it will be for our souls and peace of mind.

'What if God had suddenly consented to answer all of my queries?' asks Joni. 'Could I have even begun to handle it? It would have been like pouring million-gallon truths into a one-ounce container. Dumping a water tower into a paper cup. My poor pea brain wouldn't have been able to process it... God is never threatened by our questions. And so ... did I find the answers? Answers for deepest darkest questions about a life of total paralysis?

'Just one. But it is enough. I think I'll let Paul put it in his words: "Oh, the depth of the riches of the wisdom and knowledge of God! How unsearchable his judgements, and his paths beyond tracing out! Who has known the mind of the Lord? Or who has been his counsellor? Who has ever given to God, that God should repay him? For from him and through him and to him are all things. To him be the glory for ever! Amen"'(Rom. 11:33-36).[11]

Satan wants us to believe (and express!) wrong views about God. Every heresy is first of all a deviation in our views about God. When C. S. Lewis was losing his wife to cancer, he observed: 'Not that I am ... in much danger of ceasing to believe in God. The real danger is of coming to believe such dreadful things about him. The conclusion I dread is not, "So there's no God after all," but "So this is what God is really like. Deceive yourself no longer."'[12]

Stillbirth (3:11-19)

If the powers cannot curse the day of his conception (the argument of 3:3-10), Job now wishes that he might have died at birth (3:11,16). In an allusion to his mother he cries: 'Why were there knees to receive me and breasts that I might be nursed?' (3:12). Death would have been better than this, Job muses (3:13). At least in death Job, outcast that he now is, would share a common lot with kings and princes who currently live in great palaces. In death, their silver and gold will avail them nothing (3:14-15). In death, those who are currently abused and beaten are at peace from their tyrannical overlords (3:17-19). And if death did not take him at birth, why not now? Why must his wretched life now continue? Job wishes that he might die and be at peace from his pain and suffering.

Job's longing for death (3:20-26)

Job joins with those who **'long for death that does not come'** (3:21). Initially God had set a hedge around Job's life (2:6), but now 'The hedge has become a prison wall rather than a wall of defence.'[13] There is a suffering which makes you want to die, but you cannot. We must not be too hard on Job here. Those who have not known the combined effects of multiple bereavement and intense, unrelieved pain may wonder at the piety of wanting to die (though nowhere does Job suggest that he take his own life). People in Job's condition find it difficult to be rational, to think beyond their pain.

Job is a distressed man: sighing, groaning, fearful; he knows no peace, no quietness, no rest, only turmoil (3:25-26). He is tired of living. He sees no point to it. Everything that gave him pleasure in this world has been taken away. Life has become unbearable. 'I have had enough, Lord,' Elijah said, 'Take my life; I am no better than my ancestors' (1 Kings 19:4).

What can we say about Job's response? We need to be careful that in the detachment of our perspective we judge him too harshly. True, Eliphaz will warn Job of the consequences of bad temper (5:2), and Job will admit himself that his words were 'impetuous' (6:3) — though he pleads some justification due to the weight of his vexation. Commentators line up on every side: Albert Barnes notes that 'With all allowances, it is not possible to vindicate this language ... there is a want of proper submission and patience.'[14] The Puritan Joseph Caryl alludes to the contrast with Job's initial blessing of God and exhorts that Job should continue to 'bless, and curse not'.[15] On the other hand, Francis Andersen says, 'There can therefore be no question of disapproving what Job says.'[16] And John Hartley agrees, pointing out that 'If Job had sinned in his first speech, there would be no debate. His frequent claims to innocence would be sheer mockeries... He survives his darkest hour, since he neither curses God nor takes his fate into his own hands.'[17]

There is a remarkable restraint so far in what Job says. Though he wishes for death, he never once directly attributes his downfall to God. Job still maintains those elements of integrity which we saw in his initial response when he refused to comply with his wife's advice that he should curse God and suffer the consequences by death (2:9). This ongoing reluctance to curse God is an indication of grace in Job's heart. To desire death, not by one's own hands, but by a sovereign act of God, is not in itself sinful. To desire another course of action than the one being offered is precisely what we see Jesus himself expressing in the struggle in the Garden of Gethsemane. Whereas Job does not explicitly say, 'Father, ... may your will be done' (cf. Matt. 26:42), it is implicit in his response in this chapter. Accusations against God will come in the next speech (6:4) and after that they will fall thick and fast, but for now Job's response is remarkably free from accusations of cruelty, or injustice on God's part.

Several lessons are now worth considering.

1. Folk like Job need sympathy, not a cold diagnosis

Those of us who (bless God!) know next to nothing of the anguish of this wretched man can theologize in a detached way about the rights and wrongs of his condition, forgetting how honestly Job expresses his feelings at this point. In the first section Job 'did not sin nor charge God with wrong' (1:22), but things *appear* different here. Did Job sin in cursing the day of his birth and in wishing he was dead? It must be borne in mind that at no time did Job curse God, nor did he seek to end his own life. He comes to the very edge of the precipice, but refuses to jump. To have done so would been a grave violation. The curse that he utters appears to be a deliberate attempt to reverse the order of creation in Genesis 1:1-2:4 — turning light into darkness, day and night into non-existence.

To look for and emphasize Job's sin in this chapter is to focus on the wrong place. The chapter seems to want us to grasp the anguish and pain of this man. To enter into a diagnosis is to sit with Job's counsellors: detached, uncaring, concerned for theological accuracy at the expense of brotherly sympathy and caring.

2. *To ask too many questions of God is not safe*

He is the Potter, we are the clay. 'But who are you, O man, to talk back to God? "Shall what is formed say to him who formed it, 'Why did you make me like this?'" Does not the potter have the right to make out of the same lump of clay some pottery for noble purposes and some for common use?' (Rom 9:20-21). God's purposes are too deep for us to fathom. It was Milton who described the fallen angels as sitting in little groups discussing predestination and the counsels of the eternal God. It is almost unavoidable to demand an explanation, but it is better that we do not. This is faith's greatest test: to trust God *in the dark*. In this respect, Elihu's response is right:

> God is greater than man.
> Why do you complain to him
>   that he answers none of man's words?
>   (Job 33:12-14).

We can draw comfort, this side of the cross — something which Job could not do — that we know of one who has passed through this abyss of despair and loneliness, one who has cried, 'My God, my God, why have you forsaken me?' (Matt. 27:46; Mark 15:34). In the darkness of pain, there is one who stands beside us in our questioning of what is happening, and whispers, 'I've been this way, too.' And he accepted the Lord's will with absolute submission. That is something he wants us to do, too.

Christianity is an invitation to trust God's love at all times. Instead of answering our questions, it introduces us to the God in whom the answer to all our questions lies. It tells us to trust him *before* we get the answers. These answers will, in the main, be given in heaven, where faith becomes sight and we shall know as we are known. We look forward to that day.

Some answers, however, are forthcoming to the question:

**Why is life given to a man
whose way is hidden,
whom God has hedged in?**

(3:23).

Firstly, *God wills it.* It is enough for us to know that our Father chooses it this way.

Secondly, *our life is always better than we deserve.* Only a glimpse of the depravity of our hearts will convince us that there is mercy, even in the severest trial.

Thirdly, *God loves us.* Yes, he does! Samuel Rutherford once wrote to a lady who had lost a child, saying, 'I believe faith will teach you to kiss a striking Lord; and so to acknowledge the sovereignty of God [in the death of a child] to be above the power of us mortal men, who may pluck up a flower in the bud and not be blamed for it.'[18]

Fourthly, *the purpose of pain in the lives of the godly is to make them more like Jesus.* It is part of our calling to share in the ministry of his suffering. Every rough edge that he chisels away means a sharper reflection of Jesus in our lives.

3. Questions about our health and the loss of loved ones challenge our faith the most

It may not be our own suffering, but the suffering of one we love. It may involve having to watch a parent deteriorate into senility. It may be having to sit by the bedside of a little child with incurable cancer. It may be the pain of a random, senseless act of terrorism. Job has lost his wealth and his progeny; in addition, he bears the pain of skin ulcers, or perhaps leprosy; his embittered wife urges him to 'Curse God and die' (2:9); and Job nearly gives in. Job feels demoralized, inhuman, degraded. His dignity has been taken away.

Pain brings about the fiercest temptations. Issues which relate to personal health or the welfare of our family necessarily affect us the most. Dealing with them will not be easy. The only formula adequate enough to cover such a situation is the one given in Hebrews: 'No discipline seems pleasant at the time, but painful. Later on, however, it produces a harvest of righteousness and peace for those who have been trained by it' (Heb.12:11).

4. Christianity was from the beginning described as the way of the cross

'If anyone would come after me,' said Jesus, 'he must deny himself and take up his cross daily and follow me. For whoever wants to save his life will lose it, but whoever loses his life for me will save it.' 'Anyone who does not carry his cross and follow me cannot be my disciple' (Luke 9:23-24; 14:27). Jesus uses the picture of condemned criminals going out to execution, carrying their crosses as they went. Pain, rejection, grief and suffering — these are all part of the way of the cross.

The visions of the book of Revelation (particularly the seals and trumpets of chapters 6-11) reveal God's plan for history, which includes large-scale infliction of his wrath (judicial repudiation and sentence) on the arrogant self-sufficiency and godlessness of mankind. Christians will be caught up in these judgements, just as Israel was caught up in the Babylonian ransacking of Jerusalem. Plagues, epidemics, starvation and wholesale community ill-health are among the forms which God's wrath takes. It is part of the cost of following Jesus that we take our share of these ills. He wants us to know this so that we are not knocked out of stride by them. Richard Baxter of Kidderminster was half his life tubercular and a walking museum of other diseases — incessant dyspepsia, kidney stones, headaches, toothaches, swollen limbs, intermittent bleeding from many parts of his body and all in the days before pain-relieving drugs. Yet he remained equable, energetic, uncomplaining and outgoing to the end. The lesson is that piety and pain can and do go together and Job's response thus far proves it.

5. Job's suffering has already prompted him to pray

It may be, to use C. S. Lewis's phrase, a 'yell', but it is a prayer. In his distress he lifts his voice to God. He does what the humanist does not do — brings his frenzied aches and distresses to God. The Christian response to pain is giving to God our suffering and asking him to make of it what in his wisdom he can. By God's grace, we may even come to bear it, not just bravely and stoically, but with hope too. For 'Our present sufferings are not worth comparing with the glory that will be revealed in us' (Rom. 8:18). If our suffering is this bad, what will our glory be? Our present sufferings are working in us the beginnings of that blessed glory which one day we shall know in all its fulness (cf. 2 Cor. 4:17).

Truths of this kind help us to keep going.

4.

'Everything's going to turn out just fine!'

Please read Job 4 - 5

Chapters 4-27 comprise three rounds of speeches: there are speeches in turn from Eliphaz, Bildad and Zophar, each of which is followed by a reply from Job. The first round of speeches takes us up to the end of chapter 14:

> 1. Eliphaz's first speech (4-5) followed by Job's reply (6-7).
> 2. Bildad's first speech (8) followed by Job's reply (9-10).
> 3. Zophar's first speech (11) followed by Job's reply (12-14).

Eliphaz's first speech

Job had friends in many countries, three of whom have now gathered to 'help' their friend in his time of distress. **'Eliphaz the Temanite'** (4:1), presumably the oldest and therefore the first to speak, intends to help Job and, of all Job's 'comforters', Eliphaz is the kindest. His contribution, however, becomes more and more judgemental as it continues, and together with those of his companions, comes across as a verdict from an elders' council rather than help from a friend. These speeches are in fact a further aspect of Job's suffering! Each contribution is somewhat akin to someone 'turning the knife' in Job's wounds. These friends do not, of course, mean it that way. Their detached stance seems to suggest that in the main they were oblivious to Job's feelings. What Job thought about their contributions did not really matter. What mattered was that he be told the truth.

Essentially, Eliphaz's contribution is this: 'You are a good man, Job. So do not lose heart about this matter. You are being *disciplined* because there are some things in your life that need to be sorted out. Bear with this patiently, for it will all turn out right in the end.' His speech can be summarized under the following headings.

'Job, no one is perfect'

Eliphaz begins by acknowledging Job's **'piety'** and **'blameless ways'** (4:6). He reminds Job that he (that is, Job) has been a help to other sufferers in the past: he has **'strengthened feeble hands ... supported those who have stumbled ... strengthened faltering knees...'** (4:2-4). But now **'trouble'** has come upon Job and he is **'discouraged'** and **'dismayed'** (4:5). Now emerges Eliphaz's working theology: you reap what you sow (4:8; cf. Gal. 6:7). Couched in this seemingly accurate observation is a devastating conclusion which lies at the very heart of Eliphaz's contribution: **'Who, being innocent, has ever perished?'** (4:7); since Job is suffering, he cannot be as innocent as he makes himself out to be. Wicked men have cause to fear God's anger once it is roused: even lions are ultimately subject to God's holy indignation (4:9-10). But Job need not worry unduly, for he is not a wicked man. There is something amiss, to be sure, but it is something small. If Job is patient, he will emerge unscathed at the end of all this.

Eliphaz is a man convinced of his own self-importance, and claims his authority by an appeal to two sources.

1. The appeal to private revelations

Implicit in the fact that he is first to speak is a recognition that he is the oldest of the three friends: older and therefore wiser and more experienced. To back up his argument he claims to be the recipient of a supernatural revelation in which he has received a message from God (4:12-15). A **'form'** had stood before him, but Eliphaz was unsure of its identity (4:16). The content of the message (4:17-21) hardly needs such an extravagant mode of revelation, for the message is really quite commonplace: **'Can a mortal be more righteous than God? Can a man be more pure than his Maker?'** (4:17)[1]

This is unfair of Eliphaz. For a start, Job is not claiming that he is more righteous than God. And more than that, Job is not just suffering a little, in proportion to Eliphaz's supposed insight into Job's small transgression. Job is utterly devastated, worse off than even the dead who are at rest from pain (this world's pain, at least). Job wants to die but cannot, and Eliphaz's opening contribution has already hurt him.

Eliphaz is typical of the kind of person who insists on claiming divine support for his arguments. It is always frustrating to hear someone say in the course of a discussion, 'But God has told me!' Who can argue with that? Usually it is couched in much more subtle ways: 'I've prayed about it, and I think we should do such and such.' It often comes out into the open when folk 'feel' a call to the ministry of the gospel or missionary work. God has revealed to them their future course of usefulness. The trouble with this kind of revelation is that it binds everybody, not just the person who receives it. If God has 'revealed' to them what they should do, it becomes impossible to ask questions which imply a doubt about this proposed course of action. This remains one of the most important reasons why there are men and women in the ministry of the church who are totally unsuited to the work. Every experience must pass the scrutiny of the Word of God. 'To the law and to the testimony! If they do not speak according to this word, they have no light of dawn' (Isa. 8:20).

2. The appeal to orthodox theology

Eliphaz has been given a 'revelation' to the effect that no man is more righteous than God! This is true enough, if a little banal. There is no point in Job pretending otherwise, for no man is sinless. Not even the angels are perfect. Eliphaz suggests that God is so transcendent that he does not even have complete confidence in the angels: they are so inferior to him that he does not trust them with his secrets (4:18); much less will he trust man. Man is nothing more than a **'moth'** whose lifespan may only last a day, a 'house of clay' (4:19-20), a tent held up by a single rope (4:21). If we take a glance at some of Eliphaz's notions, we shall discover that, in the main, they are orthodox enough.

According to Eliphaz's critique, Job's remonstrations fail to take into account two factors: his creatureliness and his sinfulness.

God's transcendence. Eliphaz appeals to God's transcendence and man's smallness (4:18-21). God is incomprehensible and therefore it will never be possible to fathom his justice. It is beyond our comprehension. It is wrong even to ask questions of God. Job had better understand that his life is of no more significance than a piece of clay, or a moth. His life is a tent 'held up by a single rope'. Who is Job to question the ways of the Almighty? Implicit is a lack of submission on Job's part, a view confirmed by Eliphaz's somewhat pietistic exhortations that Job should start praying and stop complaining (5:8).

Eliphaz is far too calculating. Job insists on his right to ask questions. God will not deny him that right. Andersen comments: 'Job knows only too well that he is merely a creature. But a creature of such a God cannot be a "mere" creature. He will not be silenced by reminders that it is not for puny man to question the ways of the Almighty. His questions may be unanswerable, but he will ask them, insist on his right to ask them.'[2]

God's righteousness. Not only is God the Creator and therefore beyond impunity; he is also righteous — a factor which necessitates his judgement of every sinful deed. Behind Eliphaz's speech lies the recurring principle that Job is suffering because he sinned in some specific way. Several of his statements underline it.

'You reap what you sow' (4:8). This is true. It is a principle to which the apostle Paul appeals when calling upon Christians to mortify sin and live holy and pure lives: if you live by the flesh, you will die; if you live in the style of the Spirit, you will live (Rom 8:13). If you live one way, you will reap spiritual death; if you live another way, you will reap spiritual vitality. Just as in the physical realm, if we sow calories, we reap fat, so, too, in the spiritual realm, our spiritual health and vitality depend on how serious we are at ensuring progress in sanctification. In extolling this principle, Eliphaz was, on the face of it, perfectly orthodox.

'Can a man be more righteous than God?' (4:17).[3] Of course not! Behind it lies the truth that we are all sinners. It follows that in a very real sense we have forfeited our 'rights' before God; they have been sacrificed due to our sin. In one sense, all evil and suffering in this world are here because of sin. When it comes down to it, Job has to admit that there is no one who is really innocent — not even Job himself. Again, the universal sinfulness of man, rendering him unfit for fellowship with God and therefore for favours from God, is something every Christian wants to uphold as central to the gospel. In this, what Eliphaz said was once again true — up to a point.

'Job, you must expect suffering'

Eliphaz's insensitivity heightens as he speaks of 'the fool's' house being cursed (5:2,3). He may not be directly calling Job 'a fool'. What he means to say is that not even the righteous, like Job, can hope to escape from such suffering. Trouble does not just happen; it is the result of human action:

> **For hardship does not spring from the soil,**
> **nor does trouble sprout from the ground.**
> **Yet man is born to trouble**
> **as surely as sparks fly upward**
>
> (5:6-7).

Job must take responsibility for his condition and learn not to complain, or even ask questions of God. If he thinks that he can appeal to heaven to be released from his suffering (5:1), he had better think again.

Eliphaz now urges prayer (5:8). It is part of his philosophy that Job is essentially a pious man and if only he waits patiently on God, he will be all right. Bursting into a hymn (5:9-16) on the nature and attributes of God, Eliphaz waxes eloquent on the theme that God can change things that look impossible to man — a good point, but almost totally irrelevant to Job's case. God is supreme over nature (5:9-10) and over the affairs of men (5:11-15).

Sinners, then, get what they deserve and they should be grateful for God's corrections: **'Blessed is the man whom God corrects; so do not despise the discipline of the Almighty'** (5:17).

'Job, be patient and you will see that I'm right'

Eliphaz has made his case: Job is being chastised because of some minor infringement. What Job must do is **'not despise the discipline of the Almighty'** (5:17). If he waits on the Lord, Job will discover that the one who **'wounds'** is also the one who **'binds up'** (5:18). In fact, Eliphaz suggests, Job is much better off than he ever imagines! That God has taken the trouble to chastise him makes Job blessed! **'Blessed is the man whom God corrects'**! (5:17). What a thing to tell someone in Job's condition! And yet we meet them from time to time — folk who are aggressively cheerful in times of calamity and distress.

What Eliphaz says is perfectly orthodox and sound, but of almost total irrelevance to Job in his condition. It is, in fact, the theme of Hebrews 12:5-11. The Lord does indeed chasten us for our sin, and he does so because he loves us. God uses hurts to transform us to the image of our Saviour (Heb. 12:11; cf. Rom. 5:3-5; James 1:2-4). We are called upon to 'endure hardship as discipline' (Heb. 12:7). As J. I. Packer puts it: 'Scars tie in with sanctity. Pain has an educational effect'.[4] All this is evidence that God is our Father, for it is still true that fathers don't usually bother with their illegitimate sons. God is bothered enough to reprove his own children, because he loves them (Heb. 12:8). All this is orthodox enough. As God's children, who bear his name, we can expect trouble when we sin. But God's children suffer for reasons that have little or no connection with personal sin, and Eliphaz has left this possibility out of his reckoning altogether.

The implication in Eliphaz's counsel is, by now, explicit: Job must accept what Eliphaz says and begin to apply it to himself immediately (5:27). If he does he will be restored immediately.

A summary of Eliphaz's speech

'Since you have helped others in the past in times of difficulty,
I'm going to say something to you now. I trust you will not
become impatient. What I want to say to you is this: did you
ever know an innocent man suffer? Of course not! It's people
who sin that experience trouble like this, not righteous people.

'I know I'm right because I've had this vision: God has
spoken to me. He came to me and asked, "Can a mortal man
be found righteous in the presence of God?" All men are sinful,
including you, Job, and that's why you are suffering the way
you are.

'Don't be angry: seek the Lord and he will forgive you.
Humble yourself before him. Learn to see suffering as disci-
pline from God. And if you do that you will be really blessed.
You know that I'm right in all of this.'

Eliphaz as a counsellor

Eliphaz comes across as a man of great wisdom, but of little
compassion. It is hard not to be deeply touched by the heart-
rending cries of Job in chapter 3. To hear a man wish he had
not been born must surely be emotionally heart-rending. Yet,
Eliphaz is unmoved. He is interested only in theological
reflection. Job has bared his soul; Eliphaz is interested only in
the philosophy of suffering. Would-be counsellors, who hope
to be of some help to those suffering from bereavement and
pain, must learn to empathize and listen.

Yet, we must not be too hard on Eliphaz. He is the most
sympathetic of the three counsellors at the ash-heap. His
acceptance of Job's essential piety is to his credit. And we have
to face it: counselling the depressed is difficult: 'The first rule
of ministry to people who are depressed is that you will almost

certainly get it wrong.'⁵ He could have launched into a tirade
of rebuke at the extravagance of Job's reaction. He did not, and
deserves the credit. His cool, calculated response may well
lack compassion and warmth, and under the circumstances his
counselling technique — especially as a friend — ought to
have been different. But as we shall see, it could have been
worse — much, much worse!

Specifically, the problem with Eliphaz's contribution lies
in two directions. In the first place, *it lacks sensitivity and
compassion.* He accuses Job of being a sinner (4:7-8): suggests
he is responsible for his children's death (5:4), implies that he
is a fool (5:2) and charges Job with a lack of spiritual submission to God (5:8).

This, in fact, is a feature of all of Job's friends. As Jay
Adams points out, 'They refused to listen to Job when he
protested that their assumptions and [therefore] their conclusions were wrong. They failed to follow the biblical maxim
that leads to successful counselling: "Love believes all
things." In love, the biblical counsellor doubts the word of the
counsellee *only when the facts demand that he do so.'*⁶ Adams
goes on to point out that in starting with their own assumptions
and doubting Job's insistence that he was telling the truth, they
went on to commit a third error: they failed to uncover Job's
real problem and, therefore, could not help him with it. Instead
of providing the very help that Job needed they succeeded only
in aggravating the situation.

As a counsellor, Eliphaz is 'inept'.⁷ He fails to empathize
with Job in his excruciating pain and grief. He is altogether too
cold, too calculating, too callous. By suggesting as he does that
Job is ultimately responsible for the death of his children
(5:4,24), Eliphaz discloses a heart made of flint. We are to
mourn with those who mourn (Rom. 12:15).

In the second place, Eliphaz discloses a classic error of
misapplying a rigid theological system. This is not a criticism

of creeds, or a theological system. Eliphaz's theology was accurate and in the main we can have no argument with it. His error lies in the use he made of it. His system did not take into account the possibility that Job was 'innocent' — not that he was sinless (Job never claimed any such thing), but that he had not committed any particular sin which explained the reason for the severity of this judgement.

Eliphaz had no room in his system for the story, as recorded in John 9, of the man born blind. In answer to the query of the disciples as to who had sinned, the man or his parents, Jesus said it was neither. The reason for his suffering lay in another direction altogether. It had nothing to do with the man's past, but everything to do with his future. He had been born blind in order that the works of God might be made manifest in him, and thereby have an effect upon generations of people who would read the story and profit from it. He suffered not for any sin of his own, or any inherited guilt resulting from the sin of another; he suffered in order to bring a blessing to someone else. When we are broken up into little pieces, it is that each piece may become food for others to feed on. The ravages I am now suffering may fit me to be a channel of blessing for someone else. Death may be at work in us, in order that life may be produced in someone else (cf. 2 Cor. 4:12). Of this, Eliphaz knew nothing. His theological system was inadequate. His arrogance is thereby revealed, for he was not as wise as he thought himself to be. Those who aggressively point out theological deficiencies in others must learn this lesson: that it is possible to be perfectly sound in theology and have a heart that is as cold as ice.

We need to keep on reminding ourselves of something of which Job himself knew nothing: that the reason for his suffering lies with the account of the battle between God and Satan as recorded in the opening chapters. The battle raged on the issue, 'What will Job do when trouble comes?' All that

Eliphaz sees is: 'What has Job done to bring this crisis upon himself?' Eliphaz is correct in confronting Job — showing sympathy does not mean that sinful responses are not challenged. But his challenge is misdirected and dangerous. Eliphaz is a dangerous man who speaks the truth at the wrong time and in the wrong spirit.

5.
'Lord, I want to die'

Please read Job 6 - 7

Job's response to Eliphaz

Grief passes through a number of more or less predictable stages and Job's responses are, even today, regarded as fairly normal. First, there was *silence* (ch. 2), followed by a period of intense *questioning*, closely allied to *depression* (ch. 3). Here, in chapters 6 and 7, Job shows passionate *anger and frustration*. He is incensed, his anger fuelled by Eliphaz's ineptitude. He feels betrayed by a friend. Eliphaz's contribution has been insipid, like **'tasteless food'**, or **'the white of an egg'** (6:6). Eliphaz has failed to show even basic human sympathy (6:14-15). But Job shows no desire to argue with Eliphaz. In the main he ignores what his counsellor has said.

He begins by insisting that his initial outburst (ch. 3) was fully justified (6:2-7). Having wished that he had not been born, he now wants to die immediately (6:8-10). Next comes a section in which he expresses his disappointment with his friends (6:11-23). They have failed to show him any sympathy. He issues a challenge to them to speak straightforwardly (6:24-30). Finally, Job addresses God. Since he has no strength to hold on to, he wonders if God might just desert him, leave him alone to live the rest of his days free from pain (7:1-21). 'But there is more to this than meets the eye; for in the very act of begging God to desert him he is in fact approaching him.'[1]

'May God strike me dead!' (6:1-10)

It sounds flippant, of course, but that is because we fail to see
how Job meant what he said!

> **Oh, that I might have my request,**
> **that God would grant what I hope for,**
> **that God would be willing to crush me,**
> **to let loose his hand and cut me off!**
>
> (6:8-9).

For God, Job's death would be as simple an act as snipping a
piece of thread! And why does Job wish for death? Because he
is frightened that if the pain goes on he is going to say
something that he will regret — and to deny **'the words of the
Holy One'** (6:10) is something he wants to avoid at all costs.
Better to die now than blaspheme against God. On this level,
Job's call for God to strike him dead is an expression of his
piety, not irreverent flippancy!

Job admits his words in chapter 3 may well have been
'impetuous' (6:2), but they must be reckoned in proportion to
the immeasurable burden that he now carries. God is set
against him: it is a war and God is a chariot-riding archer (6:4).
The arrows that pierce his body are poisoned! In this sense at
least, Job shares Eliphaz's theology that God's arrows of
judgement are set against him. He feels the right to bray and
bellow like a wild animal that has been wounded (6:5-6).

'You are of no help' (6:11-30)

Eliphaz has called on Job to be patient, but Job complains that
he has no **'strength'** (6:11), all his resources are spent (6:12-
13). Job accuses his friends of lacking in **'kindness'** (6:14).

They are as ineffective as a wadi stream — empty when you
need water, but then, suddenly, too full with water from a
storm that just as quickly disappears again (6:15-21). **'Now
you too have proved to be of no help'** (6:21).

Job is angry now.[2] His grief has taken on a new shape, as it
often does. When the realization of the past sinks in, silence
gives way to feelings of resentment, and often these are vented
on those nearest at hand, particularly those from whom he
expects 'devotion' or loyalty (6:14). They fear that if they
identify with Job too closely they, too, will come under God's
judgement. So they keep their distance, treating Job as they
would someone who asked them for a loan! (6:22). In a
moment of poignancy, Job asks his friends merely to point out
the crime of which he is supposed to be guilty. That will keep
him quiet (6:24). They (thus far, Eliphaz) have treated him as
a 'windbag'! (6:26). Had they been in Job's position they
would have behaved worse. They have no right to take on the
rôle of counsellors.

**'I prefer strangling and death, rather than this body of
mine'** (7:1-16)

Job now turns from his friends to God. He is angry, bitter and
complains a lot. He suggests two reasons why God should **'let
[him] alone'** (7:16).

1. The misery of his life (7:1-5)

His life is no better than that of the workman who longs for the
shift to end that he may rest, or the hard campaign endured by
a soldier who longs for the battle to be over that he might return
to his family (7:1). And when he gets home, the nights provide
no solace, for he finds that he cannot sleep (7:4).

2. The brevity of his life (7:6-10).

'My days are swifter than a weaver's shuttle' (7:6); **'My life is but a breath'** (7:7); **'As a cloud vanishes and is gone, so he who goes down to the grave does not return'** (7:9). And in addition to the seeming futility of life, his scabs now appear to be festering with pus (7:5).

Job ponders the attention being given him. Why should God single him out? Is he a threat to the Almighty? Does Job's existence intimidate the universe? God treats him like one of the **'monster[s] of the deep'** (7:12) that need to be kept muzzled lest they break loose and cause some terrible chaos.[3]

'What is man?' (7:17-21)

The final verses of chapter 7 sound a bit like Psalm 8, but it is in the form of a 'bitter parody.'[4] Instead of expressing wonder that the Almighty takes such care of so seemingly insignificant a creature as man, Job is angry that man has become the object of his scrutiny and, yes, it has now to be said, cruelty, even sadism. Job seems to be aware of an evil eye upon him and he cries out to God to leave him alone (7:14-16). His words become wild. In effect, he says, 'If I have sinned, what harm have I done? You are too big to be hurt by a puny little thing like me; and in any case since I am a burden to you and to myself, why not be done with me?' What Job, of course, does not know is that there are more powerful creatures to be restrained than mythological sea creatures. Satan has challenged God's order. He needs to be put down. In Job's suffering, God's honour is at stake. 'In Job's temptation the stability of the universe was under attack — as the "sons of God" could have told Job — by the real "dragon" (cf. Rev.

20:2) of whom the mythical sea monster was a paganized version. The angels saw the world trembling with every tremor of Job's spirit. For if the redemptive power of God could not preserve Job in the fear of God, not only Job but the world was lost to satanic chaos.'[5]

Job insists that his outbursts, whilst 'impetuous' (6:3), are justified. He has expressed a wish to die. His friends have so far proved fickle and disappointing. The evil eye that Job perceives at the close of chapter 7 is not that of God, as Job suggests, but the devil! It is Satan who has been given power to harm him. Satan will give Job no sleep, no rest, no peace. His pressure is relentless. When Job thinks it is the Lord who hounds him so, he is mistaken. Satan is masquerading as God, for he longs for us to blame the Lord, and not him, for the evil he does in this world.

This is a message that we need to hear again and again. Paul warned the Ephesians that we ignore Satan's devices at our peril (Eph. 6:10-18). Peter was more blunt, seeing Satan as a roaring lion prowling about in order to devour us (1 Peter 5:8). He had himself experienced Satan's sharp teeth in his flesh, and but for the Saviour's intercession, he would not have recovered (cf. Luke 22:32).

A summary of Job's reply

'You accuse me of impatience, but look at what I'm going through. God has wounded me. All I want is to be allowed to die.

'But I want you to know one thing: I have not denied God or rejected my faith. You should be trying to help me; instead your words sound like treachery. If I have sinned as you say, then I want God to show me what I have done. I cannot tell you what it is. I just wish you had a little more compassion. I'm suffering for no good reason that I know and I am not going to keep quiet about it.

'Lord, if I have sinned, why do you not just forgive me?'

Job's anger

Job feels that the world is against him, his friends are against him and God is against him. He is at the end of his tether; his life is passing away in futility. His words become wild.

In one sense, there is little point in analysing the words of an angry man in too much detail. Job will himself regret some of his outbursts at the end. Anger is a basic instinct and as such, in the right circumstances, is a necessary valve for releasing tension. Paul urges the Ephesians to be angry — but at the same time to be careful that they do not sin (Eph. 4:26). 'God is a just judge, and God is angry with the wicked every day' (Ps. 7:11). God's wrath is an expression of his anger, and Calvary is its most solemn expression. It was the righteous anger of God upon sin that caused Christ to cry, 'My God, my God, why...?' And above all else, the Word of God reveals that the Lord Jesus was angry. In driving out the money-changers from the temple, zeal (righteous anger) was said to have 'consumed him', or 'eaten him up' (John 2:17). And Mark informs us specifically that he turned on the Pharisees 'in anger' (Mark 3:5).

But anger is difficult to control. We are not to be bad-tempered. James gives us salutary advice: 'But the wisdom that comes from heaven is first of all pure; then peace-loving, considerate, submissive, full of mercy and good fruit, impartial and sincere' (James 3:17). Anger must not be allowed to get out of control. Modern psychiatry encourages the free expression of verbal and physical anger as a means of therapy. Scripture, however, is full of warnings as to the effect of such a course. Ten proverbial sayings prove the point:

A fool vents all his feelings,
    but a wise man holds them back

                           (Prov. 29:11).

Whoever has no rule over his own spirit
    is like a city broken down, without walls

                           (Prov. 25:28).

The discretion of a man makes him slow to anger,
    and his glory is to overlook a transgression

                           (Prov. 19:11).

Do you see a man hasty in his words?
    There is more hope for a fool than for him

                           (Prov. 29:20).

An angry man stirs up strife,
    and a furious man abounds in transgression

                           (Prov. 29:22).

He who is quick-tempered acts foolishly,
    and a man of wicked intentions is hated

                           (Prov. 14:17).

He who is slow to wrath has great understanding,
    but he who is impulsive exalts folly

                           (Prov. 14:29).

A wrathful man stirs up strife,
    but he who is slow to anger allays contention

                           (Prov. 15:18).

A man of great wrath will suffer punishment;
    for if you deliver him, you will have to do it again

                           (Prov. 19:19).

> Make no friendship with an angry man,
>   and with a furious man do not go
> lest you learn his ways
>   and set a snare for your soul
>
>   (Prov. 22:24-25).

Job was angry for at least three reasons:

1. Job felt the loss of his dignity

Job has spoken of his condition as worse than that of a slave. Sleeplessness has added to his agitation. He feels victimized. His life seems to have little point to it. His body is racked with pain. His open, dirty sores are a constant reminder of his loss of dignity.

When a woman in her early fifties, in the peak of health, is struck down with debilitating Alzheimer's disease, robbing her of her long-term memory, she feels that every trace of her dignity is gone. When a man in approaching his retirement, having prepared for it and looked forward to it, is smitten with a stroke, rendering him unable to speak, feed himself, or perform the essential necessities of life without aid, he feels that his dignity has been taken away. 'Why me?' Job says (cf. 7:20). And we can understand why he asks it.

2. Job felt that his life was futile

Job's life is passing away more quickly than he ever imagined. There is no point in planning for the future. Indeed, his entire earthly existence now seems to have little point. It would be better for God to end his life, rather than torment him like this. 'Mercifully, God does not answer such prayers.'[6]

3. Job feels unfairly treated

Job has cried, 'I will not keep silent' any more (7:11); 'Let me alone' (7:16); 'What have I done to you?' (7:20). Towards the end of this speech he says something quite extraordinary. Like a child who is angry with its parents and storms out, Job seems to say, 'You'll be sorry when I'm gone!' (7:21). He is bruised, his relationship with God under severe strain, and he throws out one final retort to the Almighty. Knowing that God essentially cares, Job says, 'You'll be sorry when I'm gone.' Despite all that is happening to him, Job still thinks of God as one who loves him, else he would not be angry. Despite the pain, the indignity, the unanswered questions, there is a relationship between the two that Job is still conscious of — even in the darkness of his soul's present condition.

The devil is attacking Job. He is attacking his mind with doubt. He feels his days of service are finished. He longs for death. Matthew Henry says, 'Job is begging God to ease him or end him.'[7] And there is just the hint of self-pity emerging. The hardest lesson to learn is that God alone can determine what is best for us. Only he sees the beginning from the end. He is the only one who knows what it is going to take to conform each one of his children to the image of his Son. And he will spare nothing in accomplishing that goal. Self-pity, like some obnoxious salesman, keeps attempting to get in the door. To keep the door shut and bolted is what we are asked to do. If Job found it beyond him, we too will need to call upon God for strength to help us — a strength that is readily available 'to help us in our time of need' (Heb. 4:16).

6.
'Where there's smoke there's fire!'

Please read Job 8

Bildad's first speech

'Bildad the Shuhite' (8:1) takes Eliphaz's argument a step
further. Whereas Eliphaz had shown a little kindness in his
remarks, Bildad is not afraid to be blunt. Words like 'analytical', 'superficial' and 'clinical' are used to describe him. He is
a 'traditionalist', 'entirely wedded to the past', 'a moralist' for
whom everything is either black or white. Suffering is punishment, and the death of Job's children is proof of it! Eliphaz had
shown some acceptance of Job's righteous character. Job was
suffering for those sins which humans cannot avoid. Bildad,
however, does not accept Job's claim to innocence. 'There is
no smoke without fire,' is Bildad's working hypothesis. Job's
tragic condition speaks of a crime and if Job only searches his
conscience, he will discover what it is.

Like Eliphaz, Bildad shows no compassion whatsoever for
his friend. He simply ignores Job's plea for understanding and
sympathy. High on Bildad's order of priorities is to defend
God's just character. Bildad has detected in Job's outbursts a
criticism of God's handling of affairs and he is incensed.
Instead of appealing to a vision, as Eliphaz had done, Bildad
appeals to tradition for a defence of his position. In what is
meant to be a closing word of encouragement, Bildad adds that

in any case, if Job is innocent, as he insists, he will not die. His speech may be summarized under two headings.

'The death of your children says that you must be guilty' (8:1-7)

Bildad is even less polite than Eliphaz (who at least began by kind words about Job's integrity, even if they did carry sarcastic overtones). Job is a 'windbag': **'Your words are a blustering wind'**! (8:2). All three of Job's friends presuppose Job's guilt, yet there are subtle differences between them. Whereas Eliphaz extolled God's holiness (cf. 4:7-9), Bildad's emphasis lies on God's justice: **'Does God pervert justice? Does the Almighty pervert what is right?'** he asks (8:3). If Job would only look to God, he would be restored to his **'rightful place'** (8:6).

For Bildad everything is so utterly simple and straightforward: we get what we deserve. Those who prosper in this world do so because they are righteous. Those who suffer do so because they are wicked. There appear to be no exceptions to this simple rule. And even a fool can point out its inadequacy, for there are exceptionally wicked people who do very well in this world. It was, as must be pointed out many times in the course of this book, something that bothered the psalmist no end: 'For I envied the arrogant when I saw the prosperity of the wicked' (Ps. 73:3).

'Job, it is a simple matter of cause and effect!' (8:8-22)

Bildad appeals to a long line of godly ancestors to prove his assertion that God always acts justly (8:8-10). Wickedness inherits its own reward (8:9-13; cf. Eliphaz's perception in 4:8:

'You reap what you sow'). Wickedness, like a spider's web (8:14), or a plant (8:16), is a fragile thing and soon destroyed.

So 'Cheer up, Job, everything is going to turn out fine in the end!' (8:20-22).

A summary of Bildad's first speech

'You're blowing hot air again! Is God ever unjust? It's like this: if your sons were to blame, they have paid for it when their house fell on them and killed them; if you are innocent, as you insist, God will deliver you.

'Take a lesson from history: people who sin perish; those who transgress are punished. God doesn't reject the righteous, nor does he maintain evildoers.

'Look, seek the Lord and everything will turn out fine in the end.'

The justice of God

Job, in his anger, had cried out that his suffering was unfair. By drawing attention to God's justice, Bildad has now made things worse for Job, for he cannot see that he has committed any sin in proportion to the judgement that has now come upon him. In comparison with what he perceives in others, far more openly sinful than he, God's justice seems grossly unfair. Bildad cannot take this. Without any of the niceties of Eliphaz's opening speech, Bildad weighs in with an accusation that Job is nothing but a windbag (countering something Job had himself suggested about his friends, see 6:26). The sooner Job shuts up and starts acknowledging what his friends are telling him, the better!

Bildad's main thesis is that God never perverts (twists, bends, makes crooked) what is right (8:3). The word he uses can also suggest 'to falsify a weight' (Amos 8:5), or make a path crooked (Eccles. 1:15; 7:13). What Bildad means is that God allows no one to suffer who does not deserve it. Eliphaz and Bildad operate a theology of 'cash-register justice'.[1] Suffering is, without exception, brought upon those who are guilty of transgression. There is no other reason for pain in our lives.

There are aspects of what Bildad says which are perfectly true.

Firstly, *those who kept the covenant could expect to be blessed*: 'Carefully follow the terms of this covenant, so that you may prosper in everything you do' (Deut. 29:9; cf. Exod. 23:22). This blessing did not, of course depend on perfect obedience. When Israel sinned, God had laid down a pattern of sacrifices to offer (including a broken and contrite heart) as the way of obedience. But it is undeniable that there were blessings for those who followed God's way, and these blessings took the form of knowing that one belonged to God's chosen people (Deut. 28:1,9-10); freedom from war with surrounding nations (Deut. 28:7); and material prosperity (Deut. 28:3-6,8,11-12).

A crude interpretation of these passages might suggest that the godly people of the Old Testament knew extraordinary times of physical prosperity. But this is evidently not the case. To suppose that would be to fly in the face of what actually happened. Abraham, for example, is singled out as a self-evidently righteous man. Yet, he did not possess so much as a square inch of land in Israel. When it came to burying his wife, Sarah, he was forced to purchase a plot for the task. And as for Israel, she was never the most prosperous nation on earth. Her history included bondage in Egypt, forty years in the wilderness, generations of trouble with the Philistines, conquests by Assyria and Babylon and subjugation by Greece and Rome. Clearly, the blessings of which the covenant spoke were of a higher dimension than wealth and health. Indeed, the godly may enjoy the highest reaches of covenant blessings — union and communion with God — whilst at the same time knowing wracking pain and discomfort in the 'outer man'. For Job to plead with God for a reward as an incentive to keep on fearing him would, in any case, be to accede to Satan's original accusation: 'Does Job fear God for nothing?' (1:9). For Satan, and seemingly for Job's comforters, walking with God through pain is not possible.

Secondly, when the godly appealed to God's justice, as they often did in the Old Testament, it was with a view to assuring them that *God would not forsake them in their hour of need*. We find, for example, that the psalmists frequently appeal to God's justice as a source of confidence:

Answer me when I call to you,
    O my righteous God.
Give me relief from my distress;
    be merciful to me and hear my prayer

(Ps. 4:1).

Vindicate me in your righeousness, O Lord my God

(Ps. 35:24).

O Lord, hear my prayer,
    listen to my cry for mercy;
in your faithfulness and righteousness
    come to my relief

(Ps. 143:1).

Nor is this confined to the Old Testament. Paul drew the same confidence when he defined the gospel in terms, not of the grace of God, but of its *righteousness*: 'I am not ashamed of the gospel, because it is the power of God for the salvation of everyone who believes: first for the Jew, then for the

Gentile. For in the gospel a righteousness from God is revealed, a righteousness that is by faith from first to last, just as
it is written: "The righteous will live by faith"' (Rom. 1:16-
17); 'Grace [reigns] through righteousness' (Rom. 5:21).
Paul's confidence lay in the fact that God had provided the
righteousness necessary for acquittal. And having received it
by faith, Paul was assured of it for ever. It is exactly the same
thought in 1 John 1:9: 'If we confess our sins, he is faithful and
just [righteous] to forgive us our sins and to cleanse us from all
unrighteousness.' Calvary makes it mandatory that God
should bless his people! Every threat contained in the covenant, the wrath which every violation deserves, is met by
Christ. Jesus was made a curse for us. He endured the anathema of the covenant. The covenant threat (that those who sin
will die) was extinguished in him.

God's justice is a source of blessing! But Bildad applied the
rule crassly and materialistically.

A formula that knows no exceptions

If Eliphaz had hinted that Job was responsible for the death of
his children (5:3-4), Bildad tries another tack: they died
because they themselves had sinned. There is some circum-
stantial evidence to back up his claim: they were at a party at
the time of their death, and Job himself felt the need to offer,
as priest and father, a sin-offering on their behalf for fear that
'Perhaps my children have sinned and cursed God' (1:5).
God's just way means that there are no exceptions for Bildad:
sin receives its due punishment immediately: **'Does God
subvert judgement? Or does the Almighty pervert justice?'** (8:3).

A rigid application of a truth, which prevents the possibility
of exceptions, or broader analyses of the situation, is a dangerous and cruel line to take. Bildad is a man who has got hold of

half of the truth and has made it into the whole truth. It is always a mistake to do that, and always damaging.

Most of us can take personal injury better than injury to our children. A natural, built-in parental instinct takes over when folk abuse our children. To hurt them causes us more pain than anything inflicted on us personally. Bildad's arrogant, aggressive stance consigns Job's children to perdition. They died in sin and because of sin. Even if it was true, Bildad, in drawing attention to it, shows gross tactlessness.

The appeal to tradition

In an age which idolizes the latest fashions, an appeal to tradition is no bad thing. To say, 'But it has always been this way,' can often be a means of introducing sanity into an otherwise disorientated, confused jungle of ideas. Bildad picks up Job's despair as to the brevity of his life (7:6) and says, **'We were born only yesterday, and know nothing'** (8:9). It is an appeal to the past, to the long-standing tradition of another era.

There is something inherently irritating and arrogant about older folk who belittle the experiences of the young with a withering remark: 'You know nothing, son.' Bildad is like the man of the world, the man who has experienced a bit of life, to whom the wisdom of the ages has been handed down and who is dismissive of anything that the young have to say. There is something artificial about Bildad's faith. It is theoretical and 'borrowed'.[2]

Bildad's case from tradition follows three lines.

1. The papyrus

Taking Job's protestations of innocence (7:20), Bildad argues his case from 'a papyrus parable'. A papyrus may grow up overnight without water. It looks green and fresh, but it soon withers and dies in the heat of the sun. Bildad is pointing now at Job and saying, as in Jesus' parable of the soils, that the word has fallen on stony ground (8:13). Job may have started well, but he has failed to finish the race. Job cannot be sure of his own salvation and the way he has responded to his suffering has proved his hypocrisy.

The spider's web

In another parable, Bildad compares Job's protestations to a spider's web. Webs are intended to be stretched by small creatures, not six-foot tall human beings! A web's fragility proves that it is foolish to lean your weight on it. Job's reliance on his innocence is equally fragile. He cannot be as innocent as he claims and Bildad has seen, in his wisdom, that no sooner has Job leant on it than it has broken.

The gourd

Bildad's third line of argument comes from a parable of the gourd, **'a well-watered plant in the sunshine'** (8:16). Anyone who has tried to get rid of a tree too close to the house by simply sawing it down to ground level will know that it has the frustrating habit of sending up shoots again. Its roots remain alive in the soil beneath. This gourd (or 'vine'³) leaves no roots once it dies. No tell-tale shoots will appear to remind us that it once existed. Bildad is now making his most cruel attack of all. Job had made the plaintive remark at the close of chapter 7 that God would miss him when he was gone. It was his parting shot in an attempt to shame the Almighty into treating him better! Bildad cruelly suggests that once he dies, no one will recall his existence — not even God! What faith Job had is systematically attacked.

The traditionalist has spoken. Bildad's cold, analytical, insensitive application of the justice of God has allowed for no possibility that Job may be innocent and still suffer. God's justice demands that he must be guilty. That Job could be suffering *for the sake of others*, to help not himself as such, but others who find themselves caught up in trouble, is a concept outside Bildad's theological system. As such, the doctrine of the cross would be anathema to Bildad. For a righteous man to suffer in the place of others would, for Bildad, make God unjust. Bildad's theology, though sound in its beginnings, ends up denying the possibility of salvation!

As a counsellor, Bildad's methods are cruel in the extreme. For Bildad, Job is nothing but a Pharisee, a whitewashed sepulchre, a hypocrite. That is the unkindest cut of all!

7.
A place to scream

Please read Job 9 - 10

Job's response to Bildad

I have read somewhere of a doctor who thinks that every hospital should have a 'screaming room' — a place where the anger involved in grief and pain can be expressed. Job is longing to scream. It is the scream of someone in anger and despair.

Job's grief process reaches another stage here. We have already noted in response to Eliphaz's speech how Job moved on from silence, to questioning, to depression and to anger. Now he slides into despair. Job feels powerless and trapped. He has in addition a sense of being persecuted by God, that God is not merely watching him, but watching him with the intent of fastening guilt upon him. Death seems the best option and, in Job's view, it cannot be a long way off. If only God would leave him alone for the last few days of his life, so that he might die in peace, free from his burdens and pain! Job is at the point of expressing certain views about God that normally he would not even dare to think. Pain does that.

'How can a mortal be righteous before God?' (9:1-3)

Bildad's theological system was essentially devoid of any notion of grace on God's part. Blessings are merely rewards for good behaviour. And Job has seen through it. Yet, as far as Job's neighbours are concerned, their immovable opinion of Job by now is that he must be a terrible sinner. The only way he can be vindicated in their eyes is by a restoration of all his wealth and health. When Job now asks, **'But how can a mortal be righteous before God?'** (9:2), he is not asking the question Paul asked about justification. Paul asked how a *sinner* can be declared righteous with God. Job, on the other hand, is asking how a *righteous* person can be justified ('vindicated') before God. It is not his sense of sin that is uppermost in Job's mind at this point, but his sense of being in the right. He has done nothing wrong (at least not so wrong as to merit this calamity). And more and more Job wants to be vindicated in this matter. He wants his day in court with God so that he may prove that he has not committed the kind of sin that deserves the suffering he now endures.

Job is far too conscious of how small and insignificant he is in himself to defend his cause now in the courtroom of the Almighty. Previously the thought of God's transcendence had led him to ask why God should bother to afflict a frail man. Now the same thought leads him to ask why should a frail man such as Job contend with the Almighty? There is no point to it. Job has lost the sense of God's loving-kindness. God is an adversary. Satan has succeeded for the moment in making God out to be Job's enemy.

But Satan has not won — not yet: Job has not cursed God; nor will he.

The incomprehensibility of God (9:4-13)

Job's request will be granted him, for in time God will speak to Job directly. But it will not be the occasion that Job thinks it will be. For God provides no explanation for Job's suffering.

Rather he bids him yield to it, acknowledging as he does so that God is just in all that he does.

To underline the futility of arguing with God, Job alludes to God's limitless wisdom and the vastness of his power (9:4), illustrating it by references to feats of power over mountains, earthquakes and light (9:5-6). **'Who has resisted him and come out unscathed?'** (9:4), Job concludes.

Four features of God's innate sovereignty are described. Essentially God is *incomprehensible*: **'He performs wonders that cannot be fathomed, miracles that cannot be counted'** (9:10). This is a theme we shall return to often in our study of the book of Job. It is a key that unlocks its meaning. Job never is given a full explanation for his trial. Instead, he is asked to submit to God in humble acquiescence, trusting that the Lord will look after him. As Calvin points out, there are two attitudes one can adopt to God's justice (something to which, we recall, Bildad has drawn attention): 'One says, "God is just; for He punishes men according to what they have deserved." The other says, "God is just; for, irrespective of how He treats men, we must keep our mouths shut and not murmur against Him, because we can gain nothing by it."'[1] What Job (and we ourselves) must learn is that 'We must acknowledge the incomprehensible majesty of God.'[2]

Not only is God incomprehensible; he is also *invisible*. Moses was unable to see God's 'face' at Sinai, seeing only a glimpse of God's back as his glory passed by (Exod. 33:22-23). Elijah had a similar experience (1 Kings 19:12-13). 'The nearest encounter Job can have with God is a hurried passing by of a figure he cannot see or recognize':[3] **'When he passes me, I cannot see him; when he goes by, I cannot perceive him'** (9:11).

If God is incomprehensible and invisible, he is also *unaccountable*: **'Who can say to him, "What are you doing?"'** (9:12). God has no need to answer anyone but himself. 'But who are you, O man, to talk back to God? "Shall what is formed say to him who formed it, 'Why did you make me like this?'" Does not the potter have the right to make out of the same lump of clay some pottery for noble purposes and some for common use?' (Rom. 9:20-21). 'It is not for men to plead with God,' says Calvin somewhat quaintly, 'for they shall but lose time.'[4]

God is also *unrestrainable*: **'God does not restrain his anger; even the cohorts of Rahab cowered at his feet'** (9:13; cf. 26:12). If God desires to show his anger, no one is in a position to prevent him. Rahab, like Leviathan (3:8; 41:1), was a creature of the sea. Paganism believed that Rahab fought a great battle with God at creation.[5] Job alludes to mythology to underline that nothing, real or imaginary, poses any kind of threat to God's powers. He really is sovereign, no matter from which vantage-point we consider it. How can a puny creature like Job make any impression at all on one so powerful and mighty?

Job feels as though every aspect of God's being is now *against* him. God has withdrawn and in his misery Job feels desperately lonely. No one understands him. There is no one to sympathize, to put their arms around him and comfort him. These are words of utter despair.

'How then can I dispute with God?' (9:14-35)

Job feels trapped. He insists that he is essentially innocent, but no one is prepared to listen to him. His friends are arguing on a different plane altogether. And God is so powerful and majestic, Job feels it impossible to gain a hearing. In a moment of anguish, he declares, **'Even if I summoned him and he responded, I do not believe he would give me a hearing'** (9:16). This is, of course, not true. Satan has deceived Job about God. He has once again told lies about the character of the Almighty. He has, as he did in Eden, impugned God with false accusations about God's intentions.

Job would like to bring God to court and have him declare to the world that Job is 'Not guilty'. In a contest with God's justice or power, God wins hands down: **'If it is a matter of strength, he is mighty! And if it is a matter of justice, who will summon him?'** (9:19). But such is Job's terror at the prospect that he is convinced he would make a mess of it and speak in an improper way (9:20).

Pain distorts our minds. Job seems to lurch from moments of confidence to moments of sheer terror. The depths of his despair as he contemplates talking to God in court reach an altogether low point when he declares that God disposes of the wicked and the righteous in the same way: **'It is all the same; that is why I say, "He destroys both the blameless and the wicked"'** (9:22). Job is wrong, of course. That the wicked as well as the righteous die is not in dispute. But what Job fails to comprehend here, but states majestically elsewhere (19:25-27), is that even in death, God keeps a hold of his own people. Pain has robbed him of his assurance here. It is a lesson we need to bear in mind when counselling the sick and hurting: in their torment, they can often reason irrationally and contrary to the way they actually think.

'What is the point of it all?' As the pain gets worse, Job convinces himself that God does not care — that God isn't even sympathetic! These are notions bordering on blasphemy, but we have all thought them in times of spiritual depression. We only have to think of how honest the psalmist could be to remind ourselves of what we are capable of thinking:

I remembered you, O God, and I groaned;
    I mused and my spirit grew faint...
Has God forgotten to be merciful?
                                            (Ps. 77:3,9).

So what can poor Job do? There are some options to consider. First, he could try a little self-hypnosis. He can tell himself that his wounds do not itch, that the pain he feels deep down in his soul is just an illusion. **'If I say, "I will forget my complaint, I will change my expression, and smile"'** (9:27).⁶ According to Rogers and Hammerstein, 'Whenever I feel afraid, I hold my head erect and whistle a little tune, so no one will suspect I'm afraid!' The notion is about as sensible as inane smiles on the faces of pained and hurting Christians who are forced into expressions of behaviour totally contrary to their personalities. There are times when smiles just will not do, and this was one of them.

A second thought occurs to Job: he could engage in a ritual declaration of his innocence. He mentions washing his hands (9:30), a well-known ritual means of purification and a symbolic declaration of innocence (Deut. 21:6; Ps. 26:6; 73:13). It was the supreme act of Pilate at the trial of Jesus Christ (Matt. 27:24). And what would God do to Job, clean and fresh from his aromatic bath? Plunge him into a cesspool of filth so that his very clothes would shun the stench of his naked body! (9:31).

All that is left to Job is the courtroom! But how can he even speak to God? The answer lies in an arbitrator: **'If only there were someone to arbitrate between us, to lay his hand upon us both'** (9:33). In every possible way, Job feels at a distance from God. God's majesty has towered over him, making him feel small and insignificant. God's justice further threatened any attempt at a meeting of minds. If only there was some means of making contact! God cannot be argued with, as two lawyers of roughly equal standing might argue in a court of law. The only way for this to become at all possible is by the provision of a mediator.

This is the answer to Job's problem, if only he would grasp it. But the pain is too severe, the hurt inside too bitter. Job can only retreat again into despair and further irrational thoughts.

'I will say what I think' (10:1-22)

Job's speech now descends, having reached a climax at the close of the ninth chapter with a desire for an arbitrator. Since no such person was available, Job sinks into further despair. Two elements now appear as Job, insisting on his right to say what is on his mind (10:1), speaks directly to God.

First, Job *insists that the charges against him be read out* in a formal manner (10:2).

Second, in the guise of a courtroom lawyer, *he interrogates the Almighty* with a series of searching questions. Has God taken any delight in Job's downfall? (10:3). Has God misread the facts? Does he not see Job's innocence? (10:4). Has God failed to catch the guilty, taking it out on Job instead? (10:5-6). Does the Creator destroy his creation, even when he has expended such skill in its making? (10:8-17). Has God really made Job with such singular care and providence, only to stalk him like a lion for no good reason? Is Job in the grip of a God who is angry and determined to make Job his target, whether he is guilty or innocent? This is what Job now thinks.

There are no answers: just an empty silence. Job longs that God's attention be diverted from him. He just wants to be left alone. **'Turn away from me,'** he pleads (10:20).

A summary of Job's reply

'I agree with you, up to a point. God does not give his blessing to evildoers. But how can anyone be right with God? You cannot argue with him and win. Even if I was right I could not argue with the Almighty. I would still have to ask for mercy. And even if God did answer me, I wouldn't believe it. He would just give me more of the same. That's why I think this is so unjust. I say I'm innocent; he says I'm guilty — so what's the point?

'Sometimes I try to tell myself to cheer up, just forget the pain. But the pain is getting worse. It's so relentless. I'm losing this battle. I could bear it, if he took away the pain. I think then I could talk more rationally.

'I hate my life! I just want to know why God is so angry with me, that's all. Is that so much to ask? I have searched my own heart, but I cannot come up with the answer in myelf.

'Lord, you made me. Are you now going to destroy me? Why didn't you do it long ago if this is the case?'

Job's need of a mediator

One feature has now emerged in Job's quest for an answer to the problem of his suffering. Only the presence of a mediator can help Job in his plight: one as powerful as God and as compassionate and understanding as a true friend. If Job is going to make any progress at all he needs to find one, a go-between, who can bring together parties which at present are not in communication. If there is to be a meeting of minds, someone who can maintain the interests of both needs to intervene — someone whom both God and Job implicitly trust.

Moses was such a man, for he spoke to Israel on God's behalf at the giving of the law (Exod. 20:18-21; Gal. 3:19), and to God on Israel's behalf when Israel sinned (Exod. 32:9 - 33:17). But Job needs a mediator, not because he has sinned and is therefore estranged from God. He needs someone who can sympathize with his aches and pains. He needs one who has stood where Job has stood.

What Job is looking for is a 'go-between', an 'arbitrator', someone to negotiate between two parties in a dispute. The concept is familiar in modern industrial and international negotiations. The pattern that calls for his services goes something like this: things get tense; both sides feel the lack of common ground for continuing discussion; one side walks out — and at once a mediator needs to be found to set estranged parties back to the negotiating table once more. The mediator is one whom both sides trust. He represents justice, peace and goodwill. He represents each side to the other and finds a basis for restoring friendship.

But where can Job find such an arbitrator? The answer, of course, lies in the revelation of Jesus Christ as the mediator between God and man (1 Tim. 2:5). For not only does Jesus act as mediator on behalf of our sin (something which Job, too, needs). He is also one who, though God, 'is able to help those who are being tempted' and 'sympathize with our weaknesses' (Heb. 2:18; 4:15). At this point, however, Job can see no such mediator. As things develop, however, the fog in his mind clears and the mediator appears, a vision which attains its grandest expression in chapter 19 (19:25-26; cf. 16:20-21).

Jesus Christ is the answer to the problem of suffering, but as yet Job cannot see it.

8.
'Repent!'

Please read Job 11

Zophar's first speech

If Eliphaz had appealed to private revelations and Bildad to tradition, Zophar appeals to nothing except his arrogant confidence in his own importance and wisdom.

Zophar, perhaps the youngest and therefore the last to speak, is the least sympathetic of the three friends. According to Eliphaz, initially at least, *Job is a slight sinner.* Eliphaz began with an assumption that the innocent never suffer permanently: 'Who, being innocent, has ever perished? Where were the upright ever destroyed?' (4:7). Job must be one of the innocent: his sin must therefore be trivial and his suffering will be over soon. 'Should not your piety be your confidence and your blameless ways your hope?' (4:6). Job is essentially a righteous man temporarily chastised by God (5:17-18) for some imperfection inevitable in any mortal (4:17). We said that *initially* Job was in Eliphaz's eyes a slight sinner. Towards the end, however, Eliphaz's composure seems to have been unsettled and he makes the accusation that Job is a great sinner: 'Is not your wickedness great?' (22:5).

According to Bildad, *Job is a serious sinner.* He too believes in immediate retribution (suffering is punishment) but is much more blunt about it. He cites the death of Job's children as proof that God punishes the wicked: 'When your children sinned against him, he gave them over to the penalty of their sin' (8:4). Bildad doubts Job's righteousness: '*If* you are pure and upright...' (Job 8:6, emphasis added). No justification exists for this inference regarding Job's sons: it goes against the redemptive significance of the sacrifices made on their behalf; furthermore the book of Job says nothing about the profligacy of Job's sons. This is an instance of Bildad's cold, analytical approach where a principle is applied without any recourse to the facts of the case. Job's sin is serious, though evidently not as serious as that of his sons; he may yet have cause, so Bildad thinks, to hope. If he proves to be innocent, he will be rewarded.

According to Zophar, *Job is a secret sinner.* Since Job refuses to acknowledge his sin (Job 11:4) it follows that Job must be a secret sinner (Job 11:5-6). Job may well be unaware of the enormity of his crimes against God, but God's omniscience ensures that nothing escapes his knowledge. God knows more of Job's sins than he can ever imagine. Zophar finds no mitigating circumstances in Job's case at all.

In the end, all three of Job's friends are saying the same thing. 'Some comforters', Calvin comments, 'have no more songs but one, and have no regard at all to whom they sing it.'[1]

'Job, so great is your sin that God has even forgotten some of it' (11:1-6)

Zophar is furious with Job. He can hardly contain himself. He spares nothing and goes on the attack with real venom. Job has been guilty of **'idle talk'**[2] (11:3): false words, empty words, unnecessary words and mocking words (11:2-3). Bildad had called Job a 'windbag' — suggesting that his words were not to be taken too seriously, but Zophar accuses Job of sinning with his mouth. 'According to Zophar, Job is far more than a "windbag"; he is a heretic and a blasphemer.'³ Job is a 'babbler'. By mocking God with his words, he has challenged God's morality. Zophar believes that God needs him to defend his honour against Job's insults.

In a courtroom scene, Zophar accuses Job of not being fair: the accusations of the first two speakers should have silenced him: yet he goes on talking. He is in contempt of court. He will not submit to his guilt even when it is clearly proved. Zophar's pretence at being a good lawyer goes too far: he puts words into Job's mouth. True, Job had insisted on his innocence: 'I am blameless' (9:21); 'You know that I am not guilty' (10:7); but Zophar twists what Job has to say, suggesting instead that Job had said something different.

Firstly, Zophar accused Job of saying, **'My beliefs are flawless'** (11:4). Job had certainly instructed others (4:3-4), but he had never suggested that he was infallible!

Neither had Job ever said, **'I am pure in your sight'** (11:4). Yes, Job was insisting upon his innocence (9:14-21). He had even claimed that he was 'blameless' (9:20-21) — something which God had said in Job's defence against Satan's accusations (1:8; and confirmed by the narrator of the book of Job, 1:1). But that was a far cry from claiming that he was without sin at all. Sinless perfection was something that neither God, nor Job himself, had ever claimed for him.

Zophar failed to observe one of the cardinal rules of counselling: he had failed to listen to the one who was hurting. By putting words into Job's mouth, Zophar only added to Job's sense of frustration and pain. Job already felt estranged and misunderstood. Zophar's opening salvo only added to his increasing sense of isolation and betrayal.

But the real sting of Zophar's contribution was to suggest that Job needed to plead for mercy (11:5-6). The implication is clear enough: 'that not only is Job being treated fairly — as Eliphaz and Bildad have argued — but more than fairly; he is

actually getting off lightly with less than his guilt deserves'.[4]
Zophar claims authority for his insights. He is a wise man. The
word **'wisdom'** *(mashal)* is the one used in the Old Testament
to describe the teaching of a person who was wise (often
translated 'proverb', or 'parable', Prov. 1:5; 4:2; 9:9;
16:21,23). If Job could but grasp it, God has actually over-
looked part of his sin!

'Can you fathom the mysteries of God?' (11:7-12)

Zophar launches into a hymn on the sovereign wisdom of God.
'Can you fathom the mysteries of God?' he asks (11:7). Job
would have been the very first to admit that he could not.
According to Zophar, sin is sin, and however much mercy has
tempered justice, justice is still the principle on which the
universe runs. God is the regulator of retribution. God knows
who is guilty and who is not! And Job is guilty — he must be!
    The hymn itself is sound enough:

    1. God's wisdom and knowledge are *limitless*: They
go beyond all the realms of the created universe (11:8,9).
    2. God's wisdom and knowledge are *beyond human
comprehension*. His ways are 'past finding out'. God
knows sins that Job either does not remember or refuses
to acknowledge. Job may not want to admit it, and his
friends may not be able to detect it, but God has discovered something amiss in Job's life (11:10-12).
    3. God's wisdom and knowledge *ensure that justice
will be seen to be done*: God will bring the guilty to book
(11:10-11). God passes by and imprisons and brings the
guilty to court (11:10); and he passes sentence and no
one can hinder him from doing it.

All this is true, of course, but where is Job the sufferer in all of this? As George Philip comments, 'There may some truth in Zophar's sermon to Job, but there is certainly no humanity in it, and remember it is spoken to a man of ripe years whose heart has been laid bare by suffering.'[5]

The poem is a fine discourse on God's incomprehensibility, but its context needs to be understood. We must not miss the entire sarcasm and cutting edge of its intention. 'He would have made better use of his excellent doctrine of the incomprehensibility of God, however, if he had humbly recognized the limitations of his own knowledge of divine providence and had not presumed to understand Job's sufferings to perfection.'[6] Zophar was right, for this is the very truth that ought to — and will — still Job's restless spirit. In the end, pain is perfectly compatible with God's promise to bless his children. What Zophar failed to do was to implement his own doctrine. For if God is truly beyond our understanding, we have to concede that there may well be reasons for suffering other than those which we can perceive! In failing to grasp this point, Zophar only further hurt Job's already tender spirit with every word he uttered.

We catch a glimpse of this in two stinging remarks made by way of a conclusion to the hymn. First, Zophar mentions a courtroom (11:10). It has been emerging progressively from Job's replies so far that he wants a day in court so that he may vindicate himself before God (cf. 9:14-24, especially the references to 'my Judge', 9:15, and 'a matter of justice', 9:19). But Zophar now suggests that such a court would be Job's undoing: **'If he comes along and confines you in prison and convenes a court, who can oppose him?'** (11:10). God is not only the Judge but the investigator, lawyer and jury as well. He has power to lock Job up — for ever! Job just wouldn't stand a chance!

Not only does Zophar attempt to remove from Job the hope that a day in court would prove him innocent; he also becomes abusive. Citing a proverb, he draws a comparison between wild donkeys and foolish people. In effect, Zophar is suggesting that Job is **'witless'** and asinine! (11:12). Job is nothing but an 'empty-headed ass'. When arguments no longer have any force, pretentious fools like Zophar resort to defamation of character.

'Job, you must repent and seek the Lord's mercy!' (11:13-20)

There is only one thing for Job to do — *repent!* Zophar uses two pictures to suggest that Job's repentance must be thorough.

Firstly, Job must **'devote'** his heart to God (11:13). Zophar reveals a fine awareness of the spiritual nature of repentance. 'The sorrow of hypocrites,' writes Thomas Watson, 'is in their faces: "they disfigure their faces" (Matt. 6:16). They make a sour face, but their sorrow goes no further, like the dew that wets the leaf but does not soak to the root. Ahab's repentance was an outward show. His garments were rent but not in spirit (1 Kings 21:27). Godly sorrow goes deep, like a vein which bleeds inwardly. The heart bleeds for sin: "they were pricked in their hearts" (Acts 2:37). As the heart bears the chief part in sinning, so it must be in sorrowing.'[7]

Secondly, using a word which describes *covert* acts of extortion (i.e. secret sins) — a word which the eighth-century prophets used for underhand violations — Zophar seems to suggest that Job's wealth had been acquired by extortion, and adds, **'Allow no evil to dwell in your tent'** (11:14).[8]

By way of positive incentives for repentance, Zophar concludes his speech by suggesting that if Job repents, truthfully and fully, he will know instant blessing. This will include a peace of conscience — he will be able to **'lift up [his] face'** (11:15, cf. 10:15); freedom from every trial — his trouble will be so much 'water under the bridge' (11:16); and (since Job was anticipating death) long life (11:17). If Job follows Zophar's programme for instant health and wealth (pleasure, profit and position), his life will be one of unmixed joy (11:17). If not, Zophar is equally forthright: Job can expect to join the company of the wicked, for whom awaits sorrow, doom and eventual loss of every hope (11:20).

A summary of Zophar's speech

'It's time someone put a stop to your talking, Job. You want a day in court? I wish God would come down now and tell you what you are. Quite frankly, Job, you wouldn't stand a chance. He doesn't need an investigation to find out what you are. You would soon discover that, in fact, you've got away quite lightly.

'Listen to me, Job, there's only one thing for it: repent.'

Immediate retribution — right or wrong?

At the heart of Zophar's view of things was a belief in instant retribution. Zophar believed, as all biblically informed Christians believe, that at the heart of God's justice is retribution: the rendering to men what they have deserved, rewarding good with good, evil with evil.

Retribution is what we expect of God. We know in our hearts that this is what ought to be. It is why we feel such pain when the ungodly seem to prosper. It is the anguish of the psalmist in Psalm 73 that the wicked are 'not in trouble as other men' and this simply ought not to be.

It is part of Job's assessment of things, in his reply to Zophar, that 'Those who provoke God are secure' (12:6). Zophar has had the temerity to point to the empty-headed

donkey (11:12) and suggest that even it can back up his
contention that good is rewarded and evil is punished. For
Zophar everything in the garden is neat and tidy. He has
everything all boxed up. But for Job, all in the garden is not
lovely. There are thorns and briers: judges become fools
(12:17); priests are humiliated (12:19); advisers are silenced
and elders are deprived of good sense (12:20). There doesn't
seem to be any justice.

The book of Job opens by preparing us for this idea: why
else tell us that Job was wealthy, healthy and pious? It can only
be to heighten the shock that a man of such eminent godliness
should be treated so harshly. This is certainly not what some
evangelicals today tell Christians to expect if they follow the
Lord wholeheartedly. The 'prosperity gospel' (as it is often
called) is founded on the principle that godliness brings with
it freedom from disease and want. That was the propaganda
which Job's three friends, especially Zophar, tried hard to
sell: not just that God rewards those who follow him with
material, this-worldly blessings, and likewise punishes those
who do not by withdrawing these things, but that he does so
immediately.

Partly right

This view is partly right. To take the *negative* side of retribution for a moment, the fornicator who contracts AIDS reaps
what he has sown. There is no question of merely falling
victim to chance. Misconduct has been the cause of his
downfall. He has suffered *immediate* retribution. The businessman who conducts one shady deal too many and whose
business, as a result, becomes bankrupt, is likewise the victim
of *immediate* retribution.

This is what the Bible leads us to expect! The writer of
Chronicles in rewriting the books of Samuel and Kings has this
very aim in view: to bring to the foreground the doctrine that

those who disobey God can expect to be punished *immediately*! One example will suffice to prove it. The story of King Uzziah is told in Kings (where he is called Azariah) in a few short verses (2 Kings 15:1-7). The narrative is content to tell us that he was a good king and that he died of leprosy. The same story in 2 Chronicles, however, takes much longer — twenty-three verses (2 Chron. 26) — to tell the story of this hapless king, pointing out that the reason why he died of leprosy was that he became proud, usurping the rôle of the priests in the temple administrations and that as a consequence leprosy broke out on his forehead, from which he died. It was a case of immediate retribution![9]

Why does the book of Chronicles do this? The answer lies in the fact that the author (Ezra?) is writing to those facing Persian exile in the fifth century. Like their ancestors in the sixth and seventh centuries, they too were serving other gods, and the author of Chronicles wants to point out to them a history lesson: God often metes out summary judgement to those who live contrary to his laws. If they do not turn from their idolatry *soon*, they can expect to receive a similar fate to Uzziah! That is why the most famous verse in Chronicles is one which emphasizes this very theme: 'If my people, who are called by my name, will humble themselves and pray and seek my face and turn from their wicked ways, then will I hear from heaven and will forgive their sin and will heal their land' (2 Chron. 7:14).

Nor is this merely an Old Testament notion. It is precisely this viewpoint that explains why certain folk in Corinth were ill and others had died: they had shown scant regard for the Lord's Table (1 Cor. 11:30). It is also the reason why Ananias and Sapphira experienced summary execution at the Lord's hands: they lied (Acts 5:1-11).

There is also a *positive* aspect to retribution. Under the Old Covenant immediate blessings of a material kind were indeed to be expected (cf. Deut. 28:1-19). And in the New Testament also we are told that every good and perfect gift comes from God (cf. James 1:17). We are not to be moaning Christians! In criticism of those who peddle the 'prosperity gospel' we must not sin by denying that God has given us much more then we ever deserve. God does give us good days: good health, a good marriage partner, the blessing of children, days of leisure and fun. We do God a grave injustice when we do not acknowledge the good things he gives. Counting our blessings is the way to glorify God. This is not merely an evangelical cliché, but a profound and staggering truth! God is better to us than we deserve, and far better than we ever acknowledge.

Zophar, it has to be said, has pinpointed an oft-neglected truth which the modern church needs to hear: that, sometimes, God metes out his blessings and curses sooner, rather than later.

Partly wrong

Zophar's handling of this truth is misguided for at least three reasons.

Firstly, *God does not always carry out his judgements immediately.* The Chronicler, for example, points out that there are exceptions to the rule of immediate retribution: Josiah was a good king who died in tragic circumstances (2 Chron. 34-35), and Manasseh was an evil king who lived long (2 Chron. 33:1-20). There are times when God seems to delay in the execution of his judgement. This is the heart of Job's reply in 12:6: 'The tents of robbers prosper, and those who provoke God are secure — in what God provides by his hand.' This is what the psalmist observes in Psalm 73. The sins of some men go ahead of them, whilst the sins of others drag behind.

Secondly, *Zophar is wrong in suggesting that the kind of blessing/judgement people can expect is always a material one.* His point was to suggest that illness was a sign of God's

disfavour, evidence that specific sin had taken place. Good
health is, by consequence, the result of an obedient lifestyle.
This is patently false. I think, as I write these lines, of a godly
woman seemingly a few weeks away from death by cancer,
who has been told by a minister who hardly knows her that if
she only had faith she would be well again. According to this
view, her unbelief (the sin that ensures the progress of disease)
is the root cause of her trouble. This is more than mere
theological naïveté; it is cruel advice.[10] 'To be told that longed-
for healing was denied because of some defect in your faith
when you had laboured and strained every way you know how
to devote yourself to God and to "believe for blessing", is to
be pitchforked into distress, despair, and a sense of being
abandoned by God. This is as bitter a feeling as any this side
of hell — particularly if, like most invalids, your sensitivity is
up and your spirits down.'[11]

True, there is an element in the expectations under the Old
Covenant which prepared Israel for material and this-worldly
blessing, but there are shadows of the cross which fall deep
into the Old Testament also. Isaiah, for example, had warned
Israel that God's servants can expect to be tried and tested, to
suffer not because they have sinned, but as part of God's
calling in faithful service in his kingdom. Many of Isaiah's
fellow prophets, Jeremiah and Elijah for example, knew days
of pain in faithful service to God.

The New Testament explains it more fully. Jesus warned of
two areas of expectation in preparing his disciples for a life of
service: self-denial and cross-bearing. It is in this sense that
Paul could write to the Corinthians when, like Job, he felt he
was about to die under the strain, telling them that he felt he
'had the sentence of death' upon him. The Greek for the word
translated 'sentence' is 'answer', implying that in response to
his prayer for deliverance from the crushing effect of his trials,
God had given the answer, 'No' (2 Cor. 1:8-9). There were

reasons for Paul's sufferings that had to do with something other than the fact that Paul may have sinned in some way. For one thing, the sight of Paul's suffering would encourage the prayers of others (few things will make others pray more than when a friend is suffering). Then again, God's refusal to intervene immediately helped to demonstrate in graphic fashion his sovereign power. Also, when Paul was finally relieved of his burden, the thanks for his deliverance would be given to God alone (2 Cor. 1:11). It may therefore be said that suffering is one of the 'marks' of the church.

To expect that God will always intervene *immediately* with judgement or blessing is to have what we may call an 'over-realized eschatology' (a difficult term, I know, but one which helps convey the view that expects *now* all the judgements and blessings which are promised us in *the age to come*). Paul seemed to be contending with this very problem when, in his last letter (2 Timothy), he corrects those who insist that the resurrection is past already (2 Tim. 2:18) and that therefore freedom from suffering and material prosperity are to be experienced now to the full. He exhorts Timothy, who may have been tempted to give up his calling to be the Lord's servant, not to yield to the panderings of the flesh or the enticements of the world. He also warns of Demas who appears to have done this very thing. 'Discharge all the duties of your ministry,' Paul tells Timothy, by which he means: 'Don't give up your calling to be a preacher because of the allurements of this-worldly things' (cf. 2 Tim. 4:5).

Thirdly, this view is also wrong as a view of Christian discipleship, for *it suggests that following Christ need not involve suffering*. This is patently false. Christ's image is fulfilled in us by means of suffering. Paul even goes so far as to say: 'I fill up in my flesh what is still lacking in regard to Christ's afflictions, for the sake of his body, which is the church' (Col.1:24). Paul's words are worth examining closely, for they help us understand why God allows his children to suffer for reasons that are not immediately related to personal sin. Paul is not suggesting at all that there is something lacking in Christ's atonement. Not at all! But he is suggesting that Christ goes on suffering — *in and through his people*. When someone like Job suffers, Christ suffers along with him. And it is part of our Christian vocation to accept this yoke patiently and meekly. Job will, but not quite yet.

9.
'Though he slay me, yet will I trust him'

Please read Job 12 - 14

Job's response to Zophar

'Wisdom will, of course, die with you!' (12:1-12)

Job is getting tired of his friends. He really wants to talk with God about his condition.

Job's friends may have succeeded in unsettling him, but anger has a way of refocusing one's energies. In bitter sarcasm, Job suggests that his counsellors are too conceited. Their view of themselves is too inflated. **'Wisdom will die with you'** (12:2), he suggests ironically. In no way does he feel himself inferior to them for in his pain he has come to learn something that his friends do not know. He knows that it is possible in God's way of things for a righteous man to suffer. It is not always true that the wicked are judged *immediately* (12:4-6). Even the animals and birds know it (12:7-9). This is a valuable lesson to learn; indeed it is the chief lesson of the book of Job. Learn it now and learn it well, the book seems to be saying to us, and you will spare yourself further pain.

'To God belong wisdom and power' (12:13-25)

Job is not impressed by Zophar's great hymn on God's sovereign wisdom (11:7-12). He provides one of his own which surpasses it (12:13-25). **'Wisdom and power'** belong to God (12:13). God's sovereignty appears in the destructive powers of nature (12:13-16), and in the downfall of rulers of every kind (12:17-25). Everything is subject to his rule — everything from the elemental forces of nature to the highest civil and cultic dignitaries. It is in effect an exposition of something Paul would later say: 'Has not God made foolish the wisdom of the world?' (1 Cor 1:20). No one is truly wise in comparison to Almighty God — especially not these three pretentious sophists from the East!

It must be understood that Job's hymn on God's wisdom and power lacks any reference to any good purpose that God may have in his own suffering. Everything Job says here is true: God is almighty, all-wise (12:13), all-powerful (12:14-21) and all-knowing (12:22). But the veil is drawn over Job's eyes by the pain he now suffers, for he does not yet appreciate that God is all-loving, too. The hymn is inadequate as a full description of God's purposes in this world. Even the pain is being weaved into the tapestry of our life for our good and betterment (cf. Rom. 8:28). This is something Job has yet to see.

'I want to speak to the Almighty' (13:1-22)

Zophar has not been successful in frightening Job away from his day in court with God (cf. 11:10), for Zophar had got it all wrong concerning Job's intention in this matter. Job wishes, not so much to bring an indictment against God, but rather to hear what indictment God may have against him (13:23).

Having previously asked God to leave him alone, Job has found a new confidence. He wants God to **'summon'** him (13:22). He knows that the course is full of **'jeopardy'** (13:14). Nothing will shake Job now: **'I desire to speak to the Almighty and to argue my case with God'** (13:3). Job will appear before God, not to plead for mercy as Zophar has suggested, but to clear his name. Such is his confidence — not in himself so much (though that, too), but in God — that in a moment of triumph he cries: **'Though he slay me, yet will I hope in him; I will surely defend my ways to his face'** (13:15). Like the man in a darkened cell who can detect a small pinprick of light confirming that day has broken and the sun has risen, Job, though he cannot himself see it, gives expression to his faith in God even though he is suffering. He may not understand providence, but he trusts in the God of providence. Calvin comments: 'Job indicates that although he is overthrown and as it were enraged in his passions, that he has not lost all hope; it is not that he pretends to plead against God, or perhaps to alienate himself from Him, or that he wishes to vex Him by having no more to do with Him. Why not? He protests that he hopes, whatever may come of it. "Although He may kill me," he says, "and confound me, yet will I not cease to trust in Him; nevertheless I will argue my ways before His face. Behold, I must mix this vehemence which you see and which you perceive, I must mix it with the hope which I have in God." And here we have a beautiful and excellent mirror of God's working. For he lets the faithful fall, in order that their faith may be so much better tried.'[1]

'How many wrongs have I committed?' (13:23 - 14:6)

Still using the language of the courtroom, Job charges his friends with false witness against him. They **'smear me with**

lies', 'speak wickedly ... deceitfully' (13:4,7). How would they fare, he wonders, if the tables were turned and God should examine them? (13:9).

Unlike Adam, Job will not flee from God should he appear for a trial. If God should grant him a moment's respite from his suffering and stop terrifying him, Job will come before his throne and plead his case (13:20-22). Like Jacob, Job wants a wrestling match with the Almighty! It is a summons and will reach its climax in Job 31.[2] Nothing hurts Job more than God's silences. In anticipation, Job asks directly a torrent of questions (so far he has only asked such questions of his friends):

> How many are my iniquities?
> Why do you hide your face?
> Why am I your enemy?
> Will you treat me like a leaf or stubble that is driven
> to and fro?
>
> (13:23-25).

Job's case is this:

1. God has punished him for the sins of his youth and is now holding these against him (13:26-27; cf. 25:7; Hosea 13:12).

2. Life is short enough and hard enough without being hounded by God as well (13:28 - 14:6)

3. Comparing man to a tree, he says that at least a tree's roots will sprout again when it is cut down, but when a man dies, where is he? (14:7-10).

If a man dies will he live again?' (14:7-22)

Job is longing for eternal life (14:12). The question he asks here is one that many have pondered before and since:

If a man dies, will he live again?
All the days of my hard service
I will wait for my renewal to come

(14:14).

But just as mountains erode with time (14:11), so the firmest convictions of men are ground into the dust by the reality of life. 'Life is hard and then you die,' is about all Job can see at the moment. He is almost at the point of seeing something beyond death, a resurrection in which all wrongs are put right, but for the moment it is beyond him. Later, it will appear as a glorious affirmation of faith (19:25-27), but for now Job's eyes are firmly set on the ash-heap beneath him. Dust and ashes are what he is destined for, and not much more. No sooner has he glimpsed heaven, but the door slams shut on him (14:19-20).

The pain of it is excruciating. Revealing his soul at the end of the speech, Job ponders the ultimate horror: of not knowing what becomes of our family after we have died and gone to the grave (14:21).

A summary of Job's reply

(With irony) 'To be sure, wisdom will die when you die! God alone is truly wise. God alone is sovereign. He made the world in which we live and orders everything that happens. He can turn kings into paupers and make fools of judges. He can even raise up a nation and destroy it.

'There is no point in talking to you three; I want to talk to God instead.

'Since you believe that God judges sin, you had better be careful what you say, for if you speak falsely, God will judge you for it.

'In any case, I want to speak to God. Even if he should destroy me, I will still hope in him. All I want is an explanation.

'Lord, what are these sins that I am supposed to have committed? Why do you not speak to me? Don't you care about me any more? What hope do I have if you are against me?

'Lord, I just wish that you would let me die.'

The final judgement will provide the answer

Only the doctrine of the resurrection and final judgement can provide Job with an answer to his soul's discomfort. Only in the knowledge that the mediator that Job longed for would open the way for man to rise from the dead to a final judgement where all wrongs are put right can he be released from the feeling of injustice and unfairness. The judgement at the end of the age will demonstrate, and vindicate, God's perfect justice. In this world, where God has let the 'nations go their own way' (Acts 14:16), it is no wonder that evil is rampant. In such circumstances, where Satan is allowed to tempt folk like Job, 'Doubts arise as to whether God, if sovereign, can be just, or, if just, can be sovereign!... the Last Judgement will be His final self-vindication against the suspicion that he has ceased to care about the righteous.'[3]

It is a feeling we must all admit to having shared at some time or another.

10.
Trading insults

Please read Job 15

Eliphaz's second speech

When arguments lack logic, folk do one of two things: they either repeat what they have already said (only louder — a bit like those of us who find ourselves in a foreign country and cannot speak the language), or else they resort to trading insults. Job's 'miserable comforters' (16:2) appear to engage in both, beginning with insults.

Bildad has called a Job a windbag (8:2); Zophar added that he was an empty-headed donkey (11:2). Now Eliphaz joins in and suggests that Job 'empties the east wind from his belly'.[1] The allusion is coarse and unbecoming — especially to one as pretentiously wise as Eliphaz.

Eliphaz appears affronted by Job. Although he had wanted to help Job (4:6), he now appears to be more concerned about proving himself right than about giving genuine help to his friend. Would-be counsellors need to learn that if they are to be of help to those who are hurting, they had better not take offence when their help is refused. All three of Job's friends appear to take things far too personally, being more concerned for their own positions than in offering genuine relief. People who are hurting, like hurt animals, tend to lash out when touched; Job's godliness does not prevent him from a similar reaction at times and it is a demonstration of the immaturity of his three friends that they fail to anticipate it.

Eliphaz's accusation

Eliphaz accuses Job of three basic errors.

1. Job lacks reverence.

Job seems to Eliphaz to **'undermine piety'**: his words are intrinsically irreverent (15:4). Perhaps Eliphaz is thinking of Job's boldness in entering into a lawsuit with God (13:3,19-24). Is this what he means when he says to Job, **'You vent your rage against God'**? (15:13). Perhaps, but it is equally possible that Eliphaz is more concerned about himself than God: it is not that Job is irreverent towards God so much as towards Eliphaz, 'the Wise One'! It just may be that Eliphaz is filled with his own importance — he is older, maturer and therefore wiser than Job. He represents the school of wisdom. When Job had said earlier that he knew as much as he did, Eliphaz seems to have taken it as an insult (12:3). There is no room for God, or others, in those who are full of themselves.

2. Job lacks modesty.

In an earlier speech, Job had suggested a sense of fear in presenting his case before God — not because his case was poor, but that he would make a mess in presenting it (9:20). This is exactly what Job has done, suggests Eliphaz. Job's language has been over the top, lacking in dignity and propriety. It is no way for a pious man to behave. His own mouth had condemned him (15:6). But it ill behoves one who can use such a coarse expression as Eliphaz about the 'east wind' to give lectures about dignity — especially to someone who is hurting so badly. According to Eliphaz, in showing such evident lack of patience, Job is guilty of a gross moral failure. It is at once a sin against his own conscience (15:6) and against God (15:13).

3. Job lacked wisdom

Eliphaz thinks of himself as 'the all-wise one' and is taken aback by Job's confidence to call into question the received wisdom of the sages — **'the grey-haired and the aged'** (15:10). Job has claimed to know as much as, if not more than these wise men (12:2-6), maintaining in particular that the doctrine of *immediate* retribution is only half true at best (12:6). Job's counsellors have only one song to sing and they have sung it to death!

Having traded insults, Eliphaz now returns to his theme that the righteous prosper and the wicked suffer. Job cannot be innocent, for even the most perfect is marred in God's sight:

> **What is man, that he could be pure,**
> **or one born of woman, that he could be righteous?**
> **If God places no trust in his holy ones,**
> **if even the heavens are not pure in his eyes,**
> **how much less man, who is vile and corrupt,**
> **who drinks up evil like water!**
>
> (15:14-16).

He then repeats a great deal of what he had said earlier in chapter 4. Eliphaz believes in total depravity and uses his theological position to batter Job into defeat. Pain, trouble, anguish, desolation, ruin, loneliness and futility are the inevitable wages of sin (15:20-31).

Eliphaz warns of the fate of the wicked

Having thus condemned Job, Eliphaz makes sure he understands the consequences of his sinful behaviour by a lengthy
warning on the fate of the wicked (15:17-35) — a warning
which is the received wisdom of the sages (15:18). Eliphaz is
no universalist! He believes in the punishment of the wicked
after death and is not afraid to say so. He holds nothing back:
'Listen to me and I will explain to you...' (15:17). We must
not miss the point that Eliphaz intends to suggest that if Job
doesn't repent — and that, quickly — he, too, is in danger of
falling into this very punishment.[2]

There are, however, a couple of variations in Eliphaz's
words. Since Job has rebutted the notion of immediate retribution — this *may* be the way God does things at times, but by
no means all the time — Eliphaz now suggests that retribution
is sometimes *unseen*. Just because we cannot see God's
punishments does not mean that he has not inflicted them!
God's punishments may be *inward* instead of outward; it may
be that 'Despite all that external prosperity, the ungodly man
is inwardly suffering already for his unrighteousness and the
principle of retribution is already at work.'[3] Eventually, what
is now working unseen inside the wicked man will emerge and
consume him. And even if God's retribution is delayed, it is
only delayed for a short time and soon, in the wicked man's
lifetime, he will see the just desert of his actions. For justice to
be done, it must be seen to be done *in this life*, Eliphaz insists.

The wicked are those who defy God and are thus in pain all
their lives (15:20), in anxiety (15:21), without confidence or
faith (15:22), begging (15:23), terrified of death — 'the day of
darkness' (15:23) — which pounces on them when least
expected (15:24-25), even though they regard themselves as
invincible (15:26). Good-living weakens their resolve
(15:27); they find themselves homeless, vagabonds with nowhere to hide (15:28), destitute of the comfort that wealth had

once secured for them (15:29). The wicked will not escape death, **'the darkness'** (15:30), like a tree which withers and dies in the face of a strong wind or a severe drought. And like this withered tree which does not see harvest, the wicked man will be **'paid in full'** before **'his time'** (15:32). For a season, maybe, like a vine which sheds unripe fruits, or an olive tree which blossoms, the wicked may prosper. But it is short-lived and disaster is around the corner (15:33). Their doom is certain (15:34-35). In other words, **'His wealth will not endure'** (15:29); the retribution which the wicked man deserves will be seen *in this life*. The wicked are marked down for the **'sword'** (15:22), cast out as **'food for vultures'** (15:23). If Job is innocent, as he says, his pain will go away, but in his present actions Job is in danger of aligning himself with the wicked and his fate.

According to this view, what is properly to be expected in the world to come, at the final judgement, is meted out in this life. As we have already seen there were those addressed in 2 Timothy who were claiming that the resurrection 'is past already' and that therefore the blessings of the age to come have already come. This is a major theme in 2 Timothy, and one which Paul seeks to counter. As we now see, it is an error that is as old as the book of Job! According to Eliphaz, Job's theology (wisdom) is astray: there is no point in claiming innocence, for even the most upright are sinful (15:14-16). As Eliphaz had said in his opening speech in chapter 4, there is no such thing as perfect innocence, and therefore Job's claim to it is utterly misguided. We know, however, from the introduction of chapters 1 and 2 that this is not the case. Job was suffering, not because of his sin, but because of a cosmic battle taking place between God and Satan.

This would all be sound theology if it were meant to be a depiction of what awaits the unbeliever *in the world to come*, but as a description of how things are *in this world*, it is frankly silly. It was (and remains) the oft-repeated concern of the godly that the wicked seem to do very well in this world, as Job had himself expressed (12:6; cf. Ps. 37; 49; 73). Eliphaz's contribution is getting stuck in a groove, and Job is incensed by it!

A summary of Eliphaz's speech

'Job, you're full of wind! Worse than that, you're utterly irreverent. Every time you open your mouth you only manage to make things worse for yourself.

'You refuse to listen to the wisdom of the past, but I'm going to repeat it anyway: it is wicked people who experience pain all their days. They have no security and neither do they prosper; God is against them. It is all so clear. Why don't you accept it?'

11.
'What miserable comforters you are!'

Please read Job 16-17

Job's response to Eliphaz

Job's reply is a little confusing.[1] We can hardly expect him to be completely rational when his body is racked with pain and his mind tormented by bad advice. However, his reply to Eliphaz contains a key thought that eventually will help him win through to victory in his trial. **'My witness,'** Job says, **'is in heaven'** (16:19).[2]

There had been a sting in the tail of Eliphaz's contribution. Eliphaz had spoken of the deceitfulness of the wicked and had, by implication, accused Job of concealing the truth about himself (15:35). For Job's friends, the fact that he claimed to be suffering 'innocently' was not just a matter of lacking wisdom; it was evidence that Job was nothing but a hypocrite whose words could not be trusted. Job is the prey, not only of unaccountable suffering, but of insulting and unfeeling friends. They are all **'miserable comforters'** (16:2).

Job appears as a desperately lonely man. He had closed his previous speech expressing the painful thought that he would never live to see his children grow up (14:21). His sense of isolation reaches a climax in 17:6 when he sees himself as a **'byword to everyone'**. In this respect Job's experience closely matches that of Christ: 'Those who sit at the gate mock

me, and I am the song of the drunkards' (Ps. 69:12). It appears
that people living in distant lands were now openly speaking
about 'that great sinner Job'! Men spit in his face, he adds
(17:6). His sufferings are poignant: Job is suffering in every
part of his being: physically — **'You have bound me'** (16:8);
socially — **'You have devastated my entire household'**
(16:7); and spiritually — **'My spirit is broken'** (17:1).

How like Jesus Job is!

There are several allusions here that remind us of the
sufferings of Christ. We have not, so far, made much of this
connection between Job and Jesus, but it is time to draw out a
few of them.

Suffering was a part of both of their lives. Indeed every
Christian is told to expect it. Suffering is one of the ways God
makes us more like Christ. Christlikeness is the goal of
sanctification (Rom. 8:29; John 13:15).

Think of Christ's loneliness: his flight into Egypt, the
saying about the birds of the air and foxes and their holes, as
well as those times in Gethsemane and on the cross. Think, too,
of the way Christ suffered.

He suffered *physically*. He had a body like our own. It was
not superhuman. It was a body highly sensitive to pain. The
Scripture records how he suffered hunger, thirst, weariness
and exhaustion. At Calvary he endured whipping, immo-
lation, suspension in a fully conscious state. The worst of pain
is known to him.

He suffered *emotionally* too. He possessed an ordinary
human psychology (apart from sinfulness). He knew joy and
contentment, as well as the dark side of our experience. He was
'a man of sorrows and acquainted with grief'. The shadow of
Calvary falls deep into his life. Think of those passages in the

Gospels where he was 'deeply distressed and troubled' and 'in anguish' (Mark 14:35; Luke 22:44). He knew what it was to be terrified by the unfolding will of God.

He also suffered *socially*. He loved his neighbour, but his neighbour did not love him. He was condemned by established religion, an embarrassment to his family, betrayed by one of his companions, and the multitudes bayed for his blood. In one of the most revealing asides in the Gospel of Mark, we learn that the disciples were chosen to 'be with him' (Mark 3:14). Jesus, too, needed the support of human companionship!

There is more than a hint in these features of the story of Job of the Christ to come. It is not, I think, that Job is meant to be a type of Christ in the formal sense. Rather, Job is being portrayed as one in a long line of godly souls who are called upon to suffer in this world as a result of satanic abuse.

Taking up our cross

In accepting the Christian calling we take up an instrument of death and identify with it. Recognizing the place and the inevitability of trials is a mark of Christian maturity. 'Do not be anxious', Paul says (Phil. 4:6). How could he say such a thing? One answer involves accepting that the Christian life brings pain. Suffering — 'losses and crosses' to give it a Puritan expression — is part of what we must expect in the Christian life. Paul witnesses to it in a lesson he learned after the first missionary journey, 'We must go through many hardships to enter the kingdom of God' (Acts 14:22).

Paul's Christian realism demanded that hardships were among those things he urged us to expect — so much so that he infused it into his theological understanding of the Christian life. For Paul, the central truth of the Christian life was that grace had brought him into union with Christ. It is the theme of Romans 6 that union with Christ is the framework of sanctification. And Romans 6 is a summary of Paul's emphasis elsewhere: the phrases 'in Christ', 'in the Lord' or 'in him' occur 164 times in the New Testament — all of them in Paul's letters — testifying to its importance (1 Cor. 1:2; Eph. 1:1; Phil. 1:1; Col. 1:2, etc.).

It is this very truth that is captured in what Paul writes earlier in this letter to the Philippians: 'I consider everything a loss ... that I may gain Christ and be found in him' (Phil. 3:8-9). To be *in* Christ was his consuming passion. 'Union with Christ is ... the central truth of the whole doctrine of salvation... It is not simply a phase of the application of redemption; it underlies every aspect of redemption...'[3] Thus wrote John Murray, and others have concurred with his point of view that the doctrine of union with Christ lies at the very heart of the Christian life.

But this union with Christ has ongoing implications for the whole of our Christian lives. If grace has brought us into union with Christ in his death and resurrection (Rom. 6:5), grace also ensures that an ongoing communion with Christ in his death and resurrection dominates the whole of the Christian life. It is, again, what Paul has been alluding to in the previous chapter: 'I want to know Christ and the power of his resurrection and the fellowship of sharing in his sufferings, becoming like him in his death, and so, somehow, to attain to the resurrection from the dead' (Phil. 3:10-11).

One of the implications of being a Christian, of being in union with Christ, is that we share in his sufferings. We become like him in his death. Paul expounded this truth in 2 Corinthians 4:10-12: 'We always carry around in our body the death of Jesus, so that the life of Jesus may also be revealed in our body. For we who are alive are always being given over to death for Jesus' sake, so that his life may be revealed in our mortal body. So then, death is at work in us, but life is at work in you.' Paul sees a pattern by which he may interpret the whole of our Christian lives: it is a kind of repetition of Christ's life and death in our own lives. There is some kind of reduplication of Christ's life in our own. This is what Calvin saw too: 'From the beginning the church has been so constituted that the cross has been the way to victory and death the way to life.'⁴ Thus trouble goes hand in hand with a Christian testimony and it accounts for why Paul alludes in Romans 8:36 to something the psalmist had said: 'As it is written: "For your sake we face death all day long; we are considered as sheep to be slaughtered."'

This surely cuts across the grain of contemporary thinking on the nature of the Christian life. We live at a time when the Christian faith is more or less flabby, preoccupied with its pleasures and intrinsically egocentric. Words like 'consecration', 'holiness' and 'mortification' sound old-fashioned. The call for self-negation, involving an identification with Jesus in his death — 'taking up a cross', to use New Testament language — is drowned out by the clamour for self-expression and achievement of maximum pleasure. Dietrich Bonhoeffer wrote, 'The cross is laid on every Christian. The first Christsuffering which every man must experience is the call to abandon the attachments of this world. It is that dying of the old man which is the result of his encounter with Christ. As we embark upon discipleship we surrender ourselves to Christ in union with his death — we give our lives to death. Thus it begins; the cross is not the terrible end to an otherwise Godfearing and happy life, but it meets us at the beginning of our communion with Christ. When Christ calls a man, he bids him come and die.'⁵ Eight years later the Nazis hanged him.

When we affirm that the shadow of Christ's cross falls over every part of our Christian lives, we shall not be caught offguard when trouble comes: 'Dear friends, do not be surprised at the painful trial you are suffering, as though something strange were happening to you' (1 Peter 4:12). So, what should our reaction be? '... But rejoice that you participate in the sufferings of Christ' (1 Peter 4:13).

Knowing that, whatever the pain, we are sharing in Christ's ongoing ministry will aid in keeping our spirits sweet. It is to this that Paul alludes in Colossians in a breathtaking statement of the place of suffering in the Christian life: 'Now I rejoice in what was suffered for you, and I fill up in my flesh what is still lacking in regard to Christ's afflictions, for the sake of his body, which is the church' (Col. 1:24). Paul is not thinking of Christ's propitiatory work. That cannot be added to in any way. What Paul has in mind is the church-building work of the Saviour, an ongoing work whereby he takes mortal sinners into his confidence and uses them — a process which involves pain and persecution. Just as Paul learnt after Stephen's death that he was, in fact, troubling Christ just as much as he troubled Stephen, so too he was to make this a hallmark of his understanding of the Christian mission. The devil's attempts to destroy everything that is Christ's will inevitably be manifested in sustained attacks on Christ's people. In this way, 'Death is at work in us' (2 Cor. 4:12). Christian contentment begins by a recognition that we are called upon to share in this union in Christ's death.

It is was such a recognition that inspired Amy Carmichael to write:

Lord crucified, Oh mark thy holy cross
On motive, preference, all fond desire,
On that which self, in any form, inspires,
Set thou this sign of loss.
And when the touch of death is here and there displayed
On things most precious in our eyes,
Let us not wonder; let us see the answer to this prayer.

A vindicator (16:1-22)

Returning to Job, we find that there are further echoes of the coming Christ in his response to Eliphaz's speech. Following his cry for an arbitrator (9:33), Job now calls for a **'witness ... in heaven'** to vindicate his words before God (16:19).

Job's reply adds little that is new. He disputes with his comforters, calling them 'miserable' (16:2). It seems that they are more than just inept, for the word has the meaning of 'breathers out of trouble'. They are counsellors of torture, not of comfort! Instead of healing, they add to Job's pain. Instead of sharing his pain, they have sat in judgement on him from the vantage-point of those who are emotionally and empathetically at a distance. This is a stance at variance with those who deign to be counsellors and who ought, as Job goes on to suggest, to offer **'comfort'** and to **'encourage'** (16:5).

Job has heard Eliphaz's theology of 'the fate of the wicked' many times before (16:2). It had been a long sermon and Job trades in insults over its 'windy' — **'long-winded'** — nature (16:3; cf. 15:2),[6] and accompanying 'head-shaking' signs of disapproval (16:4).

A personal lament (16:7-17)

Job complains that God has **'worn [him] out'** and made him look like a godless man (16:7). His shrivelled body bears testimony to his rejection (16:8). God has become his assailant, or adversary (16:9) — a word *(satam)* which sounds remarkably like 'Satan'! Job now knows that the cause of suffering lies 'up there', beyond this world of time and space, only he names God as his adversary — God is like some wild animal that takes pleasure in torturing its hapless prey!

In a trio of metaphors, Job sees himself as having been seized by the neck and beaten, made a 'target-practice' for would-be archers, and like a breached wall of a city made defenceless by the relentless battering of an invading warrior (16:12-14). To add insult to injury, he sees himself surrounded by a mob who shout insults and gloat at his downfall (16:10).

Job is left to mourn, an act that is accompanied by the signs of grief and pain: sackcloth, dust, tears — the sign of death in his eyes (16:15-16). Job believes his wounds to be mortal (16:18). And his death will be an act of murder! Everything within him cries out for vengeance. He sees little hope for vindication this side of the grave — indeed, he has already conceded that the task is hopeless (9:14-16). But the cry of his spilt blood upon the ground will ensure that justice will eventually be done. And to ensure it, he calls upon the **'earth'** and **'heaven'** — the 'sleepless watchers of men's actions and guardians of ancient covenants'⁷ — to witness his blood shed in innocence, that is to say, his murder (16:18-19). As in the case of Abel, the spilt blood cries out for vengeance (Gen. 4:10). In Ezekiel 24:7-8 the guilt of Jerusalem remains to be punished because the blood shed on it (through murder and violence) remains unabsorbed by the rock.

Job desires a kinsman-redeemer to avenge his blood when his case is heard in heaven. He is assured of the redeemer's existence and that even now he is preparing his case, his argument for Job's defence: **'Even now my witness is in heaven; my advocate is on high'** (Job 16:19).

Who is this 'witness' who comes to Job's defence in heaven, whose function it is to mediate between God (the assailant) and Job (the victim)? What is the identity of this one of whom Job says, **'On behalf of a man he pleads with God as a man pleads for his friend'**? (16:21). It is difficult to be certain exactly whom Job had in mind, but the answer appears to be God himself, as Job seems to testify in the next chapter:

'Give me, O God, the pledge you demand. Who else will put up security for me?' (Job 17:3).[8] We have the privilege of further revelation as to the provision of Jesus Christ, the Second Person of the Trinity of God, to fulfil this rôle, but Job knew little of his identity. Job seems only to be assured that though God appears to be angry with him, his sense of justice will prevail in the end. As Hartley puts it, 'The whole drama of redemption centres around the antinomy between God's justice that is sometimes expressed in wrath toward sinful man and his love that reaches out to redeem that same sinful man.'[9]

Job's **'spirit is broken'** (Job 17:1). Confident though he may be about vindication in the life to come, he cannot muster any hope for the present. He is not hopeful of living long enough to see it here and now! The Lord's sharp shears have clipped his life so close to the roots he does not see how it can ever grow back:

> **Only a few years will pass**
> **before I go on the journey of no return.**
> **My spirit is broken,**
> **my days are cut short,**
> **the grave awaits me**
>
> (Job 16:22 - 17:1).

Many know this spirit of crushing despair that has overtaken Job: a family, shattered by divorce; an adolescent, caught in the web of drug addiction or an unwanted pregnancy; a couple, learning that their newborn child is handicapped. Like Job, we feel at times that nothing can help us here and now. Only the reality of pain seems to face us. But so long as we can do what Job did, there is hope. To know, with clearer insight than Job was ever able to perceive, that there is one in heaven who pleads for us as 'for his friend' is to have recourse to a source of power and healing that will strengthen and sustain us.

Job has yet another argument in his arsenal that he pleads in his defence: his friends, those **'mockers'** that surround him (17:2), must not be seen to prevail. Job hands them over to God's tribunal (a similar feature occurs in 27:2-6) to be charged as 'mockers'. Later he warns them specifically of punishment that awaits those who inform on friends for personal gain (17:5). The allusion is to the case law in Deuteronomy 19:15-21, where the penalty for malicious prosecution was to apply to the false accuser the punishment assigned to the crime he wrongly alleged. Job is prepared to face the risk of being found guilty, so assured is he of his innocence. He has no 'pledge' to offer. It could have been a garment, or a ring which a borrower would place with his creditor as guarantee that he would pay his debt (cf. Gen. 38:17-20, where Judah offers his daughter-in-law, disguised as a prostitute, his seal and a staff as a pledge for a goat — the payment he had offered for her 'services'). It could also be a person (cf. Gen. 43:9; 44:32-34, where Judah is a pledge for Benjamin's life). Since Job has neither property nor friend (17:3) to act as pledge, he calls on God to be his bondsman. The witness of 16:19 must be God himself.

Job's speech ends, as we have noted earlier, in a despairing account of his distress. He is without a friend, the marks of death are visible in his bodily appearance and his life is ebbing away (17:5-16). Having raised himself to such heights in his cry for a witness in heaven, he quickly descends to the depths again as his present circumstances get the better of him. We are reminded of Peter's experience on the storm-tossed waters of the Galilean lake (Matt. 14:22-36). The only relief he can expect from his pain is the community of maggots! His only recourse is to prepare himself for a home in **'the grave'** (17:13; Hebrew, *Sheol*). And there in death his hope dies with him:

'Will it go down to the gates of death? Will we descend together into the dust?' (Job 17:16). This is utter despondency. If he is to be vindicated, God must act now before it is too late and he is claimed by the forces of darkness.

A summary of Job's reply

'You miserable lot! Anyone can speak as you do but it takes compassion to help a man when he's down.

'You say that if I speak it makes things worse, but when I stop speaking my pain doesn't go away, so what's the use? I'm covered in sores, my bones ache and my kidneys feel as if they're about to burst. And worse, God has given me over to you — and all you can do is mock me! But I don't really care what you think of me: it's God's opinion of me that matters. Even as I speak I have one in heaven who pleads my cause.

'Lord, show them that I'm not guilty. I have no one else to turn to.'

God will not let us go

These closing verses are a reminder to us of how far God may let us fall. We are assured that his hold of us is secure, even when our hold of him falters. But that truth does not preclude the fact that at times he allows his children to experience real despair and hopelessness. It is, after all, the way the Saviour went, being made to feel the anguish of being forsaken by God (Matt. 27:46; Mark 15:34).

It is of the greatest reassurance to know that Job's witness in heaven is one who is touched with the feeling of Job's infirmities (Heb. 4:15). And the same is true for all of God's children! Having himself been brought to the very edge of the precipice of despair, Jesus is all the more able to help us from the resources of his omnipotent compassion. We hear him say to us, 'I have prayed for you ... that your faith may not fail' (Luke 22:32). Paul seeks to convey this same truth when, in the context of adversaries and death, he asks, 'Who is he that condemns?' (Rom. 8:34). He wants us to remember that, with Christ as our Redeemer, we have one whose concern for our welfare and future prosperity is unshakeable: it is 'Christ Jesus, who died — more than that, who was raised to life — is at the right hand of God and is also interceding for us.' He will not let us go!

John Geere described the character of an old English Puritan in 1646 as bearing the motto: '*Vincit Qui Patitur* — He who suffers conquers!' This is a fitting description of Job, though at the close of this speech he is in despair. There are better days ahead, and this is something we must never forget.

12.
The calamities of the wicked

Please read Job 18

Bildad's second speech

Bildad has been variously described as 'tetchy',[1] 'the traditionalist with the barbed tongue'[2] and as 'more concerned for his own reputation than for meeting Job's need'.[3] He is the hatchet man whose lack of modesty and propriety through inexperience and youth does not prevent him from saying exactly what he thinks. He has no patience with Job, who lacks understanding (18:2), likens his friends to brutish animals (18:3) and expects the universe to be turned on its head simply for his own benefit (18:4).[4]

There is hardly anything new in what Bildad says: it is largely taken up with a sermon on the fate of the wicked (18:5-21) — something which Job has now heard many times and which in particular had been the closing application of Eliphaz's last tirade. He offers no hope at all. Instead he paints a picture entitled 'The Dwellings of the Wicked'; it is intended to be a portrait of Job. So black and white is Bildad that some feel that he cannot possibly be describing Job at all.[5] According to this view, we are meant to find his description unconvincing. It is doubtful, however, whether Job found it so. There is evidence to suggest that Bildad's contribution hurt Job deeply.

Bildad's weapons are many.

1. The lamp

'The lamp of the wicked is snuffed out; the flame of his fire stops burning' (18:5). A lamp burning in the house is a symbol that there is life about the place.⁶ Job had already confessed that he was in the dark (17:12) and Bildad rubs salt into his wounds by suggesting that it is proof of his wickedness. When Job had bared his soul, Bildad took the opportunity to expose him further.

2. An old man shuffling along

'The vigour of his step is weakened' (18:7). Bildad draws a picture of an old man, hobbling, unable to take long strides any more: 'His athletic pace becomes a shuffle.'⁷ Like the extinguishing lamp, the vigour of a wicked man soon fades. His shortened steps make him unstable; he is prone to stumble and fall. The contrasting idea can be found in Scripture, too: 'You broaden the path beneath me, so that my ankles do not turn over' (Ps. 18:36); 'When you walk, your steps will not be hampered; when you run, you will not stumble' (Prov. 4:12).

3. Traps

> **His feet thrust him into a net,**
> **and he wanders into its mesh.**
> **A trap seizes him by the heel;**
> **a snare holds him fast.**
> **A noose is hidden for him on the ground;**
> **a trap lies in his path**
>
> (18:8-10).

Six words are employed (net, mesh, trap — two different words in the Hebrew — snare, noose) implying that escape is not possible. There is no escape for the wicked.

4. Disease and fear of death

What lies in store for the wicked person? **'Calamity', 'disaster'** and disease which **'eats away parts of his skin'** (18:12-13). The man in the picture is not only old, but diseased. He has been visited by **'death's firstborn'** (i.e. disease), like some emissary of **'the king of terrors'** (i.e. death) preparing its victims for a meeting with Death — here portrayed as an enthroned king. For this man, like the victims of a police-state, a knock at the door signals the coming of officers who tear folk away from their homes and frogmarch their victims before a merciless potentate.

Human experience everywhere knows the fear that death instils. The epistle to the Hebrews describes the redeemed as persons who had been 'held in slavery by their fear of death' (Heb. 2:15). Death is traumatic: it shocks, unnerves, unsettles the strongest of men. It is the 'king of terrors' still and its emissary, disease, though slain a thousand times, rises again and again in new guises to do its dastardly work.

5. Fire and destruction

'Fire resides in his tent; burning sulphur is scattered over his dwelling' (18:15). The occupants having been 'torn' away from their dwelling, the house is set on fire and destroyed. The fire comes from above and the picture reminds us of the stories of Sodom and Gomorrah (Gen. 19:24) and Dathan and Abiram (Ps. 106:17-18). The result is 'root-and-branch' destruction (18:16).

Even the memories are destroyed in the fire: **'The memory of him perishes from the earth; he has no name in the land.'** Bildad is thinking here of how rulers ensured their continued survival in the memory of those that followed by inscribing their exploits on tablets of stone (Absalom was to do this, 2 Sam. 18:18). Accounts could also be written down and 'remembered' in a book; much of the motivation behind the writing of the book of Nehemiah was that God would remember him (Neh. 5:19; 6:14; 13:14,22,29,31). Job may well allude to this very thing in the next chapter (19:23).

Alternatively, a means of ensuring a continued memory of one's existence was to have children. If a man died prematurely, before having children, Old Testament law provided for 'levirate marriage' (as in the case of Ruth and Boaz). Bildad declares that Job's 'memory' will fade: he will have **'no offspring or descendants among his people'** (18:19). This is his cruellest jibe, opening up sore wounds over the loss of Job's children.

Bildad has expressed his verdict and passed his judgement: Job is wicked and is even now paying the consequences. Bildad has espoused once again his view of immediate retribution: that the wicked suffer for their crimes against God and humanity here and now. It is simplistic and naïve. One wonders if Bildad had ever seen what he was recounting. The wicked are not forgotten: we still talk of Sodom and Gomorrah to this day! Bildad's world-view is the stuff of fantasy. He was shaken by Job. It wasn't only what Job had said that unnerved him; it was the nagging thought that he knew that Job was a righteous man.

Bildad appears so to overplay his hand that one suspects he is arguing from desperation rather than conviction. Everything Job stands for is an affront to his theological system. He is clearly shaken by it. And his only defence is to entrench himself in a view that, one suspects, even he does not fully believe in any more. No one in his right mind would argue the way Bildad does, and one gets the impression that here is a man more intent on keeping his own convictions intact than on offering genuine help and understanding to a friend in desperate need. Sometimes we have to be prepared to admit that we are wrong. At the very least we should have the courage to admit that we just may be mistaken.

A summary of Bildad's second speech

'Job, you are behaving like an idiot. How long are you going to argue like this? Let me spell it out to you again: wicked people are punished. They lose their health, their homes and their offspring. Do I need to say any more? Everyone else can see it, Job, except you. Are you really that stupid, or what?'

13.
Rejected

Please read Job 19

Job's reply to Bildad

Job feels rejected by his friends, by God and by society.

Rejected by his friends (19:2-5)

Arguments get heated and Job finds it hard to be patient with his counsellors. There appears to be a new intensity in his manner here. His friends have reproached him **'ten times'** (19:3) — a number of fulness (e.g. ten fingers) — by which he implies that, in their shameless verbal attacks, they have given 'a full measure'. Job now makes what can only be a hypothetical statement about his sin: **'If it is true that I have gone astray, my error remains my concern alone'** (19:4). It is not so much that Job is claiming that *if* he has sinned, that is his business; it is between him and God and nothing to do with his friends. Rather, Job is saying that his sin has not violated *them* in any way. It resides 'in his own house'. Job has done nothing to violate his friends and their personal attacks have been wholly unjustified. They seem to think that they themselves were God! (cf. 19:22).

It is also argued that the word used for 'error' in 19:4 is a 'mild word'. In other words, Job may well be suggesting here that he is fully prepared to concede that he has sinned (who hasn't?). The penalty for this 'error' lodges with him. But he has not sinned *greatly*, as they had insisted, and Job is not about to give up his claim to innocence — at least the claim that he had done nothing to deserve his particular predicament (cf. 9:21; 10:7; 16:17).

Rejected by God (19:6-12)

Job's argument is not that sin is the cause of his undoing, but that God is. **'God has wronged me'** (19:6), he insists. Similar thoughts have been expressed previously: 'He mocks the despair of the innocent... If it is not he, then who is it?' (Job 9:23-24); 'You ... search out my faults and probe after my sin — though you know that I am not guilty' (Job 10:6-7); 'God has turned me over to evil men ... shattered me ... seized me... He has made me his target... Without pity, he pierces my kidneys and spills my gall on the ground' (Job 16:11-13). This is what precipitated Bildad's question: 'Does God pervert justice?' (Job 8:3); and later Elihu's words: 'It is unthinkable that God would do wrong, that the Almighty would pervert justice' (Job 34:12). It reaches a climax at the close of this chapter when, in the course of appealing to his friends to show some mercy, he pinpoints his trouble: 'The hand of God has struck me' (19:21).[1]

Job's problem is a common one: whenever we do not see the *whole* plan we tend to assume there is a fault with it. Job is unaware of the spiritual contest in which he is a player. He therefore concludes that God is against him.[2]

Images come thick and fast: Job feels as though he is caught in a net (19:6); set upon by thugs and unable to summon any help (19:7); blocked in his path as nightfall approaches (19:8);

humiliated as a prince by some alien lord (19:9); dishonoured, uprooted and therefore without hope (19:10 — contrast 14:7-9 where the tree, though cut down, still has some hope because its roots are intact); forced like a warrior into a single-handed combat (19:11); surrounded by hosts of besieging enemies (19:12).

God is responsible for causing him grievous bodily harm. In a final picture of desolation, he pictures God as a mighty army surrounding an enemy fortress and building a ramp, together with giant catapults and battering rams to destroy him. Anyone who has ever visited Masada, on the south-west shore of the Dead Sea, cannot fail to appreciate the sense of isolation the Zealots must have felt when facing the surrounding Roman legions camped below.[3]

Job feels acute isolation; God has forsaken him. It is one of Satan's strategies to make God out to be our enemy, by 'working the soul', as Thomas Brooks put it, 'to make false inferences from the cross actings of Providence'. We see this in David's conclusions in Psalm 77. He is in distress, unable to sleep and his 'soul refused to be comforted' (Ps. 77:2). What is the conclusion that he draws from this? God has rejected him for ever, his love has vanished, his promises have failed, his mercy is forgotten and his compassion has turned to anger (v. 7). 'God can look sourly,' Brooks comments, 'and chide bitterly, and strike heavily, even where and when he loves dearly. The hand of God was very much against Job, and yet his love, his heart, was very much set upon Job... The hand of God was sore against David and Jonah, when his heart was much set upon them. He that shall conclude that the heart of God is against those that his hand is against, will condemn the generation of the just, whom God unjustly would not have condemned.'[4]

There are three remedies to this condition.

1. What we desire is not necessarily what is best for us. As Brooks says, 'Physic often works contrary to the patient's desires, when it doth not work contrary to their good.'[5]

2. Recall that God works all things together for our good (Rom. 8:28). God's control of providence is comprehensive. The individual pieces of the jigsaw may appear haphazard and without form, but when put together they compose a perfect picture. 'The motions of divine providence are so dark, so deep, so changeable, that the wisest and noblest souls cannot tell what conclusions to make.'[6]

3. All of God's dealings with us — even if he should hand us over to the devil for a season of testing — will only better help us on the road to heaven. As we have seen before, Job's counsellors engaged in a 'this-worldly' frame of reference. They neglected the notion of a world to come where wrongs are righted and injustices put right. We must recall continually that this world is not the only world there is; that life on earth *at best* is but a preparation for a larger, richer, more important and endless life beyond. It was with such a notion that Paul was inspired to face his own personal conflicts: 'I desire to depart,' he told the Philippian church, using the word *analusis* — a word used for the last rope to be cut before the ship slips its moorings and sails out into the harbour and beyond on a new journey!

Rejected by society (19:13-19)

Much more is at stake in Job's sense of isolation. He is alienated by his brothers, estranged from acquaintances, forsaken by kinsmen, forgotten by friends, ignored by his servants, rejected by his wife, scorned by children and detested by those who once loved him (19:13-19). Details of Job's

physical condition come to the surface, including: bad breath
— something which offends his wife (19:17); his appearance,
which he describes as being **'nothing but skin and bones'**;[7]
and the loss of his teeth (19:20).[8]

Bildad has not made any attempt to help Job; he has not
even been listening to him! 'A person in pain is helped the
moment he senses that he is beginning to be understood. A
dying person was asked what he looked for above all in the
people who were ministering to him. "For someone to look as
if they are trying to understand me," he remarked. "He did not
look for success but only that someone should care enough to
try."'[9]

Someone who is in pain wants to have contact with another
person who understands him. 'I saw his heart in his face,'
Shakespeare wrote.[10] One of the most important aspects of any
ministry amongst those who are suffering is what someone has
called 'the ministry of presence'. It is central to the covenantal
ministry of God with us:

> Even though I walk
>   through the valley of the shadow of death,
> I will fear no evil,
>   *for you are with me*
>
> (Ps. 23:4).

The same thought strengthened Paul in his imprisonment in
Rome when he wrote to the Philippian church, 'Yet it was
good of you to *share in my troubles*' (Phil. 4:14). Job had no
such sharer in his afflictions. He was a desolate man!

A new note (19:21-22)

It is surprising that Job calls on his friends to **'have pity on'**
him at this stage (19:21), particularly since it is followed by as

aggressive a speech against his friends as any to be found in the whole book (19:28-29). Job has not exactly paved the way for their pity, having implied their treachery (6:15), their heartlessness (6:27), their stupidity (12:2-3; 13:2), their worthlessness (13:4), their lies (13:7) and their bias (13:7-9). They were 'miserable comforters' (16:2) who had almost succeeded in tormenting and crushing him (19:2).

This is not the way to win friends and influence people! Nevertheless, desperate times call for desperate measures and, as we have noted before, we should not expect clear logical development to characterize everything Job says. If Job's friends can only stop persecuting him, he will be satisfied. He expects little from them — certainly not that they should actually take up his cause; all he wants is a little kindness. It is, perhaps, the most damning indictment of these counsellors that they showed no pity towards their friend. It is, alas, an indictment on the church since Job's day that such heartlessness has all too often been evident among its members too.

Resurrection (19:23-29)

It is equally unexpected that, following this account of Job's desolation, he should interject what is the most well-known statement of faith in the entire book. Indeed, so confident is Job at this point of future vindication that he utters a dire warning to his friends (19:28-29). We need to put it firmly in its context.

Job's longing is that his plea of innocence be recorded for future posterity: he is convinced of his own demise. If it were committed to writing on a scroll (19:23), or better still a rock (19:24), 'it might secure a hearing and possibly a kinder verdict from some future generation. By the inclusion of Job's history in the Scriptures, that wish has been realized beyond his imagining.'[11] This, at least, was a prayer that God answered. It rose, one believes, from the lowest point of Job's spiritual life. 'Out of the depths I cry to you, O Lord,' said the psalmist and Job could echo the sentiment. God hears those desperate cries!

Hope of a future vindication is one thing; future generations may or may not give him a fair hearing. It is time for Job to assess his present position.[12]

So far he has told us what he 'knows'. He 'knows', for instance, that God is his enemy (6:4; 10:8-14; 13:24; 16:7-14; 19:7-12); that he will soon be dead (7:21; 16:22), 'murdered' by God (12:15; 16:18); that he has no hope of gaining vindication from God (9:2-3, 20,28-33; 19:7); and especially that he is innocent (13:16; 16:19-21). But it is time to make clear something else which he 'knows', something which he has been struggling to elicit from his ordeal from the start: that there is a heavenly, divine Vindicator who will argue his case before God. Twice before Job has made an attempt to put this thought into words (9:33; 16:18-22). Now it reaches a climax, for here, he not only knows that his Vindicator exists, but he believes that he will be successful!

> **I know that my Redeemer lives,**
> **and that in the end he will stand upon the earth.**
> **And after my skin has been destroyed,**
> **yet in my flesh I will see God;**
> **I myself will see him**
> **with my own eyes — I, and not another.**
> **How my heart yearns within me!**
>
> (19:26-27).

What is it, precisely, that Job knows?

1. 'My Redeemer lives'

A redeemer *(go'el)* was a person's nearest relative (brother, uncle, cousin, or some other relation) whose obligation could be to buy back family property and thus retain it as part of the family inheritance (Lev. 25:25-34; Jer. 32:6-8); or to pay the necessary amount to save a kinsman from slavery (Lev. 25:35-54); or to marry a widow and provide her dead husband with an heir (Ruth 3:12; 4:1-12); or even to avenge the death of a murdered relative (Num. 35:12,19-27; Deut 19:6,11-12; Josh. 20:2-5,9). Each Israelite had to pay 'a ransom for his life' at the time of the national census; firstborn sons (who since the Passover belonged to God), and especially those in excess of the number of Levites who replaced them, had to be redeemed; the owner of a notoriously dangerous bull, which gored a man to death, was himself put to death, unless he redeemed his life by the payment of an adequate fine; and an impoverished Israelite compelled to sell himself into slavery could later redeem himself or be redeemed by a relative (Exod. 21:28-32; 30:12-16; 13:13; 34:20; Lev. 25:47-55; Num. 3:40-51).

What this illustrated was that somebody had to pay a price to set free property from mortgage, animals from slaughter, persons from slavery or death, or the deceased from dishonour *in order to keep them* (or their memory[name]) *in the family*. Job is confident that such a redeemer exists who will defend his own cause and act as a family-member indebted to maintain his honour and integrity. Job's life is forfeit; God seems already to have pursued him close to death. Should he die, as he expects to, it was the function of the redeemer to avenge the shedding of innocent blood. Even if everyone else disowns him (his 'friends' most certainly had), Job is sure that his divine Kinsman will speak a word in his favour and thereby present a legal case that will gain God's hearing. That such a divine Redeemer exists was part of Old Testament belief. Isaiah, for one, refers to God as 'Israel's King and Redeemer' (Isa. 44:6).

2. 'In the end he will stand upon the earth'

The NIV footnote suggests another possible translation, namely, that 'In the end he will stand *upon my grave.*'[13] If Job cannot secure justice in this world; if his case remains unheard by any earthly court; if, after all, he cannot even get a hearing from God here and now — there will come a time when God will stand upon the earth, stand in judgement and vindicate Job. It is a belief in justice that keeps Job going. God's judgement will be his glory. It will be his vindication of himself, and Job takes refuge in it.

3. 'In my flesh I will see God'

A problem arises here: how can Job 'see' if he is dead and in his grave, his eyes destroyed? This has led some to think that Job is now expressing a wish that he might see God *now* — while he is still alive ('in his flesh').[14] Some evangelical interpreters take it this way, as did some of the most eminent Christian fathers. Other interpreters are equally convinced that Job is expressing here a belief of what lies beyond death. Job is convinced that he is about to die (17:1). All earthly hope is gone! 'In his own esteem he is sinking into the grave, with every indication surrounding him of God's relentless hostility; every possibility of a return of God's favour to him in this life is, to his mind, utterly shut out; and yet so fixed is he in his inward persuasion of the real friendship and redeeming grace of God to him, he bursts the boundaries of time, passes the limits of the visible and the tangible and knows that the manifest tokens of the divine love, which are denied him here, will be granted him there.'[15]

On the first interpretation — that Job is making a statement about *this* life — what follows is therefore a desire on Job's part rather than a statement of belief: 'I myself will see him', meaning 'How I wish that I could see him!' And the intensity of desire is such that his heart yearns within him (a phrase so difficult to translate that one has attempted the rendition: 'My kidneys have ended in my chest'![16]).

Needless to say, this interpretation finds its fulfilment in what happens in chapter 42, when God does become his vindicator on earth, restoring his fortunes and his honour (42:10,12), and where Job is said to have 'seen' God, thus fulfilling his desire to the letter (42:5).[17]

There is some support for this view in the text of Job. There have been times when Job has expressed total pessimism about life after death:

As a cloud vanishes and is gone,
    so he who goes down to the grave does not return
(7:9).

I go to the place of no return,
    to the land of gloom and deep shadow
(10:21).

But man dies and is laid low;
    he breathes his last and is no more.
As water disappears from the sea
    or a riverbed becomes parched and dry,
so man lies down and does not rise;
    till the heavens are no more, men will not awake
    or be roused from their sleep
(14:10-12).

Where then is my hope?
    Who can see any hope for me?
Will it go down to the gates of death?
    Will we descend together into the dust?
(17:15-16)

Some find such passages incompatible with Job's uttering here a clear account of his belief in the resurrection of the body.[18] Several matters need to be taken into account.

Firstly, it would not be unusual for someone in Job's mental and physical condition to display considerable fluctuations of mood. It is quite common for those suffering from depression, or who are in pain, to have sudden bouts of despair followed by moments of resolute faith and courage. Are we really to expect a uniformity of argument in the book of Job as though it were being debated in a court of law? Surely not! As we read the book of Job we feel that we are sitting alongside Job on his ash-heap and the fact that in one chapter he is thoroughly depressed and in the next somewhat elated is perfectly natural given the circumstances — indeed, it makes Job all the more 'human' and understandable, for we too have known such times.

Secondly, these references, whilst precluding a coming back to life as Job knew it, do not in themselves rule out a resurrection to a new kind of life. It is perfectly true that Job, should he die, could not expect to come back to life as, say, Lazarus did. Pessimism about the holding power of the grave is something quite compatible with the highest Christian assurance about a future resurrection of the body.

Thirdly, any interpretation of this passage has to take in view the cumulative insights of such utterances as Job gave in 14:14 and 16:19. It has led one commentator to say that 'The hope of resurrection lies at the heart of Job's faith.'[19] This is the view more commonly accepted by evangelicals: Job is speaking here of his belief that he will be vindicated *after* his death when in a bodily state — i.e., Job is expressing his belief in a future bodily resurrection.[20] 'They who wish to parade their cleverness, cavil that this is not to be understood as referring to the final resurrection, but to the first day on which Job hoped that God would deal more kindly with him,' observes Calvin. He adds by way of comment, 'This we concede in part. Still, we shall force them to admit, whether they are willing or not, that Job could not have attained this lofty hope if his aspiration had rested on earth. We must therefore acknowledge that he lifted up his eyes to a future immortality, for he saw that his Redeemer would be with him even as he lay in the tomb.'[21] It is Job's belief that even though he must die and be consumed, he will nevertheless stand before God in a new body. He will see God as his kinsman and not as a stranger who is currently hostile towards him (19:11-12).[22]

Job's affirmation has reminded us (and himself!) that this life is not the only life there is. Life on earth is at best a preparation for a life that is richer, larger and more important beyond the grave. With the insight of the New Testament we know that, for Christians, death is not the gateway into ultimate darkness, but rather a means of meeting with Christ. He takes us through the final dissolution of the body into a fellowship that is richer and closer than ever before. After all, we are assured that in Christ we have one who is 'not ashamed to call [us] brothers' (Heb. 2:11). We are his *brothers*! He is, as it were, our Elder Brother. He, too, has passed through this experience of pain that leads to death and emerged victorious on the other side. Our Kinsman-Redeemer is one who has tasted death for us (Heb. 2:9). What we have in Job's words are the beginnings of what progressive revelation would reveal as the doctrines of the coming of Christ at the end of times, the resurrection of the body, and the final judgement.

A summary of Job's reply

'You people are the limit! You insult me all the time. Can't you do anything else? God has wronged me! And when I cry out, nobody answers. It is true: he has taken everything that I have. My servants will not listen to me any more; even my wife has turned against me. All I want is some kindness from you.

'If only my words could be written down! But I know that my Redeemer lives and one day — yes, one day, he will make everything right again. I know this to be true.'

A ray of hope in the depths of despair

One observation remains to be made. We have seen Job plumb the heights of spiritual affirmation in God's justice that will finally vindicate him. We have also observed him in the very depths of despair and confusion. Can a single individual express such hopeful thoughts amidst such darkness? Robert Davis, a minister of a large, thriving church in America, writes of his own experience of Alzheimer's Disease. In the course of just seven months and his retirement from ministry, he described his experience as 'a combination of medical, psychological, mental, and spiritual changes that tossed me around like a cork in the ocean. During this time I had a special mountain-top experience that drew me as close as I have ever been to the sunshine of Christ. During this same time I had the blackest times, in which there was not even any moonlight — times when I was convinced that Christ had forsaken me to be consumed by the terrors of blackness.'[23]

Afflictions are 'God's archers', Calvin comments,[24] to which the best response is one of submission: 'Let us be content to walk whithersoever he leads and directs us, assuring ourselves that his only will must be to us the infallible rule of right: whereas we see Job so overmastered of his affections, let us understand that it is a right hard thing for us to submit ourselves to the single will of God, without asking a reason of his works, and especially of those works that surmount our wit and capacity.'[25] In dealing with the issue of suffering, Calvin suggests again and again that the purpose of the book of Job is not to provide explanations for it, but to show that submission is the way of wisdom.

Despite the confusion of Job's thoughts, he remained convinced of God's existence.

Janet Zorick, a Lutheran Christian, lost her husband in a terrible fire in a crowded building. She, too, had been in the fire, but her husband had saved her. She escaped, but her husband did not. For some time afterwards, Janet could not get over it. She recalled his words: 'One of us has to get out for the kids.' She glanced at the blackened watch handed to her afterwards. She remembered the strange fact that her husband's charred body only had one shoe on. How could God allow such a thing? Janet came to the conclusion that she *had* to believe in God: 'There has to be a hereafter or what's the use of anything?' she said.

That is the point that Job is making. Through the tragedies of life, there is an over-arching providence, a benevolent hand at work that sweeps all of human history to a climax: the mystery of the new heavens and the new earth. In that process great upheavals take place, but every single one of God's children will be brought safely to him to live with him for ever.

It is this vision that keeps us going through days of darkness. It is what sustained Job in his hour of need.

14.
Sinners in the hands of an angry God

Please read Job 20

Zophar's second speech

When Jonathan Edwards preached his famous sermon, 'Sinners in the Hands of an Angry God,' to his New England congregation it is said that his listeners clung on to their pews until their knuckles were white, fearing lest they should fall into hell. Those who listened to Zophar's sermon may well have done the same — all, that is, except Job. He did not see its relevance to his case.

Job's warning of a sword (19:29) has made Zophar's blood boil. He is **'troubled'** and **'greatly disturbed'** (20:1). Zophar feels 'rebuked' and 'dishonoured' by it (20:3). He feels compelled to speak from the storehouse of his great **'understanding'**! (20:3).The trouble is that he has only one song to sing, and in truth it is not a song at all, but a dirge on the fate of the wicked! Taken in the abstract, it is an almost perfect sermon, one of remarkable consistency and pointed application. Having made a balanced first speech in which he had depicted both the fate of the righteous and the wicked, he now focuses excusively on the negative.

The destruction of the wicked (20:4-11)

The joy of the wicked is a hollow thing: it does not last (20:5). This is not quite the Christian thought expressed in the lines: 'Solid joys and lasting treasures, none but Zion's children know.'[1] Zophar is more concerned to point out the negative than the positive. Immediate punishment of the wicked is part of his world-order. Job cannot be an exception. His pride may ascend to the heavens, but as they say, 'The higher you climb, the harder the fall!' (20:6). The wicked man will be consumed like fuel (**'dung'**) in the fire (20:7). He will vanish like a dream (20:8), like a man who disappears (20:9). His wealth and youthful vigour will expire along with him (20:10-11). He returns eventually to what he is — **'dust'**.

Wrongdoing yields no ultimate profit (20:12-23)

Preachers worth their salt are prone to use illustrations to get their point across. Zophar is no exception, here using a sustained metaphor (eating) to keep together what he wants to say. Thus he refers to the **'mouth'** (20:12,13), **'tongue'** (20:12), **'stomach'** (20:14,15) and **'belly'** (20:23) and to such acts as savouring (20:12), swallowing (20:14), spitting and vomiting (20:15) and sucking (20:16), to foods such **'honey and cream'** (20:17) and speaks of things tasting **'sweet'** (20:12) or **'sour'** (20:14). The point Zophar is trying to get across is one summed up by a proverb: 'Food gained by fraud tastes sweet to a man, but he ends up with a mouth full of gravel' (Prov. 20:17). A wicked person savours his evil deeds like a little child who sucks the last juices out of a sweet so as to taste all the flavour. And as 'sweet-suckers' know, the sweet eventually dissolves.

Sin often comes sugar-coated and it is part of Christian maturity to recognize that things which appear sweet on the outside can be full of deadly poison inside. Should the morsel be swallowed, it releases its emetic into the system, causing vomiting.

There is no escape for the wicked (20:24-29)

Perhaps recalling that Job had said himself that God was attacking him like a warrior in battle (16:13), Zophar changes the picture from food to a more military one. There is no escape for the wicked from the ultimate punishment of God. Even if he should escape one weapon, another catches him (20:24). Eventually the evildoer and all that he has gained will be consumed by the fire and flood of God (20:26,28). Zophar seems to be directly contradicting Job's affirmation earlier when he cried out, 'Even now my witness is in heaven' (16:18), by adding that there is no point in Job asking for a trial, for the very earth and heaven will rise up and testify to his iniquity (20:27). **'Such is the fate God allots the wicked,'** Zophar concludes and it is clear that he means Job to take it personally to heart (Job 20:29).

Zophar has nothing more to say. These are his final words to Job. He seems to have made up his mind about his friend and given him up as a lost cause. He doesn't even bother to call Job to repentance, such is his conviction that he is utterly lost and doomed. Zophar has come across like a record where the needle has got stuck in the groove. In a forlorn attempt to get something concrete into his charges against his friend he seems to have a particular grudge concerning Job's wealth. He just cannot get it out of his mind that Job must have acquired it by ill-gotten means (cf. 20:10,18,21,22,26,28). It may well be that Zophar is guilty of envy. It would not be the first case of a preacher who has castigated his audience for something that lies more appropriately at the door of his own heart. When we are engaged in judgemental counselling of this sort, we need to make sure that our motives are pure. One cannot help suspecting that Zophar's were not.

A summary of Zophar's speech

'Job, you are making my blood boil! You are insulting and arrogant. What I am saying is known by everyone — except you it seems! Evil people perish quickly. They get what they ask for in the end. They may prosper for a little while, but eventually it catches up with them. God judges people like that. That's all I have to say.'

15.
The wicked prosper and the righteous suffer!

Please read Job 21

Job's reply to Zophar

In Job's speeches to date, he has been keen to give his own defence, often breaking off into a prayer. The time has come, however, for a direct rebuttal of his friends' remarks. It is possible to see Job quoting directly from what his friends have said, showing, at the very least, that he has been listening to what they have had to say.¹ He begins by pleading with his friends to pay attention: **'Listen'**, **'bear with me'**, **'look at me'**, **'clap your hand over your mouth'** (21:2,3,5).

Job asks for some genuine **'consolation'** (21:2). Though he is anxious to gain the hearing of all his 'friends', he appears to want Zophar's attention in particular suggesting (in the singular and not the plural) that after he has finished his speech, Zophar can return to his mocking (21:3). Job was clearly hurt by what Zophar had said. 'Sticks and stones may break my bones, but words will never hurt me,' is a childish rhyme that never did ring true to life. Words can and do hurt deeply. It is why the Bible takes such pains to counsel us about the use we make of our tongues (cf. James 3:1-12).

It might be helpful if we take note of some of the things that Job has specifically noted (see table).

Reference in Chapter 21	Quotation from friends' speeches	Friends' thesis analysed	Job's rebuttal
21:7	5:5; 15:20; 20:15-18	The wealth of the wicked is of no advantage to them.[2]	Their wealth is real and lasting (21:7); it even provides for their offspring (21:8).
21:7; 21:13	20:11	Zophar had asserted that the wicked die prematurely.	Job insists that they 'live on' (21:7). Indeed, as they grow old they increase in power — a word which 'can refer to both physical prowess, managerial efficiency and material prosperity'.[3] 'They spend their years in prosperity and go down to the grave in peace' (21:13).
21:8; 21:11	18:19	Bildad had suggested that the wicked die childess (as Job was about to do).	Job says that 'They see their children established around them, their offspring before their eyes' (21:8), and 'They send forth their children as a flock; their little ones dance about' (21:11).
21:17-19	18:5; cf. 5:4; 20:10	The wicked are blown away like chaff.	'How often?' Job responds sceptically. The friends have an answer for this: sometimes God punishes their children instead. Eliphaz and Zophar had said this (5:4;

Reference in Chapter 21	Quotation from friends' speeches	Friends' thesis analysed	Job's rebuttal
			20:10; cf. 21:19). Job finds this notion inherently unjust. A man should suffer the consequences of his sin himself.[4]
21:19-21	5:4; 18:19; 20:10,21	God will punish the children if he doesn't punish the evildoer.	The children of the wicked are often more powerful than the wicked themselves (21:8); this doctrine is morally unacceptable (21:19-21).
21:22	4:17; 11:5-9; 15:8-14	Job's friends call into question his right to pursue this constant querying of God's ways in the death of individuals. Job should not question God's ways.[5]	Death is the great leveller; both the good and the evil die. It says nothing about their standing with God (21:22-26).
21:28	15:34; 18:21; 20:28	'Show us, if you can, a wicked man dwelling in a fine house. It cannot be done!'	There are many travellers who will tell you that there are many wicked people who dwell in luxury. Not only so, but they die in luxury also. Their funerals are splendid affairs (21:31-33). Their ill-gotten wealth ensures that their graves are looked after for generations to come.

Job is unimpressed by what his friends have had to say. True though their words may be in another context, they are irrelevant as far as Job is concerned and therefore **'falsehood'** (21:34). His friends have proved faithless. Job feels that he deserves something better. They have broken their trust. They have been disloyal. It is something which he has said of them before (13:1-12; 16:2). **'How can you console me?'** he asks (21:34). Job would eventually find his consolation, but not from these men. 'Great hearts can only be made by great troubles,' Spurgeon wrote. 'The spade of trouble digs the reservoir of comfort deeper, and makes more room for consolation.'⁶ It is obvious that Zophar and his companions had known little of suffering in their own lives. They were not in a position to offer such cold advice to their suffering friend. One cannot help gain the impression that at the close of Zophar's speech, he is so carried away with his own eloquence that he has forgotten all about Job! It may not be too harsh a judgement to conclude that Job's companions loved the sound of their own voices.

'How long, O Lord?'

Zophar's point was to suggest that the wicked only enjoy the fruit of their sins for a short time. If God's retribution is delayed for a while, *it is only for a while!* But Job finds this premise faulty.

Job describes the wicked in terms of their blasphemy. He portrays them as saying to God,

> **'Leave us alone!**
>   **We have no desire to know your ways.**
> **Who is the Almighty, that we should serve him?**
>   **What would we gain by praying to him?'**
>   (21:14-15).

And are they judged? No! The wicked **'spend their years in prosperity and go down to the grave in peace'** (21:13). They **'live on'** to old age (21:7), contrary to what Zophar had suggested (20:11); they see **'their children established'** (21:8), contrary to what Bildad had said (18:19); their homes are places of safety (21:9), contrary to what Eliphaz had implied (5:24); and their livestock (i.e. their financial security) **'never fail to breed'** (21:10). This may be a little exaggerated, but it is how we often perceive things to be.

At the end of the day, whether one is good or bad appears not to make any difference (21:22). The prosperous and impoverished die together and it seems to make no difference to God (21:23-26). Even in death, their graves are maintained and secure (21:32). In other words, the godless never appear to suffer too much.

A summary of Job's reply

'Listen to me, I know I'm being impatient, but that is surely understandable! My body is shaking because of what's happening to me.

'What you keep on saying just isn't true. I have known many wicked people prosper and become very powerful. They prosper; their families prosper, even after they have gone. They have all they need and they seem never to be in trouble. They even insult and ridicule God and get away with it. I tell you, I have seen it.

'It's rare for a wicked man to be judged in this world. "But their sons are punished," you say. But God ought to punish them and not their sons.

'What you say is nonsense — it stinks! It's just not true.'

An assessment of Job's reply

Job's reply is true, *but only up to a point.* God does shower his gifts of common grace upon the wicked as well as the righteous. But there is a purpose behind his activity. Paul points out what this purpose is: it is meant to lead the wicked to repentance. 'Or do you show contempt for the riches of his kindness, tolerance and patience, not realizing that God's kindness leads you towards repentance?' (Rom. 2:4). God 'causes his sun to rise on the evil and the good, and sends rain on the righteous and the unrighteous' (Matt. 5:45) for an evangelical end.

Job was not the only one to complain about God's ways. Habakkuk complained about it in his day:

How long, O Lord, must I call for help,
   but you do not listen?
Or cry out to you, 'Violence!'
   but you do not save?

(Hab. 1:2).

Why does God allow certain things to happen? Why do such terrible things happen to good people? Why doesn't God answer our prayers? Habakkuk had called for God to act, but called into question God's timing.

Habakkuk's complaint was that King Jehoiakim, an ambitious, cruel and corrupt leader, had brought Judah to the brink of disaster by his alliance with Assyria. It was time for God to punish him. But God seemed to be silent to the prophet's cries. It looked as though he had forgotten his people. But this was not the case. Eventually, in his own time, God would raise up the Chaldeans who would punish the Assyrians.

One would expect the wicked to be punished, but it is Job whom God has struck (21:9; cf. 19:21; 9:34). And Job is troubled by it. Why? Because he still believes that God is in control, inflicting his punishment on Job (21:9). And, what is more, it is God who lies behind the wicked's prosperity: **'Their prosperity is not in their own hands'** (21:16). Deep down, despite the seeming chaos, Job does not abandon his belief that God is in control of all that happens. Despite all his arguments, it is the secret of his calmness, his 'patience' or perseverance. No matter how rich and secure the wicked may be, Job will have none of it. Even in his misery Job would not exchange places with the wicked — not for all their riches!

An anatomy of the soul

When Calvin came to write a commentary on the book of Psalms he wrote by way of introduction: 'I have been wont to call this book, not inappropriately, an anatomy of all the parts of the soul; for there is not an emotion of which anyone can be conscious that is not here represented as in a mirror.'[7] He might as well have been thinking about Job, for in this book also we are given a glimpse into every aspect of Job's soul. Every feeling imaginable is expressed somewhere or other in these chapters.

Throughout history, people have turned to Job to help them in times of difficulty. They may not always have found answers to their questions — Job didn't! But they have been helped simply by knowing that others have expressed the anxieties and perplexities that they have been too frightened to mention.

There is a unity about the Bible's message, and Christians recognize it immediately. The experiences of Moses, David and Elijah are our own experiences. We are 'a million miles away' from Job culturally, socially, geographically, and perhaps even spiritually. But we instinctively recognize something in what he writes that is true of our own situation. We make allowances for Job's time and circumstances, but we find parallels all along the way. Whenever we are tempted to feel that we are unique, that no one else has ever known the trials we are suffering, the doubts we experience, the fears that keep us awake at night, the feeling of deep-seated anger that rises within us when badly treated — then we discover, as we read Job (or, as Calvin said, the Psalms), that we are not unique!

One thing we should note is the honesty of Job. He expresses his depression, his fear, his hurt. He does not try to hide his feelings. Some of us do. Others of us, who have different temperaments, are far more quick to express the way we feel. We ought not to be too critical of each other for that. We are far too hasty in judging someone who is phlegmatic, for example, because he is not bouncing about like Tiger. Not everyone is a Tiger! Some of us are Eeyores!

Job, like Asaph in Psalm 73, has 'had the feet taken away from him' (cf. 'My feet had almost slipped,' Ps. 73:2). He was almost gone. He is angry that the wicked are prospering and the godly (like himself, of course) are in deep trouble. Who hasn't felt that at some time? Why should I suffer? What have I done to deserve this?

Job, like Asaph, does not comprehend the ways of God in the world and as a result he is badly shaken. It is the problem of theodicy![8] Here he is practising the godly life, avoiding sin, meditating on the things of God, spending time in prayer, and so on. He has kept clear of the polluting effects of the world. And yet all day long he is plagued and chastened every morning. Everything seems to be going wrong. He is obeying the demands of a righteous life and things are getting difficult. Nothing seems to be going right at all. But worse than that, he sees that the ungodly are prospering. They are not in trouble. They live well and die well. They are deceitful and blasphemous; they are successful in every way and stand out in fatness. They speak with such arrogance! Pride covers them like a garment.

The book of Job teaches us (as does Psalm 73) the following lessons:

1. To be confused by God's dealings with us ought not to surprise us in any way

'My thoughts are not your thoughts, neither are your ways my ways' (Isa. 55:8). We cannot possibly know the mind of God. God is great, ultimately unknowable. He is essentially incomprehensible. 'God is not the sort of person we are; His wisdom, His aims, His scale of values, His mode of procedure, differ so vastly from our own that we cannot possibly guess our way to them by intuition or infer them by analogy from our notion of ideal manhood. We cannot know him unless he speaks and tells us about himself.'[9]

2. To be troubled about God's dealing with us is not a sin

That seems a trite sort of thing to say and not very helpful, but there are those who seem to be always clear about how God works. Think of the contributions of Job's three counsellors. They were very sure about God's dealings. If you are in trouble it is because you have sinned. It is as simple as that. Well, Paul was never as clear as that. 'We are perplexed,' he admits (2 Cor. 4:8). Think of Joseph in Egypt: do you not think he was in perplexity?

3. Trouble is a period of great temptation

Whenever trouble is present, Satan is present somewhere. Even if the trouble is a chastening from God (and in Job's case we are informed that it was not), the devil will use it to make you distrust God. This was something that even Jesus was subjected to. In the wilderness he took on Satan and his cohorts in order to gain for us the final victory over the kingdom of darkness. Temptation is incredibly powerful.

4. Trouble need not defeat us entirely

This is what the book of Job is ultimately about. Peter was reassured that in his fall Jesus had prayed for him (Luke 22:31). God will keep his own, even though he may test them.

16.
Job: one of the greatest sinners on earth

Please read Job 22

Eliphaz's third speech

There is always a tendency in any debate to overplay one's argument. Fact blurs into fantasy in the interest of winning a quarrel. Job's friends have long since forgotten Job *the man*; they are far more concerned now to prove themselves right. Having come this far, and sighting victory, they become merciless in their counselling methodology. In fact, it is difficult to see any method at all. At first all three had something distinctive to say. In the second round of speeches all three concentrated on the fate of the wicked. Now, in this third round, Eliphaz appears to contradict his earlier position, Bildad only gets the preface of his speech out and Zophar doesn't speak at all! In the midst of it all, thoughts of Job's feelings seem to have no bearing on what they now say; they are going to indict Job as the worst sinner on the globe, no matter what.

All of this reflects, sadly, on our own attempts at helping others when, far too often, we are more anxious to prove ourselves right than to offer real, genuine help to those who hurt. And those of us with clearly defined theological positions are most vulnerable here. We had better learn something from these men.

'Is not your wickedness great?'

If Eliphaz began in a courteous manner, the evidence of it is now quickly vanishing. As the oldest and wisest he had expected his words to be accepted without question by Job. His diatribe that sin causes suffering has gone unheeded. Job has had the audacity to flatly contradict it. The very foundation of Eliphaz's theology has been questioned. It is time to get nasty. **'Is not your wickedness great? Are not your sins endless?'** Eliphaz asks (22:5).[1]

Eliphaz has now become personal. Gone are the niceties of formal debate. Job is a great sinner! Agreeing with Satan, Job's three friends accuse him of being a hypocrite. God's champion, the one in whom God's grace had been so evidently exhibited, in point of fact belongs to the devil. God cannot possibly be punishing Job for his **'piety'** (22:4). It has to be, therefore, because Job is a sinner — *a great sinner*! The sooner Job admits it, the better. Job had better stop thinking that in some way he is something special in God's eyes and own up to the fact that he is a sinner.[2]

This was Eliphaz's point in his opening speech. If Job is to be delivered, it will be because his hands are clean (22:30). But whereas Eliphaz had started by suggesting that Job was *not* a great sinner, he has by now changed his mind. Job is amongst the greatest of sinners on earth! It hardly aids our confidence in this man's counselling ability when in the course of his argument he changes his point of view so radically . As Clines comments, 'These are the most specific, most harsh, and most unjust words spoken against Job in the whole book, and it is strange to find them on the lips of Eliphaz, out of all his friends.'[3]

What sin has Job committed? Eliphaz shows the power of his imagination by inventing an entire catalogue of transgressions: oppression of the poor (taking a poor man's clothing as a pledge against a non-existent debt and refusing to return it at night, 22:6);⁴ refusing **'water to the weary'** and withholding **'food from the hungry'** (22:7); showing no mercy to widows and orphans (22:9).

Job's case, whatever the facts may have been, is not helped by the fact that he had been a very rich man. Eliphaz knows the public's envy and distrust of the rich and plays on these feelings. In the opinion of the majority, Job was bound to be guilty. Eliphaz is only confirming what most people would have thought of Job in any case.

Secret sins

Having sown the seeds of doubt, Eliphaz goes into top gear. He deliberately misquotes what Job has said and turns it against him. Most of us have heard clever interviewers do this on the media, deliberately putting words into someone's mouth. It makes us want to shout: 'But wait a minute, he didn't say that!' Job had attributed a certain saying to the wicked in his reply to Zophar (21:14-15), and Eliphaz promptly turns it against him. He accuses Job of having said that God neither knows what Job is doing, nor can he do anything about it:

> **Yet you say, 'What does God know?**
> **Does he judge through such darkness?'...**
> **They said to God, 'Leave us alone!**
> **What can the Almighty do to us?'**

> (22:13,17).

It was Zophar who had originally accused Job of being a secret sinner (11:5-6). Now Eliphaz joins him in suggesting that the real cause of Job's downfall lay in hidden sins that even Job may not be conscious of. The whole argument is now confused, since he has already charged Job with being a great (and presumably open) sinner.

In Eliphaz's eyes, Job has nothing but contempt for God. Job has said, of course, nothing of the sort, but truth is little valued in the heat of an argument. In a cutting remark, Eliphaz suggests that folk are actually glad that Job is suffering: in their eyes, it is no less than he deserves (22:19).

A call to repentance

The final section (22:21-30) at first glance appears a little strange following what Eliphaz has just said. Basically, it is a call to submission: to be at peace with God (22:21); to hear and consequently hide God's Word in his heart (22:22); to return to the Almighty, and turn away from wickedness (22:23); to find delight in the Lord rather than in material things (22:24-26); and to engage in a life of prayer and obedience (22:27). On the face of it, it appears orthodox enough.[5] 'This ...,' comments Smick, 'could not be improved on by prophet or evangelist.'[6] Eliphaz seems to be calling upon his 'friend' to repent and seek the face of God. He calls upon Job to listen carefully to his words, implying that they are God's words:

Submit to God and be at peace with him;
   in this way prosperity will come to you.
Accept instruction from his mouth
   and lay up his words in your heart

(22:21-22).

This is the confidence we often think we have: that our thoughts are God's thoughts. Eliphaz's private visions of the night (chapter 4) have now assumed authoritative proportions. Eliphaz's theology is now confirmed: the evidence of a man's righteousness lies in his health and wealth. The result of Job's supposed lifestyle of *profit* and *pleasure* (22:3-4) is to be found in his present *poverty* and *pain*. The message of the 'prosperity gospel' is that God wants us to prosper and be happy; if we give to him, he will give us our heart's desire: health, wealth and happiness. Job's evident lack in these areas is a signal of God's displeasure — a displeasure caused by gross sinfulness on Job's part. Job's only source of hope lies in immediate repentance. It is a song we have heard before, and we shall hear it again.

The irony should not be missed that it is Eliphaz and his companions who will need the intercession of Job in order that *their* sins might be forgiven (42:7-9). Eliphaz reminds us of the Pharisee — all pomp and show, but failing to see that outward circumstances are no reflection of the condition of the heart before God.

A summary of Eliphaz's third speech

'Job, if what you are saying is true, then why are you suffering? Surely it's not because you are so holy?

'No, face up to it, Job, it's because your wickedness is so great. You have robbed the poor, stripped them naked, refused to give them food and water. You must also have been extraordinarily mean to widows and orphans. This is why God has set traps all around you.

'You keep on saying that God is far away, and that he cannot see what is happening to you, but this is just a way of saying that God cannot see the wickedness which you do. I see it clearly now: you are following an evil path, you deny God's power, and his goodness!

'Job, you had better repent quickly! God is speaking to you through me and he is saying to you that the road down which you are travelling ends in destruction and misery. If you repent, God will restore you. He will even give back to you the riches you have lost. Better still, he will restore to you the joy that you have lost.'

17.
Deserted by God

Please read Job 23 - 24

Job's reply to Eliphaz

Sometimes it is best just to ignore the foolish, unhelpful contributions of misguided friends. Instead of replying to Eliphaz's charge, Job seems to continue where he left off at the end of chapter 21. It is a speech in which Job reflects on the apparent injustice of God's dealings with the righteous (chapter 23) and with the wicked (chapter 24).

Job's pain, his **'groaning'** (23:2), has pushed him to the edge of self-control. He feels the weight of God's hand upon him: **'His hand is heavy'** (23:2). The same expression is used of the people of Ashdod in Samuel's time, when the Philistines had captured the ark and taken it from Ebenezer to Ashdod. 'The Lord's hand was heavy upon the people of Ashdod and its vicinity; he brought devastation upon them and afflicted them with tumours' (1 Sam. 5:6).

There are times when God seems far away. It is just such a time for Job; he feels totally deserted. He knows that his Redeemer lives (19:25), but he cannot find him (23:3). Job is more anxious than ever to present his case before God (23:4-5). When Job is finally given the opportunity to do so in the closing chapters, he becomes silent, indicating that Job is 'not so anxious to prove his innocence by powerful rhetoric as he is to renew communion with God'.[1]

Job feels abandoned by God. He is experiencing what our forefathers would have called 'spiritual desertion', the feeling that God has forgotten us. It is the sense of isolation felt by the psalmist in so many of the lament psalms:

> How long, O Lord? Will you forget me for ever?
>   How long will you hide your face from me?
> How long must I wrestle with my thoughts
>   and every day have sorrow in my heart?
> How long will my enemy triumph over me?
> Look on me and answer, O Lord my God.
>   Give light to my eyes, or I will sleep in death;
> my enemy will say, 'I have overcome him,'
>   and my foes will rejoice when I fall
>
>   (Ps. 13:1-4).

David seems to be walking through a tunnel in this psalm (there is no light, v. 3). In the same way, Job is surrounded by darkness and gloom: he is in **'darkness ... thick darkness'** (23:17). He cannot see where he is going, or what the point of it all is. Both are asking the question: 'Why is it that God seems to have forgotten me?'

We sometimes speak of God's presence with us in our lives. We feel his nearness and it is a source of great encouragement. Job's experience is the reverse:

> **If only I knew where to find him;**
>   **if only I could go to his dwelling!...**
> **But if I go to the east, he is not there;**
>   **if I go to the west, I do not find him.**
> **When he is at work in the north, I do not see him;**
>   **when he turns to the south, I catch no glimpse of**
>   **him**
>
>   (23:3,8-9).

Job no longer felt God's nearness. He felt spiritually depressed, lonely and abandoned.

The sense of being forgotten tends to make us feel humiliated. It is a feeling of being small and totally insignificant. Job did not know which way God was looking; he could not perceive the smile on his face. He was in a tunnel. God had forgotten him and hidden himself from him, yet God warned his people that they should never forget him (Deut. 8:11,14,19). He would later reveal himself as the one who cannot forget his people:

> Can a mother forget the baby at her breast
>   and have no compassion on the child she has borne?
> Though she may forget, I will not forget you!
>   See, I have engraved you on the palms of my hands
> (Isa. 49:15-16).

Why does Job feel like this? Chapter 24 gives us the full answer. The wicked are prospering. Unlike Samuel, God does not have a regular circuit for judging people (24:1-2). Cruel and greedy men therefore roam the land unchecked. Job gives voice to a catalogue of vices that threaten to undo society and reduce it to chaos. His description is reminiscent of the end of the opening chapter of Paul's letter to the Romans. The list includes: farmers who move boundary fences and thus allow their livestock to graze on land which does not belong to them; merciless treatment of orphans, widows and the poor; murderers who come out at night and perform their evil work; adulterers who watch for dusk and think no one will see them as they give in to their lusts (24:2-17). Such evildoers are deserving of God's curse, and Job calls for it (24:18-25).

There are important lessons to be learnt in this response of Job's as to the way we are meant to deal with the sense of desertion by God that sometimes overtakes us.

For one thing, Job has already begun the healing process by identifying the problem. Whenever we begin to speak to God about being abandoned, we are no longer at the lowest point: the tide has turned; we are on the way up.

This can be seen in Job's words of faith that follow. They seem to rise as a direct result of his having identified the problem. He is **'terrified'** by his ordeal, to be sure (23:16); but he is not **'silenced'** by it (23:17). What looks so agonizingly fatal is in fact a sign that in Job's life there beats a heart of faith. To speak as candidly as Job does throughout these chapters, and here especially, is a sign of *life*! Watching over every meticulous detail of Job's life is a God who loves him and cares for him. And deep down, Job knows it! He even says as much: **'But he knows the way that I take...'** (23:10). Depressed and confused as Job is, there are signs here that he is on the mend. Why, he is even talking about the Lord and how much he knows and cares for him!

Seeing things God's way

Have you ever felt like Job? I am sure that you have. I, too, have had such days when God seems far away. And at times like these it difficult to remain objective. We tend to view everything from our own point of view — a darkened point of view.

This is why we need light. And Job found it outside of himself. Rather than focus on the turmoil in his own heart, he begins to look at the situation as God would see it. He puts it this way: **'When he has tested me, I shall come forth as gold'** (23:10). He is acknowledging that even though his life is filled with darkness and trouble, he is not asking that these be removed. That would be our instant request, would it not? Job realizes that their removal may not be in his best interests. They may be, after all, the very means of his blessing.

Job is concerned to *understand* what is taking place. He wants to be able to see that there is a purpose to what is happening to him. He knows there is, of course; but he wants to be able to see it.

Imagine that you were born in a part of the world where there was no Bible. One day you discover a page of John chapter 19, with the details of the crucifixion, death and burial of Jesus Christ. Would it inspire you with any hope? Probably not. Unless you had access to chapter 20, which records the resurrection of Jesus Christ and the knowledge that he is still alive, you would be unable to interpret the full significance of Jesus' death. Interpreting providence is like that: one needs to see the whole picture. Job's response is very moving: 'I don't know what's happening; *but he knows!*' 'In the grip of the mystery of God's providential dealings with us', comments John Murray, 'this is the very acme and apex of faith. To put it very simply, it means that our resting-place, as we may be faced with the mystery of God's secret will, is "I do not know, but I know that God knows." The judge of all the earth will do right.'[2]

Bowing the knee in humble submission

What emerges here in Job's struggles with pain is something that forms the very core of the book of Job. Time and time again, Job faces the impenetrable mystery of God's ways. We have met it before and we shall do so again before we finish this book. In the end, *there is a mystery to God's ways that we can never fathom.* He is, and will ever remain, incomprehensible to us.

God is sovereign. As Herman Bavinck wrote in the introduction to a work on the doctrine of God, 'Mystery is the vital element of dogmatics.'[3] Ultimately, God dwells in unapproachable light (1 Tim. 6:16). God is great, Scripture says (Deut. 7:21; Neh. 4:14; Ps. 48:1; 86:10; 95:3; 145:3; Dan. 9:4), by which it means that he is greater than we can ever fathom. We lack the capacity to fully understand God. Though we insist that what we do know of God, we know truly, it remains true that what we know of him, we know but a little. It is to this point that Job speaks so eloquently in this chapter:

> **But he stands alone, and who can oppose him?**
> **He does whatever he pleases.**
> **He carries out his decree against me,**
> **and many such plans he still has in store**
>
> (23:13-14).

But there is another truth that emerges that is of equal importance. Job could not plumb the depths of God's ways, but God could and did. *God is not a mystery to himself.* He knows what he is doing. And in this truth Job rested with increasing ease.

This was a truth in which Jeremiah found comfort, too. Living as he did at a time when Judah was visibly collapsing and Jerusalem was being threatened by Babylonian troops, Jeremiah was witnessing the destruction of the church of God. In chapter 12, he utters a complaint: 'Why does the way of the wicked prosper? Why do all the faithless live at ease' (Jer. 12:1). What is of importance for us to know here is the way Jeremiah helps himself out of a potentially painful bout of spiritual depression. 'Yet you know me, O Lord' (Jer. 12:3). I may not understand, but I know that he does. This assurance is the source of Job's strength here too. 'When we say that God is almighty,' writes Calvin, 'it is not only to honour him, but to rest upon him, that we may be invincible against all temptations. For inasmuch as God's mighty power is infinite, he can well maintain and preserve us.'[4]

His Word in our hearts

Job's healing came as the result of an open acknowledgement of his feelings to the Lord. What Job discovered was that even in the darkness he had not lost his faith completely. God's face may have turned away, but his promises remained the same. And Job pleads them: **'I have treasured the words of his mouth more than my daily bread'** (23:12). Job had sought to keep God's law (23:11). But God's Word also contains gospel. What Job is anxious to receive are the blessings that God has promised; he wants God to be faithful to his own word. To that end Job had sought to know God's Word.

Three lessons are forthcoming.

Firstly, we need to see *the value of the Word of God in the healing process* of those who feel spiritually abandoned. Secular counsellors often suggest that Scripture is the cause of the trouble. Their advice is that we get rid of the Bible! The right advice, however, is to learn what God's Word has to say, and to discover how relevant it all is. Disciplined, thoughtful Bible study will pay enormous dividends. It will change the way we think, and that in turn will change the way we live *and feel.*

The Christian counsellor Dr John White records a personal testimony that seems appropriate just here. He speaks from the vantage-point of a trained psychiatrist and shows himself a competent pastoral theologian. Encouraging those who are depressed to engage in 'solid, indicative Bible study', he goes on: 'Years ago, when I was seriously depressed, the thing that saved my own sanity was a dry-as-dust grappling with Hosea's prophecy. I spent weeks, morning by morning, making meticulous notes, checking historical allusions in the text. Slowly I began to sense the ground under my feet growing steadily firmer. I knew without any doubt that healing was constantly springing from my struggle to grasp the meaning of the prophecy.'[5]

Secondly, we should *seek to know God's Word in advance*. 'I have hidden your word in my heart that I might not sin against you' (Ps. 119:11). When trouble comes, it is too late to start learning what God has to say. Like some of God's creatures, we must learn to hide stores of food for long, cold winter months. 'Then let us mark well,' Calvin adds, 'that we have never profited well in God's school, till his word be so deeply rooted in our hearts.'⁶

Thirdly, Dr White underlines the need for patients in the grip of severe depression *to see that the situation is not entirely hopeless*. 'Often I read the third chapter of Lamentations,' he tells us. Why? Because 'The crux of Lamentations 3 is the poet's refusal to relinquish hope in God.'⁷ This is exactly the source of Job's strength. However deep he sinks, he knows that God will do what is right. This is a great principle, if we will only learn it. God's Word is there to help us and it is full of hope and encouragement.

Job's perseverance

Does the fact that God is sovereign, that no one can oppose him (23:13), mean that we can live as we please? Is there any point in our doing anything at all, since God's will is sure to be done? Fatalism, which these questions reflect, lies behind a great deal of misunderstanding in relation to the sovereignty of God.

True faith will expose a 'work produced by faith' (1 Thess. 1:3). And this work of faith is the result of obeying what God wants us to do. 'The way of godliness is just this,' wrote John Murray, 'that when the rod of God strikes most hardly and mysteriously the saint of God cleaves most closely to the revealed will of God.'⁸

Job's patience is his endurance. He goes on living for God through the trouble that comes upon him. Two things enable him to do so:

1. A good conscience

He appeals to this when he says, **'My feet have closely followed his steps; I have kept to his way without turning aside'** (23:11). 'Conscience,' declared the Puritan Richard Sibbes, 'is either the greatest friend or the greatest enemy in the world... A sincere heart, a conscience that hath laboured to obey the gospel, and to keep covenant with God, it can look God in the face.'[9] It is a valuable companion (cf. 1 Tim.1:5,19; 2 Tim. 1:3; 2 Cor.1:12). Godliness is a matter of keeping a good conscience towards God. It is one of the greatest blessings imaginable to have a conscience that is at rest. There is no better friend.

'At the hour of death,' Sibbes continues, 'what a comfort it is that we have this answer of a good conscience, especially at the day of judgement, when we can look God in the face.'[10] John Bunyan, in his famous account of crossing the Jordan, tells of how 'Mr Honest in his lifetime had spoken to Good-Conscience to meet him there, the which he also did, and lent him his hand, and so helped him over.'[11] Simeon was able to look death in the face with such peace because he had a good conscience towards God (cf. Luke 2:29).

2. His troubles are a test

Job has come to what is the most valuable lesson of all. He has come to see that his troubles are a test from which he will emerge victorious and triumphant (23:10). He is being refined so that all the dross can be removed.

Moses likened the experiences of Israel in the wilderness to that of an eagle deliberately pushing her fledglings out of the nest (Deut. 32:11). As they drop through the sky the eagle swoops down and catches them again on its wings. It is a deliberate act designed to teach them to fly. It appears at first cruel, but its design could not be better suited to help them grow and mature. At every step, God is with us in our trials. Though he may allow us to fall through the sky, he is ready to catch us before we hit the ground.

There were things about God and his ways that Job needed to learn; and he could only learn them in the crucible of suffering. God is determined to draw Job as close to himself as possible. He cannot see that now, but in time he will appreciate it. This lesson is wonderfully illustrated by C. S. Lewis: 'Imagine yourself as a living house. God comes in to rebuild that house. At first, perhaps, you understand what he is doing. He is getting the drains right, and stopping the leaks in the roof, and so on: you knew that those jobs needed doing, and so you are not surprised.

'But presently he starts knocking the house about in a way that hurts abominably and does not seem to make sense. What on earth is he up to? The explanation is that he is building a quite different house from the one you thought of — throwing up a wing there, putting up an extra floor there, running up towers, making courtyards. You thought you were going to be made into a decent little cottage; but he is building a palace. He intends to come and live in it himself.'[12]

A summary of Job's response

'If only God were near, that I could find him so that I might present my case before him! He wouldn't turn away an upright man. But I can't seem to find him anywhere.

'When will it all end? And it looks as if there's more to come. I cannot take any more of this.

'Why doesn't God come and judge the wicked, as you say he does? Evil folk seem to be prospering. God seems to tolerate all sorts of evil. But me, who treasures his Word more than food, he punishes! He does judge the wicked in the end, but why doesn't he do so right now?

'I don't understand any of this.'

18.
God's majesty and man's depravity

Please read Job 25

Bildad's third speech

Bildad's final contribution is a bit like the last gasp of a dying man. He has nothing new to say and ends up repeating what has already been said. It is a hymn of praise, a brief doxology, extolling the majesty of God in comparison to the sinfulness of man. 'The speech is reverent but irrelevant.'[1] For Bildad, man's insignificance cannot possibly occupy the attention of such a sovereign God. But for Job, God's very omniscience — his boundless capacity for knowledge — implies that he can, and does, give man his individual attention. Bildad and Job are worlds apart.

Everything stated in this hymn is true: God rules over everything, establishes order in heaven and earth and radiates purity (25:2-4). Power, peace, perfection, purity — God's attributes trip off Bildad's tongue with poetic ease. By comparison the creation is imperfect. And what about man? He is nothing but a 'maggot' and a 'worm'. It is a classic statement of man's depravity. And in itself, Job would not disagree with Bildad's analysis. It is the conclusion that Job finds exceptionable.

A hopeless theology

Bildad's theology reminds us of William Golding's book, *Lord of the Flies*, in which he depicts a group of choirboys stranded on a desert island. The main character, a boy nicknamed 'Piggy', is driven to ask questions about the nature of man: is he an animal or a savage? In a moment of extreme mental disturbance, he thinks he hears a pig's head say to him, 'Fancy thinking the Beast was something you could hunt or kill! You knew, didn't you? I'm part of you.'

The problem with Golding's analysis of man's depravity is that it offers no room for redemption. This is precisely the problem with Bildad's theological system. Bildad speaks of depravity, but offers no hope. The Bible speaks of depravity, but offers a way of salvation from its consequences.

Golding reflects a modern view of man's depravity, one which is based on the fact that man is no different from the rest of creation. He is, to use Bildad's description, **'a maggot'**! (25:6). As maggots eat their way through life, devoid of conscience or self-awareness, man is basically the same.

The opening chapters of Job have revealed how Satan plays a vital part in Job's downfall. But for Bildad, as for modern man, there is no devil who tempts him.

Man is not just an animal. He is not the end-product of an evolutionary chain that links him with maggots. Man was made in the image of God and lived in that pristine condition for a time in Eden. Man's depravity is the result of his having fallen from this high position. But if man was created in God's image, it is possible that by some divine power this image may be restored. It is this possibility that is denied in Bildad's theology.

The primary message of the Bible is not one of human depravity. This is only part of a much larger message, the gospel, which announces that God has found a way to justify sinners and remain just at the same time. It is the message that culminates in the coming of Jesus Christ, to live and die on behalf of sinners, and offer his life as a ransom for their sins. Bildad's message, like Golding's (and we may add all moral crusades which denounce society's evils without offering any cure), only leads to cynicism and despair. This diagnosis of the problem in Job's life offers no remedy.

The Bible's message of sin is just as dreadful as Bildad's. In fact, it is worse! We are much more sinful than we ever imagine ourselves to be. But we are told this about ourselves so that we do not make the fatal mistake of depending on ourselves for our salvation. The Bible shows us our total depravity in order to show us that there is nothing in ourselves to give us the slightest cause for encouragement. The sole ground of our hope lies in our Redeemer, Jesus Christ — the very one in whom Job has expressed such confidence (19:25-27).

A summary of Bildad's third speech

'God is absolutely sovereign. There is no one like him. No sinner can be right with God. If the moon is dark by comparison, how much more is man, who is nothing more than a maggot!'

19.
'Let there be ... and there was'

Please read Job 26

Job's reply to Bildad's third speech

Bildad had a reputation for wisdom, but he has shown himself bankrupt of ideas. Job is angry. In words of deepest sarcasm, Job thanks Bildad for his contribution. What help, what strength, what sound advice Bildad has given! (Job 26:2-4). Worse than this, Job resents the tone of Bildad's words: a **'spirit spoke from your mouth'** (26:4). The inference is clear: Bildad's contribution was inspired — by Satan! Thinking themselves all-wise, Job's 'friends' have become stooges in Satan's sinister attempt to undo the effects of the grace of God in Job's life.

Job needed help, but has received only additional pain and grief. His 'friends' have treated him with contempt, failing to see him as a friend, or even a person. They have systematically stripped him of his sense of dignity.

God's power in creation

Following what appears to be a pause, Job resumes his reply (26:5). According to one commentator, 'Chapter 26 is one of the grandest recitals in the whole book ... excelled only by the Lord's speeches.'[1]

Job extends his belief in God's power to include the realms inhabited by the dead also: **'The dead are in deep anguish, those beneath the waters and all that live in them'** (Job 26:5). Job descends into the underworld of the dead, down into Sheol[2] and on down into the furthest reaches of hell. These realms are **'naked'** and **'uncovered'** to God (Job 26:6). Even though Sheol is deep (11:8, according to Zophar), dark (17:13, according to Job), and a prison from which there is no escape (7:9, again according to Job), once there, it is not possible to hide from God. Even hell — and Sheol can sometimes mean this, as it possibly does here — is only hell because of the *presence of God*! John gives us the fullest revelation available to us when he says that the ungodly 'will be tormented with burning sulphur *in the presence of the holy angels and of the Lamb*' (Rev 14:10, italics added). In a sermon delivered in 1742 on the subject of hell and its punishments, Jonathan Edwards warned that the godly and the ungodly will both spend eternity 'in the immediate presence of God... God will be the hell of the one and the heaven of the other.'[3]

And God is sovereign over this world also. He has made it and continues to uphold it. Job could give as eloquent a song on God's sovereignty in creation as any of his friends (26:5-14).[4] Job has spoken about creation before (9:4-10; 12:16-25), and will do so again (28:1-28). The elements included in this account are: sky, empty space, earth, water, clouds, moon, light, darkness, the heavens and the sea. Some of the vocabulary is taken directly from the Genesis account: **'empty space'** in verse 7 is the word translated 'formless' in Genesis 1:2. Job is thinking of the creation of the entire universe in these verses. God's hand is visible everywhere: in the night sky, in the mountain ranges that disappear into the clouds, in the storms on the sea.

God is sovereign over every imaginable enemy and foe, even **'Rahab'** (26:12; cf. 9:13) and **'the gliding serpent'**

(26:13, a possible reference to Leviathan, of which more will be said in our comments on chapter 41[5]).

The importance of the doctrine of creation in our everyday lives cannot be overstressed. 'A correct and complete doctrine of creation is the answer to all the problems that burden this present hurting world'.[6] Two truths relating to the doctrine of creation help us in difficult situations.

1. Creation is a mystery to us

There is far more in it than we can ever hope to comprehend. God creates 'out of nothing' *(ex nihilo)*; we can never do that. All around us, every day, we see things that are a mystery to us. Indeed, so 'good' is creation that all through time we see a trail of man's idolatry of creation, worshipping the creature more than the Creator (cf. Rom. 1). Such confusion is what Agur complains of:

> I am the most ignorant of men;
>   I do not have a man's understanding.
> I have not learned wisdom,
>   nor have I knowledge of the Holy One.
> Who has gone up to heaven and come down?
>   Who has gathered up the wind in the hollow of his
>   hands?
> Who has wrapped up the waters in his cloak?
>   Who has established all the ends of the earth?
> What is his name, and the name of his son?
>   Tell me if you know!
>
>   (Prov 30:2-4).

When things happen that are a mystery to us, we should not be surprised; the very world in which we live is a mystery to us.

2. The world is not self-sustaining, as God is

It needs to be upheld all the time. This is the special ministry of Jesus Christ (Col. 1:17; Heb.1:3). Without it, every creature, including ourselves, would cease to be. Paul's word to the Athenians highlights this truth: 'And he is not served by human hands, as if he needed anything, because he himself gives all men life and breath and everything else... "For in him we live and move and have our being." As some of your own poets have said, "We are his offspring"' (Acts 17:25,28).

Knowing that God created the world around us, and ourselves as part of it, is basic to true religion. God is to be praised as Creator. He is to be trusted as the sovereign Lord who has a plan and purpose covering every situation and detail. Realizing that 'Moment by moment we are kept in his love' is the only way to live. Godliness starts with a view of God as the one who made us and upholds us. That is what kept Job sane through his trials. He now focuses his thoughts here for this purpose. Calvin comments on 26:14, 'Who then can understand the thunder of his power?': 'For when a man applies his whole study to know God both in heaven and earth, and would fain glorify him in all his works: if he thinks it possible to know all, surely he dishonours God. Can we do God a greater dishonour than to go about to enclose his mighty power within the capacity of our own wit? It is more than if a man would take upon him to shut up both sea and land in his own fist, or to hold them between a couple of fingers: surely it is a greater madness.'[7]

A summary of Job's reply

'What a great help you are, the lot of you! How you have opened my eyes! Your wisdom has saved me from sure destruction!

'Yes, God is great. He has accomplished mighty things. He has put the earth where it is and set it on its course. He oversees the weather and the movement of the sea. But he says nothing to me.'

20.
'How can I get God to hear my case?'

Please read Job 27

Closing arguments

Commentators are in disagreement as to whose words are recorded in chapters 25-28. Some are of the opinion that Bildad's speech, having ended at the close of chapter 25, takes up again at 26:5-14. Some also believe that chapter 27:2-12 is Job's reply, but that the rest of chapters 27 and 28 is not from Job at all![1]

Since Zophar has not intervened, Job continues to speak to all the friends in 27:1 - 28:28: the 'you' in verses 11-12 is plural, so Job is not merely replying to Zophar here.

This is Job's closing discourse to the friends. He has one more speech (like the closing argument in a trial case) addressed to God (29-31) and once this section is over, Job only has a few short sentences left to speak by way of an epilogue at the very end of the book (42:2-6).

Job's assessment of the friends' contribution so far has been that they have spoken nothing but 'nonsense' and 'falsehood' (21:34). This is now reaffirmed; Job is adamant: **'I will never admit you are in the right'** (27:5); their contribution is so much **'meaningless talk'** (27:12).

Job is going to defend his case (**'I will maintain my righteousness...'** 27:6) to the end, in the belief that God is just. We have seen in chapter 26 how Job believed in God's power, despite the fact that he did not understand how it operates. Likewise, here in chapter 27, Job expresses a belief in God's justice even though he does not comprehend how this operates either.

One of the strangest things about all that Job's friends have said is that not once have they ever spoken to God directly. Job, on the other hand, prays to God, complains to God and even fights with God. We have already noted (in our comments on chapter 23) that this was part of Job's healing process. How did Job appear so calm and 'patient' in his ordeal? The answer lies in his prayer life. Jacob's struggles in prayer left him permanently lame, but they also changed him spiritually: he became a prince with God!

Job is prepared to risk everything he has on God's character: his **'life'**, his **'breath'**, his **'nostrils'**, his **'lips'**, his very **'soul'** (Job 27:2-4). Every ounce of Job's confidence for himself is based on God's character. He is even prepared to enter into a solemn oath to prove it: **'as surely as God lives'** (27:2).

The Old Testament did not forbid the taking of oaths, but it did forbid the false use of the name of God (Lev. 19:12). Jesus seemed to change all of this by saying, 'Do not swear at all' (Matt. 5:34). Many Christians have felt that this statement in the Sermon on the Mount forbids all oath-taking, and at first glance it appears to be the correct view. However, Jesus was himself prepared to speak under oath, breaking his earlier silence, during his trial: 'The high priest said to him, "I charge you under oath by the living God: Tell us if you are the Christ, the Son of God." "Yes, it is as you say," Jesus replied' (Matt. 26:63-64). This appears to show us that Jesus felt the binding nature of being under an oath. What Jesus forbids in the Sermon on the Mount is *false* oath-taking. The Pharisees were not fulfilling their oaths, using as a pretext that they had sworn by 'heaven', or 'earth', or 'Jerusalem', or even one's own head!

Knowing God's character is vital if we are to remain upright through spiritual trials. Growing in our knowledge of God will require the patience that Job manifested. He could not understand what God was doing to him: **'God ... has denied me justice, the Almighty ... has made me taste bitterness of soul'** (27:2); but he was still prepared to trust him.

Paul recognized that those who desire to make progress in knowing God would need to be 'strengthened with all power according to his glorious might,' so that they might have 'great endurance and patience' (Col. 1:11). One of the very things God was doing with Job was bringing him to a deeper knowledge of himself. Job was to testify at the end of his trial:

> My ears had heard of you
>   but now my eyes have seen you.
> Therefore I despise myself
>   and repent in dust and ashes.
>
>   (42:5-6).

God may ask us to pass through similar valleys to Job, and we shall need to be as patient as Job was if we are emerge as he did. Holding on to God, even when his ways appear to make no sense, is the secret of Job's life. Job may well have problems with seeing God's justice in his life: 'God ... has denied me justice' (27:2); but everything in him says that to abandon God now would be suicidal. He must hold on, even when it makes no sense. In all his searching for meaning and purpose, Job is discovering that there *is* no one else to whom he may turn.

How important it is to believe in justice! It is important for someone who has been the victim of a terrible crime to desire justice. There is relief when criminals are found guilty and victims are able to close certain doors and begin to pick up the pieces of their lives again. When a guilty person is let off, victims feel cheated, robbed of something essential to their well-being.

It is important to believe that God is just, too. And there are two sides to God's justice: he will punish what is wrong and defend what is right. The fact that God is implacably opposed to sin and will punish it, in whatever form it appears, is what we sometimes call 'God's retributive righteousness'. From the very start, God warned of the consequences of disobedience: 'But you must not eat from the tree of the knowledge of good and evil, for when you eat of it you will surely die' (Gen. 2:17). This is a principle that is endorsed in the New Testament: 'All who rely on observing the law are under a curse, for it is written: "Cursed is everyone who does not continue to do everything written in the Book of the Law"' (Gal. 3:10).

But there is another aspect of God's justice, one in which the Christian can find comfort. God will always be true to himself and to his word. The psalmist often expressed confidence in God's righteousness:

Answer me when I call to you,
    O my righteous God.
Give me relief from my distress;
    be merciful to me and hear my prayer

                                        (Ps. 4:1).

Vindicate me in your righteousness, O Lord my God;
    do not let them gloat over me

                                        (Ps. 35:24).

O Lord, hear my prayer,
    listen to my cry for mercy;
in your faithfulness and righteousness
    come to my relief

                                        (Ps. 143:1).

In each of these psalms the psalmist is expressing his confidence that God will keep his covenant promise: they are

Abraham's seed and heirs of the promise of salvation. This is what we sometimes call 'the remunerative righteousness of God'.

In pleading his innocence, Job, as we have said many times, is not claiming sinlessness. He is merely claiming that by grace he loves God, trusts him implicitly and calls on him to vindicate that he is a child of God.

Imprecations

Job's belief in God's justice now leads him to call forth a curse on his enemies (his friends!). To charge someone wrongfully made a person liable to the punishment for that crime. Hence, Job wants his friends to be regarded by the same epithet they have applied to him — **'wicked'** (27:7). The words trip off Job's tongue: they are **'enemies'**, **'adversaries'**, **'godless'**. They have no right to call upon God (27:10).

In a passage that is very much like some of the things that Job's friends have been saying, Job now applies the truth of God's righteous retribution upon his (and as Job sees it, God's) enemies. It involves a curse on the family (27:14-15), wealth (27:16-17,19), home (27:18) and eventually life itself (27:20-21). Eventually, the wicked man will be carried away (27:21-23).

Many liberal commentators have attempted to reconstruct this chapter so as to make verses 7-23 become the 'lost' third speech of Zophar. Much of what Job has to say sounds like some of the things that have come from his three friends. But there is a crucial difference. Job's friends consistently talked about *instant* retribution. Job was suffering *now* because he had sinned and God was punishing him for it. Job, however, recognizes in this passage that it may well be that the ungodly may prosper for a while. Eventually, however, retribution will catch up with him. As Calvin puts it, 'God's judgements are not executed ordinarily in this present life, although we have now and then some sign of them'.[2]

Christians have always had trouble with imprecations in the Bible. They feel that it is somehow unworthy of a Christian to pronounce curses. We are not meant, so it is widely thought, to be judgemental. Those who do so are thought to be harsh, bitter, uncharitable and, well, 'unchristian'! A Christian is guided by love and cursing is out of keeping with it.

A moment's reflection, however, will expose the vacuity of such thinking.

1. The concerns of God's kingdom are ever paramount

It is true that the New Testament gives an explicit warning not to curse: 'Bless those who persecute you; bless and do not curse' (Rom. 12:14). Paul is, of course, only reflecting the teaching of Christ in the Sermon on the Mount: 'But I tell you: Love your enemies and pray for those who persecute you' (Matt. 5:44). We have no right to seek our own personal advancement or victory over our enemies, whoever they are, and whatever they may be doing to us. It is God's kingdom that must be advanced, no matter what; and if that involves our personal suffering so that it be advanced, then we are called upon to yield submissively to it. 'God's kingdom,' argued Johannes Vos, 'cannot come without Satan's kingdom being destroyed. God's will cannot be done in earth without the destruction of evil. Evil cannot be destroyed without the destruction of men who are permanently identified with it.'[3] When we become Christians, we surrender all our rights to him.

2. The basis of imprecations (cursing God's enemies) must never be personal revenge

'Do not take revenge, my friends, but leave room for God's wrath, for it is written: "It is mine to avenge; I will repay," says the Lord' (Rom. 12:19). The cursing of God's enemies is a way of desiring the fulfilment of God's covenant: a word which includes the cursing of his enemies (Deut. 28). God is implacably opposed to the impenitent and will eventually destroy them. Job is prepared to suffer and to endure without personal revenge or hatred so long as it is in the service of the kingdom of God. 'If we show ourselves to like well of God's truth,' comments Calvin, 'we must maintain it out of hand, and all such as set themselves against us, must be our enemies, and we must detest them, assuring ourselves that there is no more agreement between truth and untruth, than between fire and water.'[4]

3. The goal of cursing in a biblical way should be the conversion of our enemies

This sounds blatantly false, for the end of God's curse is the destruction of God's enemies (cf. 2 Thess. 1:6-10). However, the temporal judgements of God are designed to lead sinners to repentance (Rom. 2:2-4). Paul's way of putting it is quite astonishing: 'God's kindness leads you towards repentance' (Rom. 2:4). The verb 'leads' is the same verb employed in the eighth chapter of Romans to describe the ministry of the Holy Spirit in the heart of the Christian: 'Those who are led by the Spirit of God are sons of God' (Rom. 8:14). It is as though God pulls at the sleeve of the unconverted and says, 'This way!' No judgement is too great if it causes sinners to seek the Lord. We need only think of what happened to Nebuchadnezzar (Dan. 4), or Saul of Tarsus (Acts 9).

Can you pray this prayer: 'Clouds and thick darkness surround you; righteousness and justice are the foundation of your throne. Your holiness is like a fire that consumes. It will consume your enemies whoever they are. The whole world trembles before you; everyone sees your glory even though they may deny it. Bring to shame all who worship idols. Lord, come in your power and show forth your glory. Establish your kingdom by bringing your judgements to bear upon the wicked who oppose you. Curse them that they may seek after you ... and if they will not, O God, then destroy them. Let all the world know that you, and you alone, are God'? If not, then turn to Psalm 97 and think again. Maybe your praying is not as biblical as you have thought!

4. We have here the basis for considering what will eventually happen to the unrepentant

God's covenant ensures that the wicked will eventually be judged for their sins. It is a sobering thing to read the description given in verses 14-23 of this chapter and think of what will happen to unbelievers at the end. In particular there is a warning that the prosperity of the wicked is not their final destiny (27:19-23). Martin Luther once remarked, 'There are three conversions necessary: the conversion of the heart, mind, and the purse.'[5] On the wall of the Court of Women in the temple at Jerusalem were thirteen brass receptacles, in the shape of trumpets. It is a sobering thought that Jesus must have sat in front of these trumpets and listened to the rattle of coins as they were ceremonially deposited in these trumpets. He heard the sound of a 'mite' sacrificially given by a widow as she came to worship and made note of it (Mark 12:41). He used the occasion to talk about sacrificial giving, no doubt as difficult to talk about then as it is now. We love money too much and Jesus warns us of the consequences of it (Luke 16:13; Matt.19:24; Luke 6:30; 12:15,33). 'It is', Jesus warned, 'easier for a camel to go through the eye of a needle than for a rich man to enter the kingdom of God' (Matt. 19:24). Our hearts have room for only one master, and for far too many, that master is Mammon. It will be their doom.

A summary of the argument so far

It might have been expected that Zophar should intervene at this point. He is the only one of the three not to have given a third speech. It seems that he has nothing to say. Perhaps Job's warning as to the fate of the wicked has got to him.

Have you grown a little tired of all the arguments put forth so far? There has been a certain sameness to the speeches. Hardly anything that Job's three friends have been saying has been of any real value (and these have taken nine of the first twenty-seven chapters). The three counsellors have insisted that Job is in the wrong and is suffering for it. Job has insisted that he is not in the wrong at all, but that God's treatment of him has been wrong. It has been increasingly difficult to maintain Job's integrity. Job has protested his innocence too much. As time has gone on, Job's health has been steadily deteriorating; his demeanour has shown less and less of the sanguine quality of the early chapters. Judgements of Job must be tempered. His response outstrips any response we ourselves would give in such circumstances. He is one of those of whom we are not worthy (Heb. 11). Nevertheless, we must interpret Job by the revelation given to us at the close of the book when he confesses that he has been guilty in the way he has responded to his trial (40:4-5; 42:2-6).[6]

It is time for Job to cut himself free from these people and think for himself. It is time to reflect on his predicament in a new way. There are times in our trials to get alone with God and talk it out with him. The remedy for Job is to reflect again on the God who controls his life. The answers, if indeed there are any, are with him. It is time to shut one's ears to the counsellors and think about God. It is here that healing comes to Job. It is the theme of the next chapter.

21.
A hymn on God's wisdom

Please read Job 28

Job contemplates God's wisdom

If we were watching a drama unfold on a stage (and the book of Job is a little like that) we could say at this point that we have come to an 'intermission'. After the dire warnings on the fate of the wicked in the previous chapter we feel as though we need a break to let the dust settle. What better way to settle the nerves than to sing a hymn of praise to the Almighty? For chapter 28 is just that: a magnificent hymn in praise of God's wisdom.[1]

'Unless you become familiar with the wisdom of God,' writes Sinclair Ferguson, 'you cannot make much real progress in the Christian life.'[2] And he is surely right. Twice, Job asks the question: 'Where can wisdom be found?' (28:12,20). It has been a failure to understand the *ways* of God that has caused Job the most trouble. Job desires to know *why* his life is as it is. And Job is not the only one who wants answers to life's most perplexing questions: we all feel the need for some kind of meaning to be given to our lives. Disillusioned students at university, confronted by ideas and theories that question the very foundation of what they have always thought, find themselves at sea. What they need is wisdom. Folk in pain, discovering that their life's ambitions have been shattered, cry out for wisdom. Young people faced by choices, some of which will lead them in the wrong direction, need wisdom. But where can it be found? This chapter provides us with an answer that transcends the confines of Job's particular difficulties.

The answer lies in contemplating God's wisdom: his decision, his decree, 'his eternal purpose, according to the counsel of his will, whereby, for his own glory, he hath foreordained whatsoever comes to pass'.[3] Every event is ordered by God (Eph. 1:11) and this is part of what we mean when we refer to the 'wisdom of God'. What we shall find in this hymn is that God is all-powerful, all-knowing and all-wise (28:20-28). God's wisdom, Job discovers, is something that is enormously powerful. 'Omniscience governing omnipotence, infinite power ruled by infinite wisdom, is a basic biblical description of the divine character,' as J. I. Packer put it.[4] It is not the first time that Job has thought about it: 'His wisdom is profound, his power is vast' (9:4). 'To God belong wisdom and power...' (12:13). It is a testimony that others will confirm: 'Wisdom and power are his' (Dan. 2:20). 'Now to him who is able to establish you ... the only wise God' (Rom. 16:25,27). But it is time to examine what Job has to say.

The genius of man (28:1-11)

From the very beginning, man's ingenuity and skill were evident. Lamech, the fifth generation from Cain (whose name means 'metalsmith'), had three sons, one of whom was called 'Tubal-Cain'. It is said of Tubal-Cain that he 'forged all kinds of tools out of bronze and iron' (Gen. 4:22). Clearly, the exploitation of earth's natural resources, as commanded by God (Gen. 1:28), and the consequent skills of mining and metallurgy were technological skills which man gained quickly. Job now gives us a detailed account of mining technology used in his own time.

He speaks of mining, tunnelling, smelting and forging. Three techniques are known to have been used: a kind of open-cast mining, especially on exposed river-beds, quarrying into exposed vertical rock surfaces, and deep-shaft mining. The reference to 'fire' in verse 5 possibly alludes to a process whereby a fire was lit in a tunnel. As the walls of the tunnel became hot, water was poured on it, causing the rock to crack. The fallen stones would then be taken to the surface. The science need not detain us, for Job has another point to get across. Man's evident skill and ingenuity, even his persistence, are self-evident. Men were prepared to be killed in the search for precious metals and gem-stones, searching 'the farthest recesses for ore in the blackest darkness' (28:3). His skill outwitted even the 'falcon' and the 'lion' (28:7,8).[5] No other creature is as curious, courageous or clever as man.

Had Job been writing today, he might have used the skills involved in modern surgery, or worldwide communications, or micro-chip circuitry, or even manned space flight. He might also have talked about the making of the Channel Tunnel! The point of this description of man's ingenuity is to point up the fact that despite it all, man is no nearer to finding the answers to the fundamental questions of life: 'Who am I? What am I here for?'

Job has already asked, 'What is man?' (7:17; cf. Ps. 8:4). The question is even more pertinent when we remember Bildad's assessment of man as a 'maggot' or 'worm' (25:4-6). Where can we find wisdom to answer such questions? The philosopher, Arthur Schopenhauer, was sitting one day in the Tiergarten at Frankfurt, looking, so the story goes, a little dishevelled. A park-keeper, mistaking him for a tramp, asked him, 'Who are you?' The great philosopher replied somewhat bitterly, 'I wish to God I knew.'

The biblical answer as to what man is lies in an analysis of the expression 'in our image' in the creation statement: 'Then God said, "Let us make man in our image..."' (Gen. 1:26). The divine image, or likeness, of God in man is seen in many areas, including man's self-conscious rationality (his ability in original thinking), his ability to make moral choices, his capacity for relationships of love and his thirst for God. It is also seen in man's dominion over the resources and powers of the earth, as prescribed in Genesis 1:26.[6]

This last point is pertinent here, for it appears to be what Job is alluding to: the image of God in man lies in his powers of ingenuity and artistic creativity, especially in mining and metallurgy.[7] God has given to man the creative and ingenious skills to ransack the world's natural resources.[8] Man is able to research, investigate and analyse how things are; he is able to devise means to retrieve and create; he is able to appreciate what is beautiful. This is part of what man is: wise beyond the capacity of any other creature on this planet. It is a derived wisdom, a pale reflection of the wisdom of man's Creator, the one to whom this hymn is a song of adoration and worship. The Bard has never been bettered: 'What a piece of work is a man! how noble in reason! how infinite in faculty! in action how like an angel! in apprehension how like a god! the beauty of the world! the paragon of animals!'[9]

The value of wisdom (28:12-19)

What is the value of wisdom? Can it be bought? What steps must man take in order to attain it? These are the questions Job turns to in the second part of this hymn. Man spends his entire life searching for wisdom, but to no avail (28:12-14). He most certainly cannot purchase it (28:15-19). If it were possible, modern man might attempt to issue shares in wisdom. Imagine it: privatized wisdom! In a sense, that is just what man does. Every personal credo for living life to the full is an advertisement for a personal view of wisdom. But each attempt to express it runs into the ground. In the West, modern man is learning the hard way that wisdom does not lie in the pursuit of power, sex and money.

The Bible, on the other hand, has a great deal to say about the attainment of wisdom. The first nine chapters of Proverbs are a sustained series of exhortations to attain it:

> Wisdom is supreme; therefore get wisdom.
>   Though it cost all you have, get understanding…
> Hold on to instruction, do not let it go;
>   guard it well, for it is your life
>
> > (Prov. 4:7,13).

Solomon even personifies wisdom, and lets her speak for herself:

> Blessed is the man who listens to me,
>   watching daily at my doors,
>   waiting at my doorway.
> For whoever finds me finds life
>   and receives favour from the Lord.
> But whoever fails to find me harms himself;
>   all who hate me love death
>
> > (Prov. 8:34-36).

Wisdom is what we need: 'Be very careful, then, how you live — not as unwise but as wise, making the most of every opportunity, because the days are evil' (Eph. 5:15-16). Paul's chief request in prayer for the Colossians was that they should be given wisdom: 'For this reason, since the day we heard about you, we have not stopped praying for you and asking

God to fill you with the knowledge of his will through all spiritual wisdom and understanding' (Col. 1:9). James promises: 'If any of you lacks wisdom, he should ask God, who gives generously to all without finding fault, and it will be given to him' (James 1:5).

The need for wisdom is the theme of the Book of Ecclesiastes. Just look at life without God. What is it like? An aimless cycle of recurring events (Eccles. 1:4-11); an endless series of events over which we have no control (Eccles. 3:1-18); an unlimited sequence of deaths, unrelated to the quality of the lives that have been lived (Eccles. 3:19-21; 9:2-6). There seems no point to it: 'No one can comprehend what goes on under the sun. Despite all his efforts to search it out, man cannot discover its meaning. Even if a wise man claims he knows, he cannot really comprehend it' (Eccles. 8:17).

So what is the point of working: to make money, to start a business venture, to study and make oneself wise? (Eccles. 1:3; 2:11,15; 5:11). None at all, if God isn't in our hearts, if he is not the reason for which we live. This is the theme of Job 28, too. Life without God is meaningless. It is to no purpose. In a world without God as our focus, there is no wisdom under the sun.

The source of wisdom (28:20-28)

Wisdom is not found in the land of the living (28:21), or that of the dead (28:22).[10] Having exhausted all human resources, and even those beyond the grave, Job has only one source to fall back upon — God! The source of wisdom lies in the one who is all-knowing (28:23), all-seeing (28:24) and all-powerful (28:25). It is the wisdom of the Creator (28:26-27). It is the word of his will, the revealed know-how of the one who knows how!

We have already noted Calvin's summary of wisdom as consisting in knowing God and knowing ourselves. It is the first part, knowing God, that Job is concerned to speak of here. He has, we need to remember, already begun the process of knowing himself as he responds to the growing crisis in his life.

Wisdom comes from knowing God and being in a right relationship to him: **'The fear of the Lord — that is wisdom, and to shun evil is understanding'** (28:28; cf. Ps. 111:10; Prov. 9:10). This is the very quality that has marked out Job from the very beginning (1:1). Reverence to God is the primary quality that makes us wise. Not till we have become humble and teachable, standing in awe of God's essential holiness and majesty, willing to have our own ways and will turned upside down, can we become truly wise.

What does it mean to *fear* God? We have already examined this subject in the opening chapter. We are now, however, in a position to examine it a little more closely, conscious as we now are that Job is speaking from the experience of suffering. At least two things emerge.

1. Knowing God

Job's sanity has been maintained in his trial, despite the ineptitude of his counsellors, because he knows God. Things have happened to him that are essentially incomprehensible. In terms of human wisdom, life bears no meaning for him. It is only as he focuses on God, the God who essentially loves him, the God of promise and covenant, the God who knows what Job does not know, that Job is able to maintain his equilibrium. God has a purpose in all of this that Job does not comprehend, but he casts himself on God alone to give meaning to his life, and we too must rest in a knowledge of the one who says to us, 'Trust me.'

For Job knowing God meant knowing the Intercessor, Advocate, Mediator who sits at God's right hand (9:32-34; 16:19-21; 19:25-27). 'I know that my Redeemer lives...' Job has discovered the secret of life: knowing Jesus Christ (in Job's case, in type and shadow). It is in Christ that God's wisdom is essentially displayed. He is 'the wisdom of God' (1 Cor. 1:30). Writing to the Ephesians, Paul affirms that the multi-faceted wisdom of God is revealed 'according to his eternal purpose which he accomplished in Christ Jesus our Lord' (Eph. 3:11). God's wisdom, the wisdom he wants us to know, is demonstrated in what Christ has done for his people.

2. Awe of God's ways

Having spoken to the Ephesians about God's wisdom having been revealed in the gospel of Jesus Christ, Paul goes on to speak of his own sufferings (Eph. 3:13). He is in prison and he urges his friends in Ephesus not to be discouraged by this. 'Because of what I have told you about the wisdom of God, don't get discouraged about my sufferings,' seems to be what Paul is saying. You can understand why they might have been discouraged! Paul was their leader. Nevertheless, they were not cast down. Why not? Because, if they could see God at work in their salvation through Jesus Christ's death on Calvary, they must also trust him to be working for their good in their ongoing, everyday lives, too.

That is Job's point. Reverence of God means being in awe of his ways. God's tapestry is wonderful — yes, full of wonders! I may not understand it, but I have to accept it. It is the wise thing to do. I must bow in humility before his will: 'With humility comes wisdom' (Prov. 11:2). This is, in part at least, what Job means by 'shunning evil'. It is to walk in obedience to what God has revealed: both in the natural revelation of the created world, and in God's Word written and infallibly inspired. 'Let us learn to be inflamed with such zeal,' preached Calvin on this passage, 'to profit in the holy Scripture, as we may preserve the doctrine that is contained there, before all our own fancies, and before all the vanities of this world that carry us away.'[11]

Samuel Rutherford, who foresaw something of the troubles that were coming to a fellow Christian, Jean Brown,[12] had this to say: 'We ... must set our face against what may befall us in following on, till He and we be through the briers and bushes, on the dry ground. Our soft nature would be borne through the troubles of this miserable life in Christ's arms; and it is His wisdom, who knoweth our mould, that His bairns go wet-shod and cold-footed to heaven ... time will eat away and root out our woes and sorrow. Our heaven is in the bud, and growing up to an harvest.'[13]

22.
'The Lord gave ...
and took away'

Please read Job 29-31

Job's final summing up of his case

Job is no longer talking directly to his friends, but to God: **'I cry out to you, O God'** (30:20). The section is reminiscent of the final stages of a dramatic court case where the barrister is giving his summing up, his 'closing arguments'. This is Job's case, for good or ill. With these words he stands or falls. Job is speaking almost entirely about himself and the pathos and sense of hurt expressed in these chapters make this one of the most moving sections of the entire book.

The three chapters can be summarized as follows: Job's former happiness (chapter 29); Job's present sorrow (chapter 30); Job's final protestation of innocence (chapter 31).

Job's former happiness

It is quite common in times of trial to think back on how things once were. 'If only things were like they used to be!' we say to ourselves. Job is doing that in this chapter. His mind lingers on halcyon days, when the sun shone and everything seemed to be so wonderful. Thoughts like these can, of course, be a sinful way of expressing discontentment with the present. But they can also be therapeutic. 'Count your blessings, name them one by one...,' says the old hymn, and it is wise advice. We do not reckon up the blessings of God enough. Were we to do so, it would transform our spiritual lives.

Four particular blessings (29:1-6)

1. God's care for him

God **'watched'** over him (29:2). As they made their way to Jerusalem, conscious that marauders and bandits might well be lying in wait for them in the hills, pilgrims found reassurance in the knowledge that their help came from the Lord who watched over them even while they slept (Ps. 121:3,4,5,7,8). At one point in Psalm 121, the way God watches over his people is described in terms of providing a 'shade': 'The Lord is your shade at your right hand' (v. 5). The same thought is expressed in Psalm 91, where the godly find safety beneath the 'shadow' of divine 'wings' above and around them (Ps. 91:1,4). The symbolism is that of a broody hen fussily protecting her brood; the point is to underline the covenant promise of the Lord's unfailing presence with his people — especially in times of trouble.

Job's way of describing God's watchfulness over his servant is to remind himself of how reassuring a light can be to a little child who is afraid of the dark: **'... when his lamp shone upon my head and by his light I walked through darkness!'** (29:3). Job can recall times when he was afraid of nothing because the Lord was with him.

2. God's friendship

To have God watching us is one thing; to have his **'intimate friendship'** is another (29:4). Once again we find the same thought expressed by the psalmist: 'The Lord confides in those who fear him; he makes his covenant known to them' (Ps. 25:14). The Lord is intimate with his people. He takes them into his confidence and reveals secrets to them that are hidden from the rest of mankind. When God asked, 'Shall I hide from Abraham what I am about to do?' he was revealing to us an astonishing truth: that Abraham was God's friend (Gen. 18:17-19). It is a truth that every disciple of Jesus holds dear that he should ever regard us as his 'friends' (John 15:14).

But the intimacy we have with God through the gospel is closer than even friendship! Following the resurrection, Jesus called his disciples 'brothers' (John 20:17). Blood is thicker than water, they say, and being part of a family is important to us. Those who have lost touch with their own family often feel cut off, isolated in a hostile universe. It is important to us when we know that another shares with us the same genetic structure, the same parents, the same background, the same memories. In Jesus, we have one who shares with us our experiences. He is our Elder Brother.

3. God's provision

In words that remind us of the opening chapter, Job speaks of the blessings of **'children'** (29:5), herds and crops (29:6). Such was the abundance of the **'cream'** (i.e. curds) and **'olive oil'**, Job tells us, he could have bathed in them. 'They will celebrate your abundant goodness and joyfully sing of your righteousness,' says the psalmist (Ps. 145:7). The grace of God reveals itself to us in terms of an 'abundant provision ... through the one man, Jesus Christ' (Rom. 5:17).

What Job is giving expression to here is the fulfilment of the terms of the covenant (Deut. 28:11). But the real blessing was not the abundance of material things, though this was a part of it; it was, rather, the presence of God!

4. God's presence

'The Almighty was still with me' (29:5). Nothing is more
reassuring than to have God's presence with us. It is the very
essence of God's covenant with us that he repeats, again and
again, 'I will be *with* you' (cf. Gen. 39:2; Exod. 3:12; Josh.
1:5,9; Isa. 43:2,5; Matt. 1:23; 28:20). At present, Job has lost
the assurance of God's presence. His friends are mocking him,
just as the psalmists' enemies did when they said, 'Where is
your God now?' (Ps. 42:3,9,10; 43:1-2). But *then*, in those
wonderful days before the trial, God was with him, and he
knew it!

John Wesley, when he was dying, was visited by many of
his friends. Each one was anxious to help and encourage their
friend and many cited to him some of God's promises in the
Scriptures. Wesley is said to have uttered the words: 'Yes, all
these promises are true, but best of all, God is with us.'

A man of honour (29:7-17)

Rich men were more often despised than respected. The
wealthy were often held in suspicion as to the means by which
they had acquired their wealth. Eliphaz, as we have seen, has
made such an accusation about Job (22:5-11) — something
which Job will vigorously deny (31:16-23). Whatever the
reason behind Eliphaz's charge (was it perhaps jealousy?),
Job appears to have enjoyed the respect of the whole city of
Uz. Indeed, he was held in considerable honour among the
people.

A visit to a Middle-Eastern city, even today, will reveal that
the entrance to the city is where people gather. Carpets are
spread out, goods are displayed and a market is quickly
established. People gather at the city gate to transact business

and exchange news. In ancient times, it was at the city gate that the city elders met to conduct their business and make the important decisions. At almost any time, citizens could be gathered to act as a jury. It would be led by an elder (acting as judge) to rule in a matter of some dispute. Thus Amos speaks of 'establish[ing] justice in the gate' (Amos 5:15).[1]

Job was evidently a city elder, a member of the ruling council of Uz. It may be that all adult men were regarded as elders in small towns and villages, but more than likely, in larger towns and cities, like Uz, they were elected in some way on the basis of age, wisdom, ability and respect. The respect in which he was held is evident as young men stepped out of his way and the old men **'rose to their feet'** (29:8). It was customary to stand in the presence of older men (Lev. 19:32). Not only that, but city officials, government and army officers signalled for silence as he passed by (29:8-10). And this was because he had a reputation for helping the poor, the fatherless and the widow (29:12-13), even seeking out cases unknown to him personally (29:15-16). This is what James calls 'pure religion' (James 1:27).

Job's life had been determined by the principles of **'right-eousness'** and **'justice'** which he had worn as his clothing (29:14). That this is not just Job's exaggerated self-appraisal is seen by the statement that all men **'spoke well of [him]'** (29:11).

A further section outlining Job's qualities as a city elder comes at the end of the chapter (29:21-25). Three particular qualities emerge.

1. Wisdom (29:21-23)

Of only a rare few can it be said that folk wait on their every word with expectancy, as they did to Job.

2. Moral rectitude (29:24)

Job is described in terms of his priestly function: his 'smile'
and the **'light of [his] face'** were a blessing to them. The
words are similar to the priestly blessings of Numbers 6:24-
25:

> The Lord bless you
>   and keep you;
> the Lord make his face shine upon you
>   and be gracious to you...
>
> (Num. 6:24-25).

3. Leadership (29:25)

Job was the **'chief'** of the city of Uz. Evidently he was more
than just an elder. As 'chief' he would lead them into battle
against marauders, speak at times of civic importance, organ-
ize in times of catastrophe and deprivation. Job — the city
mayor of Uz! Job was indeed like a king or general bringing
strength and encouragement to the people (29:25).

Youthful aspirations (29:18-21)

No one wants to die young. Indeed, young people hardly give
death a moment's thought: it is for some other day. As a young
man, Job took his health for granted. He expressed a desire to
live long and prosper. Job speaks here about his **'nest'**, adding
a homely touch that speaks of the delight his home must have
meant to him (29:18).

Job was musing as to what might have been: to live to a ripe
old age, having flourished — Job had hoped to flourish like a
tree planted by a riverside (29:19; cf. Ps. 1:3) — and then to die
in one's own home, surrounded by those who care. It is what

we would all wish for ourselves.[2] The images are vivid: Job imagines himself full of the vigour of a sapling growing by supplies of water, and as strong as a warrior with **'bow'** in hand (29:19-20).

There are some things that we never learn the value of until we face the prospect of losing them, or even worse, waking up to the fact that they have gone already. Health is one of them. Peace of mind is another. Dignity is a third.

Job has lost all three. Their deprivation is causing the most strain on Job's faith and relationship with God. In particular, his confidence in God's love is being tested. 'Curse God and die!' Job's wife had urged. It was proving to be a more alluring challenge as each day passed. The physical discomfort, the indignity of sitting on a rubbish-tip, scraping discharged matter off himself, has made Job feel dehumanized and demoralized. What happened to Job has called into question his deepest ambitions.

Perhaps Job needed to learn the lesson that we are not in charge of our lives. We may aspire to live long, but it is God's prerogative to grant it. We must all be ready to die *at any moment!* Yesterday's Christians lived by this principle better than today's, living as they did by Bishop Ken's motto: 'Live each day as if thy last.' We must budget wisely for several years (Ps. 90:10), but God may call us sooner — and it will be a promotion if he does.

Calvin wisely comments on this aspiration to live long: 'If God send us any prosperity, let us not be too sleepy: but let us consider this mortal life is subject to all the changes we can devise... And although the whole world seem to favour us, and that we have a hundred thousand shoulders to bear us up: yet must we nevertheless think, that there is no settledness here below, but that all things are transitory, so as all things are changed in the turning of a hand... For there is nothing easier with a man, than to make himself believe, that he shall always continue in a happy state, when he is once in it.'[3]

It is the same thought that led the psalmist to say of the wicked man: 'He says to himself, "Nothing will shake me; I'll always be happy and never have trouble"' (Ps. 10:6). This is the reason why Jesus warns those who are preoccupied with building great structures for themselves in this life: 'God said to him, "You fool! This very night your life will be demanded from you. Then who will get what you have prepared for yourself?"' (Luke 12:20). 'Let us call upon God,' urges Calvin, 'and wait at his hand for whatsoever it shall please him to send us.'[4]

Job's present sorrow

Job has been day-dreaming. For just a moment or two, he has forgotten the pain of the ash-heap, remembering instead the glorious days that had been. How quickly things had changed! It had, of course, been only a short time, but it must have seemed like a lifetime ago now to Job. Death, ill-health, financial ruin, a moral lapse — these can destroy the equilibrium of our lives that we so much cherish. Perhaps a pain brought him back to reality. Perhaps, too, it was the sound of someone cursing him that made him open his eyes to his situation again. He heard something and **'They mock me,'** he said to himself, twice! (30:1,9).

The attacks of men (30:1-15; 24-31)

Job has fallen from respect to disgrace in the eyes of the people. Instead of adulation, he is the butt of insults from the kind of men he would not formerly have trusted to work his dogs (30:1). He describes them as scavengers and outcasts (30:3-8). They are like animals: note the verbs **'roamed'**

(30:3) and **'brayed'** (30:7). Gangs of social misfits, who spend the nights roaming the streets, spend their energies taunting him. Job is a **'byword'** among them (30:9). As we have seen before, insults do hurt and the tongue, James reminds us, is a 'a fire, a world of evil among the parts of the body. It corrupts the whole person, sets the whole course of his life on fire, and is itself set on fire by hell' (James 3:6). Job is evidently deeply hurt by the trade in insults.

The tongue can be used to put a little child to sleep, or be an ambassador encouraging peace between warring parties. With it a barrister upholds the cause of truth in a court of law, and a general lifts the spirits of his men as they prepare for battle. But it is a volatile instrument, as Job knew right well. He had been the victim of verbal cyanide, of a relentless warfare of insults. Job felt bruised and battered. An American journalist, by the name of William Norris, who specialized in simple rhymes, once wrote:

If your lips would keep from slips,
Five things observe with care:
To whom you speak; of whom you speak;
And how, and when, and where.[5]

Job had been the victim of false witness. Street gangs and sophisticated counsellors had borne false witness against their neighbour in contravention of the commandment of God (Exod. 20:16). Commenting upon this commandment, Thomas Watson wrote, 'God has set two natural fences to keep in the tongue — the teeth and the lips; and this commandment is a third fence set about it, "Neither shalt thou bear false witness against thy neighbour".'[6]

In addition to the verbal abuse, Job has also been the victim of emotional, psychological and physical attacks. They **'detest'** him and **'spit'** in his face (30:10). If Job had dreamt of earlier days when his 'bow' in his hand was the symbol of his strength, now his bow is snapped (30:11). His manliness has been taken away. His body is weak (30:13). He is a helpless victim: they have set snares for his feet, laid siege to his walls and destroyed all routes of escape (30:12-13). Soon, the walls will be breached (30:14).

Victims of paralysing accidents, from disease to redundancy, can identify with Job. There is a loss of dignity that comes in such circumstances. Job feels as though he has no strength: his **'bow'** is **'unstrung'** (30:11).

One of the things that unsettles us as we see photographs of the Jewish pogroms in Europe is the way men, women and children were handled with such indignity. Herded into freight cars, forced to line up naked, deprived of basic amenities, tortured and brutalized, these people lost their dignity before the killing ever started. It is this sense of dignity, that it should not be this way, that troubles Job. His wounds stink and exude something offensive (30:30). No one wants to come near him (30:24). The only sound to come from Job is that of wailing (30:24,29,31).

Those who suffer like Job know what he means. They sympathize with his sense of frustration and hurt. We are made in God's image, to reflect something of his glory, but it is hard to imagine it in the form of a grown man reduced to senility, dribbling and incontinent. Where is the grace in his form? We can readily appreciate it in the outline of a golden retriever, or a dolphin, or a butterfly — but in Job in his current circumstances? We are designed for dignity and we must not forget that. True, we are sinners — a fact that should humble us. But we are also, by faith in Jesus Christ, redeemed sons of God and co-heirs with Jesus — a fact that reminds us of our essential, God-given, dignity. It is recalling the greatness of what we are — 'Now we are the children of God, and what we will be has not yet been made known...' (1 John 3:2) — that is so difficult when our bodies, minds and spirits are twisted out of shape by pain. Job is expressing just how little sense of dignity he now feels.[7]

What God has done (30:16-23)

The pain that Job has felt, as he now summarizes the entire episode thus far, lies not so much in what street gangs have done, or even the ineptitude of his friends; it is much worse than that. It is that in all the pain, God has done it (30:11). Job's life is ebbing away (30:16). His resources are gone. Hope is vanishing. All he has now are days and nights of piercing pain (30:16,17). **'The churning inside me never stops'**, he says (30:27).

How much pain can a human being take? How much can a family watch? Job's pain is continuous (30:16-17), humiliating (30:18-19), merciless (30:20-21), violent (30:22) and deadly (30:23). The metaphors are gripping: Job feels that his soul, his very vitality, has been poured out like water from a jar. Every part of his body aches. It is, as Hartley put it, 'as though God has grabbed him by his clothing and pulled it so tightly about him that every part of his body screams out in agonizing pain (30:18).'[8]

'Pain as a sensation is closely associated with anxiety, worry, fear, anger, depression and other types of emotion. When a patient becomes fearful or anxious he tends to report that his pain is more intense; conversely when he becomes relaxed and not anxious about the pain-producing stimulation he tends to report his pain as less intense. The total experience of pain involves a complex blending of unpleasant sensations with emotions.[9]

A telling illustration of some of the psychological aspects of pain is found in the Lamentations of Jeremiah:

Is it nothing to you, all you who pass by?
  Look around and see.
Is any suffering like my suffering
  that was inflicted on me,
that the Lord brought on me
  in the day of his fierce anger?
From on high he sent fire,
  sent it down into my bones.
He spread a net for my feet
  and turned me back.
He made me desolate,
  faint all the day long

                                        (Lam. 1:12-13).

Job has spoken of his pain as being 'unrelenting' (6:10).
Elihu will later speak of a 'bed of pain' (33:19). Jeremiah says,
'I writhe in pain' (Jer. 4:19) and speaks of 'unending pain' (Jer.
15:18).
  It is God who has done it!

I cry out to you, O God, but you do not answer;
  I stand up, but you merely look at me.
You turn on me ruthlessly;
  with the might of your hand you attack me.
You snatch me up and drive me before the wind;
  you toss me about in the storm

                                        (30:20-22).

'You... You...'!, Job cries. It appears as though God is watching, stony-faced, unmoved, unsympathetic, a torturer, cruel
and dispassionate.
  One of the Bible's words to describe what happened to Job
is 'tribulation'. Its root meaning lies in the word 'thresh'. It is
the process whereby wheat is thrown about in the wind to
extract the grain. 'Simon, Simon,' Jesus warned Peter, 'Satan

has asked to sift you as wheat' (Luke 22:31). What Job describes here is exactly the same process. It is always painful and difficult. Paul tells us that 'Tribulation produces perseverance' (Rom. 5:3). He has been tossed up in the air as the grain is tossed in threshing (30:22). But a character is emerging in Job. He will never be the same again. He is learning more and more about the Lord and his ways; learning to trust him, to lean on him, to call on him, to cry to him in pain. God has set up Job as his champion against Satan. And though the champion is bleeding from the scars of the battle, he *is* winning. God has chosen him, just as Jesus predicted, so that he might bear fruit (John 15:16). In that light, all the beating and flailing seems worthwhile. And Job is soon to acknowledge it himself.

Job's final protestation of innocence

Job began his summing up by recalling the blessings of God he had known in the past (chapter 29). He has since added the testimony of his present circumstances, which are almost too painful to record (chapter 30). The question, the one that has been with us from the beginning is, of course, why is Job suffering? At least, this is Job's question. It is not, as we shall come to see in the conclusion, the question that the book of Job is particularly anxious to answer. In fact, Job is never given a satisfactory answer to the problem of his suffering. For now, however, Job is still asking the question, and as far as he is concerned, the answer cannot possibly lie in the fact that he is a great sinner. He has refuted the allegations made by his friends again and again. It is time, now, to lay this charge to rest once and for all.

   In chapter 31 Job proceeds to list a whole series of sins and then to deny them. The form that the denial takes needs to be examined. Job is doing something here that would have been quite common at the time. In order to deny his involvement in a certain crime he calls down a curse from God if he is found out to be telling an untruth. Behind it lies the idea in Job's mind that he has entered into a **'covenant'** (31:1) with God, expecting that obedience will bring its reward. In Job's eyes, God seems to have abandoned the rôle of 'Job's protector' and, instead, has become his enemy.

Basically, Job is entering into an oath of loyalty and commitment to follow God with all of his heart. It is an oath of covenant obedience which Job claims to have been in effect before the trials ever started. So sure is Job of his innocence, he is prepared to have his life considered retrospectively. His friends would have cautioned otherwise, of course. When Job asked, 'How many wrongs and sins have I committed? Show me my offence and my sin' (13:23), Eliphaz had suggested that his fault lay in oppressing the poor (22:5-11). Job has already refuted this charge, protesting his innocence (29:11-12).

There is one more thing that Job can do. According to the custom of the times, he could enter into an oath, a legally binding statement whereby a defendant swears his innocence on condition that, if found out to be guilty, a curse (an agreed penalty) would be implemented. We are familiar with curses, or imprecations, being uttered against others,[10] but here the curse is being pronounced upon oneself: '*If* I have committed such and such a sin, *then* let the following penalty come upon me.' It is similar in form to what the psalmist says:

> If I forget you, O Jerusalem,
>   let my right hand forget her skill!
> If I do not remember you,
>   let my tongue cling to the roof of my mouth
>
> (Ps. 137. 5-6).

You have to be very sure of yourself to engage in this kind of oath.

Job cites an entire list of ten sins: lust (31:1-4), dishonesty (31:5-8), adultery (31:9-12), oppression (31:13-15), neglect of the needy (31:16-23), greed (31:24-25), idolatry (31:26-28), vindictiveness (31:29-30), parsimony, or meanness (31:31-32), hypocrisy (31:33-34) and exploitation (31:38-40). When we have examined each one, we shall have to come back and ask what exactly we mean when we suggest that Job is innocent, or **'blameless'** (31:6). For now, it is sufficient for us to bear in mind that Job is not claiming absolute perfection. Equally, however, his protest goes too far. Job appears blind to the deceitfulness of sin. There appears to be 'a remarkable depth of self-righteousness in him'[11] at this point. It is something which Elihu will point out in the next chapter.

Lust (31:1-4)

Job begins by telling us that he has made a 'covenant' with his **'eyes not to look lustfully at a girl'** (31:1). Here he anticipates our Saviour's words in the Sermon on the Mount: 'But I tell you that anyone who looks at a woman lustfully has already committed adultery with her in his heart' (Matt. 5:28).

These verses inform us of Job's knowledge of the power of temptation and his determination to overpower sin in his life. If we are honest, there are at least two things that we should admit to in our lives: first, our failure to deal with our sin; and second, how inadequately we go about it. Job is addressing both issues here, and revealing a remarkable affinity to our Lord Jesus Christ's repeated insistence upon overcoming our sinful tendencies. 'Pluck it out!' 'Cut it off!' 'Deny!' were Jesus' commands. By carefully controlling what he *saw*, Job is acting along similar lines. For Job, as well as Jesus, positively growing in grace was impossible without negative handling of sin.

Several elements are worth noting in Job's method here.

1. Sin must be dealt with

The first is that Job feels a need to deal with sin. He is evidently
conscious that were he to neglect scrutinizing what he saw, he
would certainly fall into sin. However self-righteous Job may
appear to be in this chapter, he is certainly aware of the
potential within him to fall into sin. He concedes that his heart
and mind are battlegrounds of conflict between the flesh and
the spirit. Sin will not go away of its own accord. Job
recognizes the need to do something if sin is to be conquered.
What was true of Job is true of each one of us. However
advanced we may be, we are never in a position of not having
to deal with temptation. The moment we forget this is the time
when we are sure to fall. We are all of us sick and damaged,
deformed and scarred by sin to a far greater extent than we ever
realize, and certainly more than we ever admit. We delude
ourselves into thinking we are strong, when we are not. When
my teenage son woke us all in the middle of the night insisting
there were uninvited guests in his room it soon became clear
that he was hallucinating and suffering from a fever. No matter
how much we insisted there was no one else there apart from
ourselves, we had the unnerving suspicion that he thought we,
and not himself, were the ones who were not quite right.
Similarly, Christians delude themselves into self-confident
assertions that they have got the better of some particular
weakness and that it no longer has any power over them.

2. The heart and mind must be guarded

The second is that Job recognizes a need to guard his mind and
thereby his heart. The man who *looks* lustfully at a woman
commits heart-adultery. It is a sin to *think* about unlawful

sexual relationships, whether they be heterosexual or homo-sexual. By restricting what he allowed himself to look at, Job was in effect protecting what his mind dwelt upon. The eye, to borrow a phrase from Bunyan, is the gate through which all kinds of evil things gain access. And sexual relations have become the gate through which many Christians walked to their destruction! The secret of holiness lies in the mind. It is what Paul is alluding to when he tells us that those who live in a sinful way do so because they allow their minds to think in a sinful way. Conversely, those who live according to the principles of holiness do so because their minds walk in step with the Spirit (Rom. 8:5). Ultimately, what we allow our-selves to think upon determines the condition of our lives. Behind it lies the principle that sin is committed well before it finds its fruit in outward acts. Even the thought of lust is sin.

Job recognized that sin needs to be starved of oxygen; it must not be allowed to take root and develop. It was to point out this that James wrote, 'Each one is tempted when, by his own evil desire, he is dragged away and enticed. Then, after desire has conceived, it gives birth to sin; and sin, when it is full-grown, gives birth to death' (James 1:14-15).

3. Practical steps must be taken

A third principle follows: that practical steps are necessary to advance in holiness. Sin needs to be mortified, not modified! We toy with the idea that so long as we can indulge in some modified form of a particular sin, we will make up for it by increased prayer and Bible study! Job, instead, was prepared to walk around wearing blinkers rather than indulge in this kind of casuistry. If your right eye is offending you, Jesus suggested, then there is only one course of action left: gouge it out! (Matt. 5:29). It is all very well to talk about holiness; even to desire holiness. But holiness can only be attained as we

implement practical steps in our daily lives. Watching what we
see might mean for us such things as turning off the television,
or refusing to purchase certain magazines and newspapers.
Whatever it may mean in practice, it is only as we do these
things that we can be in a position to say that we are serious
about wanting to be holy! Will you pray: 'Turn my eyes away
from worthless things'? (Ps. 119:37).

4. Life must be lived in the light of God's presence

A fourth principle is equally important: we are to live our lives
with God's approval constantly in mind. It is to live, as our
forefathers might have put it, *coram Deo*, before God. Job
asks, **'Does he not see my ways and count my every step?'**
(31:4). It was the thought that the all-seeing, all-knowing God
was aware of his every thought and action that motivated Job
to holiness. Job, if he has taught us anything at all thus far, has
taught us that God is great and is to be feared. God is awesome!
Jesus could not have made it clearer: if you yield to sinful lusts
you are yielding to something which eventually leads to hell
(Matt.5:29-30). That is exactly Job's point: **'Is it not ruin for
the wicked, disaster for those who do wrong?'** (31:3). Fix
your mind on that!

Dishonesty (31:5-8)

To be called a liar is deeply insulting, for liars cannot be
trusted. Truth is sacred and precious and we feel that it is a
measure of the corruption that pervades our society that truth
is often held to be a malleable commodity. Job insists that he
has avoided **'falsehood'** in every area of his life — a pretty
bold claim you might think! The word he uses is used elsewhere in the Bible to cover improper speech, including the

wrong use of God's name (Exod. 20:7), false testimony in court (Exod. 23:1; Deut. 5:20) and the utterances of false, uninspired prophets (Ezek.12:24;13:6-9,23; 21:23,29; 22:28). These things are lies (Ps. 144:8,11).

The prohibition against falsehood is enshrined in the ninth commandment. Falsehoods are intrinsically untrue and those who trade in them are insincere and untrustworthy. It is the thought expressed in Psalm 24, where we are told that the godly man is the one 'who has clean hands and a pure heart, who does not lift up his soul to an idol or swear by what is false' (v. 4). Lies are Satan's currency, a part of his image (cf. John 8:44). It was a lie that lay behind the downfall of Adam and Eve in Eden, and the betrayal of Jesus (Gen. 3:4; Matt. 26:59-68). So universal is lying that it is ample evidence of man's fallenness. Lying insults our neighbour and God, who hates 'a lying tongue' and a 'false witness who pours out lies' (Prov. 6:16-19). And Job wants to have nothing to do with lies and dishonesty. There is no godliness without truthfulness. Everyone who 'practises falsehood' is excluded from the city of God (Rev. 22:15).

But what kind of falsehoods does Job have in mind? The curse he envisages for infringement, crop-failure (31:8), might suggest that he is thinking of shady business practices. This was Eliphaz's charge, as we have seen many times, and the fact that Job keeps harping back to it may suggest how deeply it had hurt him.

Have you ever traded in falsehoods — half-truths, exaggerations, lies? A woman began praying thus: 'Lord, you know I have this weakness for exaggerating things...', at which point the minister broke into the prayer and said, 'Call them lies!'

Job claims that he is **'blameless'** (31:6). His hands are clean (31:7). Truth is sacred!

Adultery (31:9-12)

Job has already mentioned lust (31:1-4). Now he goes further
to include adultery and seduction (31:9-12). God's law forbids
adultery (Exod. 20:14). The Old Testament penalty was death
(Lev. 20:10).

The passage is full of double meanings: **'if I have lurked
at my neighbour's door'** (31:9) hints at illicit sexual inter-
course, as does the expression, **'then may my wife grind
another man's grain'** (31:10). Sex is for marriage and for
marriage *only*! And marriage is based on trust and fidelity.
Break these two principles at your peril! Casual sex abuses
another's dignity and person, however willing he or she may
be. In these days we need to remind ourselves that adultery,
whatever form it takes, is sin. Perhaps also it needs emphasiz-
ing that a life without sex is as fulfilling as one with it. Jesus
lived a perfect life as a celibate, and Paul a single life throughout his ministry (though he may have been married at one
time).

The Bible is full of peaks and troughs of spiritual experience, but few valleys are deeper than the experience of David
with Bathsheba (2 Sam.11). One of the things that emerges
from the story is that sin is never simple. Adultery was only a
part of the shame that came upon David. He knew who
Bathsheba was — that she was married to another — and
David's adultery involved both *covetousness* and *theft*. And
when Bathsheba's pregnancy was discovered, David became
embroiled in *lies* and *deceitfulness* in attempting to make
people think the baby was Uriah's. Ultimately, it led to
murder, and few things could underline the seriousness of
adultery more than that. Furthermore, adultery breaks our
relations with God. That is why Job speaks of it as 'a fire that
burns to destruction' (31:12).[12]

This expression reminds us of the way another Bible writer
warns of the danger of adultery:

Can a man scoop fire into his lap
    without his clothes being burned?
Can a man walk on hot coals
    without his feet being scorched?
So is he who sleeps with another man's wife;
    no one who touches her will go unpunished

(Prov. 6:27-29).

Adultery is playing with fire!

Oppression (31:13-15)

'Then we see here a general doctrine common to all men: which is, first that such as are advanced in any authority, must know that God's setting of them in that state, is not to give them the bridle to vex others, and to trample them under their feet; but it behoves them to refrain themselves always in lowliness and mildness.'[13]

Job had a 'large number of servants' (1:3). But he testifies to the fact that even his servants have human rights worthy of respect. Two come to the surface: the right of a servant to take his master to court (31:14); and the right of women (**'maid-servants'**) to justice, just as much as men (**'menservants'**) (31:13).

In Britain we look back to the Magna Carta, which King John signed in 1215, and which King Henry III reissued ten years later. Among its many provisions was a guarantee of a fair trial by one's peers. The Americans look to Thomas Jefferson's 'Declaration of Independence', drafted in 1776, in which are contained the famous words to the effect that it is 'self-evident' that 'All men are created equal and that they are endowed by their Creator with certain inalienable rights,' especially the rights of 'life, liberty, and the pursuit of happiness'.

Human rights are based upon the fact that we are all God's creatures: we are all made by him: **'Did not he who made me in the womb make them? Did not the same one form us both within our mothers?'** (31:15). As John Stott summarizes it, 'Human rights are at base the right to be human, and so to enjoy the dignity of having been created in God's image and of possessing in consequence unique relationships to God himself, to our fellow human beings and to the material world.'[14]

Three things emerge from the fact of man's creation by God: *dignity*, in that every human being bears, to some degree at least, the image of God (Gen.1:26); *equality*, in that God shows no partiality in his treatment of those whom he has made (Deut.1:16-17; 10:17; 16:18-19); and *responsibility*, in that it is our responsibility to be prepared to forego our rights for the sake of others. In this, Jesus is the supreme example (Phil. 2:6-7).

What Job testifies to here is the same as what Paul exhorts in the New Testament: 'And you, masters, do the same things to them, giving up threatening, knowing that your own Master also is in heaven, and there is no partiality with him' (Eph. 6:9). We are our brother's keepers. We belong to the same human family and share a responsibility towards each other. Christians should be at the forefront in setting an example by their attitude to those whom they employ. 'Remember the prisoners as if chained with them, and those who are mistreated, since you yourselves are in the body also' (Heb. 13:3).

Neglect of the needy (31:16-23)

We have returned once more to Eliphaz's charge that Job had abused the poor and helpless (22:7-9). Twice Job has taken up this charge, castigating those who are guilty of such a thing (24:1-12) and denying that he himself has ever been guilty of

it (29:12-16). Once again he refutes the accusation. He has
been generous in supplying food (31:17) and clothes (31:19-
20) to the needy. Why? Because he fears God (31:23). And
here we come across something which appears as almost
incidental: that amongst Job's children there were orphans
whom he had fostered (31:18).

'Religion that God our Father accepts as pure and faultless
is this: to look after orphans and widows in their distress...'
(James 1:27).

Greed (31:24-25)

Again, it was Eliphaz who had suggested that there was a mean
streak in Job (22:24). Job resolutely denies it. He has not
placed his **trust in gold; or said to gold, "You are my
security"'** (31:24).

Beware of putting all your confidence in this world's
treasures, Jesus warned, for you might discover one day that
they are gone. 'Do not store up for yourselves treasures on
earth, where moth and rust destroy, and where thieves break in
and steal. But store up for yourselves treasures in heaven,
where moth and rust do not destroy, and where thieves do not
break in and steal. For where your treasure is, there your heart
will be also' (Matt. 6:19-21). By 'treasure', Jesus meant the
things we tend to prize most dearly. And far too often it is
money. Hence the frequent warnings: 'But woe to you who are
rich' (Luke 6:24). 'You cannot serve both God and Money'
(Luke 16:13). 'Again I tell you, it is easier for a camel to go
through the eye of a needle than for a rich man to enter the
kingdom of God' (Matt. 19:24). 'A man's life does not consist
in the abundance of his possessions' (Luke 12:15). 'Sell your
possessions and give to the poor' (Luke 12:33). 'Give to
everyone who asks you, and if anyone takes what belongs to
you, do not demand it back' (Luke 6:30).

Bank in heaven and not on earth! It was when Zacchaeus began to do just this that Jesus declared: 'Today salvation has come to this house' (Luke 19:9).

> Take my silver and my gold;
> Not a mite would I withhold.

Consecration often begins by sanctifying the purse.

Idolatry (31:24-28)

To 'blow a kiss' is a gesture of endearment in today's society. In Israel, it was a symbol of worship and therefore was forbidden, as two passages in the Old Testament clearly indicate: one in which the Lord assures a depressed Elijah that he is not alone; there were over 7,000 others like him hidden in Israel 'whose mouths have not kissed [Baal]' (1 Kings 19:18); and another in which the prophet Hosea castigates Ephraim for Baal worship, human sacrifice and 'kiss[ing] the calf-idols' (Hosea 13:2). Job concedes that had he been guilty of such idolatry, 'blowing a kiss' to wealth, or to the **'sun'** or **'moon'**, his actions would be worthy of judgement — but, of course, he has not (31:27).

Few in our society could echo Job's words here. The worship of money is something we have already noted in our comments on the previous section. Wesley once said, 'If you have any desire to escape the damnation of hell, give all you can; otherwise I can have no more hope for your salvation than that of Judas Iscariot.'[15] Calvin makes the point that Job is portrayed here as actually talking to his money. Such is the power of riches that it seems to take on the very form of a person who communicates with, and seemingly controls, our hearts.

Vindictiveness (31:29-30)

It may be natural to feel some sense of satisfaction when an
enemy suffers, but it is wrong:

> Do not gloat when your enemy falls;
>> when he stumbles, do not let your heart rejoice,
> or the Lord will see and disapprove
>> and turn his wrath away from him
>>>> (Prov. 24:17-18).

Can we really love those who are hostile to us? The world's
principles will encourage us either to ignore them, or else to
retaliate. But Job understood the principles of the kingdom of
God that provide us with motives designed to encourage us to
follow a different path: our Father shows love to his enemies
every day in giving the sun and the rain to the righteous and the
ungodly alike. He would be within his rights to retaliate
against sinners for the dishonour done to him. Instead he
shows mercy and patience. Job has evidently done the same.
He has not abused his tongue to pronounce a premature death-
curse on an enemy (31:30).

Meanness (31:31-32)

No guests at Job's table had ever gone away hungry. The
'stranger' and the **'traveller'** had been shown the utmost
hospitality at Job's home (31:32). Nor is this some idle boast
on Job's part, for his own 'household' could verify his claim.
Job had been a witness to the grace of God at work in his life.

God's people are to 'practise hospitality' (Rom. 12:13).
And the motivation is staggering: for everything done to one
in need of hospitality is done for him who on the great

Judgement Day is going to say, 'For I was hungry and you gave me something to eat, I was thirsty and you gave me something to drink, I was a stranger and you invited me in' (Matt. 25:35). And the rewards are equally staggering, for Abraham, Gideon and Manoah all discovered that by showing hospitality to strangers, they had in fact entertained angels without realizing it (Gen.18; Judg. 6; 13; cf. Heb.13:2).

Hypocrisy (31:33-34)

Job had not attempted to conceal his sin in any way, for there were no sins of any magnitude in his life (31:33). Job is not afraid of exposure, as many in public life are. No 'news-hound' will unearth some dirt about Job and jeopardize his standing. There is no hypocrisy in Job. He has practised what he preached. The Holy Spirit has already disclosed to us who read of Job that his life was 'blameless and upright',[16] not that Job was sinless but faithful in terms of the covenant. He was what folk in these parts call 'a godly man'. There was a harmony between Job's profession and his life. He was not a hypocrite, as Satan, and, recently, Job's friends had suggested.

Adam had attempted to hide his sin in Eden, and there is a possibility that verse 33 should be rendered: 'If I have covered my transgressions as Adam...' By hiding himself in the garden, Adam had entertained the idea that God was unaware of his transgression. This is a constant ploy of Satan's. Adam was the first to show hypocrisy and he has passed this tendency on to us all. As Calvin comments, 'Surely the Devil wins much at our hands, when he makes us cloak our faults: for if we acknowledge them, we must needs be ashamed of them. But if we have once covered the evil, we think all is safe and take leave to fall asleep...'[17]

'There seems nothing which is so displeasing to Christ as hypocrisy and unreality,' comments J. C. Ryle.[18] 'The

Christianity which is from the Holy Ghost,' he adds later, 'will always have a very deep view of the sinfulness of sin. It will not merely regard sin as a blemish and misfortune, which makes men and women objects of pity and compassion. It will see in sin the abominable thing which God hates, the thing which makes man guilty and lost in his Maker's sight, the thing which deserves God's wrath and condemnation. It will look on sin as the cause of all sorrow and unhappiness, of strife and wars, of quarrels and contentions, of sickness and death, the blight which has blighted God's fair creation, the cursed thing which makes the whole earth groan and travail in pain. Above all, it will see in sin the thing which will ruin us eternally, except we can find a ransom, lead us captive, except we can get its chains broken, and destroy our happiness, both here and hereafter, except we fight against it unto death.'[19]

Exploitation (31:38-40)

One final denial comes from Job: he has not been guilty of any abuse of his land. The law made specific demands on landowners: the land was not to be sown with two kinds of seed (Lev. 19:19), it was to receive a rest every seventh year (Exod. 23:10-11; Lev. 25:2-7; 26:34-35), and in particular, no blood was to be shed on it, for if it was the land would cry out for vengeance — as the death of Abel highlighted (Gen. 4:10-12; cf. Num. 35:33-34). Job has not been guilty of abusing these laws: he has not eaten its produce without paying fair wages to those hired to perform the labour involved (31:39). As a businessman, Job pleads his innocence. At work, as well as at home, Job has demonstrated the faith which he professes. If he has not, he is prepared for the curse pronounced in Eden to fall upon his land (31:40; cf. Gen. 3:17-18).

There is a point which emerges from this chapter that we must not miss. It is that our lives are to be governed *in every part* by the rule of God's Word. It is not enough for us to have a clear conscience in one or two areas; we must be prepared to have God's law applied comprehensively. As Calvin, somewhat quaintly, puts it, 'Job touches not some one virtue alone, but comprehends generally the whole rule of good life which God has given us. And in very deed it is not enough for us to have performed a piece of the law (if at leastwise we were able to do it). But it behoves us to endeavour to rule and frame our life throughout according to all things which God commands.'[20]

A call for a fair hearing

Job ends his list of sins — of which he has insisted his total innocence — by calling upon God to give him a fair hearing. He informs the heavenly court that he has appended his signature to this 'oath of innocence': **'I sign now my defence'** (31:35). Interestingly, Job's word for 'signature' is, in fact, a letter *taw,* the last letter of the Hebrew alphabet. It is the equivalent of an illiterate person putting an 'X' on the dotted line.

In addition, Job adds that he will go to God's presence wearing this document of his innocence with full public display, striding into the Almighty's presence **'like a prince'** (31:37). Some commentators think Job is arrogant here.[21] However, Job seems to be insisting that certain allegations made against him were entirely false. As has been said many times, Job is not sinless. 'He means not,' adds Calvin, 'that he had been utterly clear, so as there was no fault to be found in him,' adding that Job had already confessed himself to be a sinner, but not a hypocritical one (cf. 31:33-34).[22]

This is Job's last word on the matter. **'The words of Job are ended'** (31:40). The only words that he will utter after this are words of repentance (40:4-5; 42:2-6). These, as we shall see, interpret for us Job's protestations of innocency.

A summary of Job's speech

'How I wish I could go back to those days when the Lord and I walked together in fellowship! I remember the times when I walked out to the gates of the city and people showed me respect. Princes would stop talking. Everyone acknowledged that I was blessed. I used to give money to the poor, and helped the underprivileged. I even represented people in court.

'But now everyone is against me. Even those needy people I once helped treat me as dirt. And when I ask God for help, he does not hear me. I have tried to do what is right, but it has been to no avail. Everything is going wrong. The jackals are waiting for me to die. My skin is black and my bones burn with fever.

'But I will not give in to sin. If I have lied, let God cause my crops to be uprooted. If I have yielded to another woman let my wife become a slave. If I have mistreated my slaves, then let me be taken to court. If I have been mean to those in need, then let my shoulder be dislocated and my arm be cut off at the elbow.

'No, I have not sinned as you say.'

23.
Suffering is God's discipline

Please read Job 32 - 33

Elihu's first speech

Another character enters at this point: Elihu, the youngest of all the contributors (32:4). He was not mentioned in the opening prologue, and his sudden appearance here might lead us to expect that perhaps there is someone after all who understands Job. These chapters have been described as 'the most interesting and the most difficult' in the book of Job.¹ It is important to remember that Elihu is as ignorant of the heavenly contest between God and Satan as were Job and his three friends. His contributions are therefore necessarily flawed. Without the full picture every attempt at analysing Job's suffering will come short of the truth. Commentators who fail to take this point into consideration necessarily fail to convey the full import of Elihu's words.

Elihu appears confident of his own ability. His contribution promises much and does rise above the level of his three predecessors. Much of it is well-worn ground, but it also contains an advance on what has been said before: Job is not necessarily suffering for anything he did in the past, but in order to bring out the latent sin hidden within his heart. Suffering is God's discipline. Eliphaz had touched on this concept briefly in his opening speech, but had failed to make anything of it. A ray of light begins to shine in these chapters which prepares the way for the (definitive) speeches of God.

We may ask what is the reason for Elihu's inclusion at all. We might have expected God to reply immediately after Job's dramatic pleas in chapters 26-31. But God does not reply that quickly. He makes Job wait. 'God acts in his own time; he is not at human beck and call.'[2]

An angry young man (32:1-5)

Elihu is an **'angry'** young man ('angry' occurs four times in the Hebrew of the opening verses — 32:2 (twice),3,5): he is angry with both Job and his three friends.

He is angry with Job because he went too far in his protestations of innocence. Job is guilty of **'justifying himself rather than God'** (32:2). In protesting his innocence, Job has made God out to be in the wrong! It is a most serious charge.

Elihu is partly right. No one is absolutely innocent and in a manner reminiscent of Hamlet's words to Ophelia, it may be said of Job, 'The man doth protest too much.' It has come to a climax in a lengthy protestation in Job 31:1-40. Job is dumbfounded that God has visited him with the curses, rather than the blessings of the covenant (Deut. 28:18,31,35). 'God seems to Job to have forsaken the suzerain's role as protector, and strangely turned enemy against an obedient vassal.'[3] But Job in this chapter also exposes a remarkable degree of self-righteousness. His blindness to the depravity of his heart exposes, not a fatal flaw (i.e. that he was unregenerate), but a serious spiritual need, and when Elihu points this out, he underlines that one factor in Job's sufferings was its exposure. Calvin's assessment is that 'Job had gone too far, although he had a just and reasonable quarrel; the others had resisted God, although they had used good reasons; for it was the wrong purpose.'⁴ In other words, Job has a good case expressed badly; his three friends have good arguments, but use them badly.

Elihu is also angry with Job's three counsellors. He is angry with them because they have singularly failed in convincing Job that God was not in the wrong. They have, by now, fallen silent, partly because they are disgusted that Job seems to be justifying himself (32:1), and partly because there is no more to be said. It is interesting to note that they are no longer called 'friends' (as in 2:11; 19:21; 42:10), but **'three men'** (32:1). None of them has answered Job's fundamental question as to *why* he was suffering. All three, in varying degrees, have been intent on finding the reason for Job's suffering in his sinful rebellion towards God. The remedy, as far as they are concerned, lies in Job's immediate repentance.

Elihu has been a listener to this debate, but out of deference to their age (and implied wisdom) he has refrained from intervening so long as the three men were in dialogue with Job. Now that they are silent, he can refrain no longer. He is bursting, **'like bottled-up wine,'** to make his views known (32:19).

Elihu's pedigree is impressive. His name, which is similar to Elijah, means 'He is my God'. His father's name, **'Barakel'** (32:2), means 'Bless, O God' and the fact that he was a **'Buzite'** identifies him as a descendant of Abraham (Buz being one Abraham's sons, Gen. 22:21). These facts seem to imply that Elihu's appearance is meant to signify that he is here to defend God's honour.

A number of very different opinions have been held with regard to Elihu. Some regard his contribution as long-winded and self-opinionated. Certainly, he mentions himself a great deal. He says of himself that he is **'full of words'** (32:18). In chapter 32 alone, he uses the word 'I' nineteen times, and 'me', 'my' and 'mine' thirteen times. And he is fairly severe on Job, accusing him at one point of being a rebel (34:37). Since no reply is given to him, some have regarded Elihu's contribution as an editorial addition to the book of Job made at a later date.

Others have drawn different conclusions. George Philip, for example, says, 'Some scholars suggest this indicates that the Elihu section is no real part of the Book of Job. It seems better to say that Elihu should never have opened his mouth. It takes grace to know when to be silent, and after all, in chapter 37:23, Elihu confesses he does not understand God.'[5]

Others, however, have noted that his theology is far more God-centred and orthodox. In particular, he notes that God sometimes uses suffering to teach us. Towards the end he gives a magnificent picture of God's power in the world of nature. It seems that he acts as a kind of bridge that leads us to God's own contribution in chapters 38-42. He has his flaws — he speaks, after all, from a heart filled with anger: against Job because he saw him as justifying himself rather than God (32:2); and against Job's friends because they had provided no answer (32:3).

Counselling from an angry heart can be dangerous. There are times when it is right to be angry, but on such occasions the devil is near: 'In your anger, do not sin ... do not give the devil a foothold' (Eph. 4:26-27). Anger can easily give place to a display of bad-temperedness, even violence. 'Never open the door to the devil. When you lose your temper you open it wide; it could not be wider. Nothing opens the door more widely than anger, and for this good reason. The moment you are controlled by your temper you are no longer able to reason, you are no longer able to think, you can no longer give a balanced judgement, for you are altogether biased on one side and against the other side... Is there anything that leads to more trouble than anger? Things said in anger and in a bitter moment! You would almost cut your tongue off, if you could, to get them back; and sometimes, though forgiven, they leave permanent wounds and scars. What havoc is wrought in the world by sinful anger!'[6]

But not all anger is wrong and youthful rage has been the cause of many a protest against the injustices and prejudices seen in the world. Though they may not see the whole picture, young people can often pinpoint a failure that others have grown accustomed to and are cynical of changing. Elihu has a point that needs to be heard.

'Listen to me' (32:6-22)

There are aspects of Elihu to admire.

1. Elihu is a good listener

He has listened carefully to what the other three had to say. Like a good listener, he let them have their say without inter-ruption (32:11). He paid the closest possible attention (32:12). True, he was now like fermenting wine in new wineskins, **'ready to burst'** (32:19), adding that although he has obeyed protocol by keeping his tongue at the roof of his mouth, he can wait no longer: words are already being formed on his tongue (33:2). But he has gained our respect by waiting patiently.

2. Elihu is courteous[7]

It was, and still is, a mark of the East that deference is given to age. Typical of the received wisdom of the times is the following: 'How fine a thing: sound judgement with grey hairs, and for greybeards to know how to advise! How fine a thing: wisdom in the aged, and considered advice coming from men of distinction! The crown of old men is ripe experience, their true glory, the fear of the Lord.'[8]

Though older than Elihu, Job's three friends had singularly failed in communicating wisdom (32:9,12,15-16). Neverthe-less, Elihu was ready to give them their place. We note, then, his deference for age and experience (32:6-7). This is not typical of youth in the Western world of today. Biblical wisdom would have us recapture that respect due to those who have experienced more, learnt more, observed more than we have, for as Calvin says, 'When God lets a man live a long time in the world, He gives him grace to be able to profit those who are younger.'[9] Paul exhorts Timothy not to be subject to the lusts of youthfulness (2 Tim. 2:22) — not that Timothy was guilty of 'debauchery, playing, adultery, drunkenness, or other dissolute actions. Timothy was such a mirror and pattern of all holiness in himself that Saint Paul even had to exhort him to drink wine (1 Tim. 5:23); and yet he speaks to him about the lusts of youth. And why? For since he was young, he could still be too hasty in some things... For young people, since they have not experienced the difficulties which are in many things, step forward boldly, for they do not count the cost of a thing; nothing is impossible for them. Youth, then, always carries presumption with it, and it is a far too common evil...'[10] Young people can learn from Elihu.

3. Elihu seeks to give some glory to God

Elihu takes no credit for his 'wisdom' for himself. It is the Spirit, the **'breath of the Almighty'** that endows wisdom (32:8; cf. 33:4). He is not claiming special revelation (as Eliphaz did in his opening speech). Every living person may tap into this source of wisdom. A human spirit endowed with wisdom from the Spirit of God is truly wise.[11]

Many critics are not kind to Elihu. They see him as an egocentric, brash young man, full of himself and with nothing of any relevance to say. True, he is young, confident, inexperienced, talkative and obviously angry, but none of these precludes him from making a contribution. Elihu is bold enough to challenge the received wisdom of the day and perhaps it takes someone of his temperament to do that. After all, the received wisdom of the day would have Elihu say nothing at all!

4. Elihu is passionate

He **'must speak'** (32:20), but without showing partiality. There is nothing dull or merely academic about Elihu. He means what he says, even if he isn't altogether right. There are few things worse than a dull preacher. And disinterested counsellors are soon revealed for what they are. So passionate is Elihu that he warns Job that he does not know how to flatter (32:22). Job had better prepare himself for some straight talking!

Suffering is God's chastening: a warning to keep us away from danger (33:1-33)

Elihu is wordy in the extreme. It has taken him twenty-four verses to say, 'Look out, I'm going to speak!' and he still hasn't started yet. He has still to come to the main point of his first speech. He has been called 'Endless Elihu'!

Having addressed the audience generally, he now turns directly to Job and requests his personal attention (33:1-7). Unlike the other three friends, Elihu refers twice to Job by name in his first speech (33:1,31). This may reflect his 'brash character',[12] but he is to be commended for his willingness to speak without fear or favour of man. Preachers and teachers of Scripture must be, to borrow Jeremiah's phrase, 'as bold as brass' (cf. Jer. 15:20). And those who receive instruction from others must not chafe when reproved of their sins. They must not be bitter when their sins are uncovered.

Words are already forming in Elihu's mouth (33:2). He pleads his integrity (33:3) and then launches himself into the case for the prosecution with himself as the prosecuting counsel: **'Answer me then, if you can; prepare yourself and confront me'** (33:5; cf. 33:22); the words translated 'answer' and 'prepare' are taken from the legal world. But he does not want Job to be terrified by the prospect: on at least two occasions Job has been paralysed into silence at the thought of pleading his defence before God (9:34; 13:21). Elihu, on the other hand, is but a fellow human being like himself, created and fashioned by the same Spirit (33:6). Job has nothing to fear by this exchange.

Here, initially at least, Elihu shows a gentler spirit than the three friends. He seems conscious that he is in no way better than Job; he is a fellow creature.[13] Those who are not conscious of their own sinfulness will have little compassion towards their neighbours. 'When they wish to rebuke those who have failed they go at it with such violence that they make the wretched wanderers stray further rather than bring them back to the right way... Therefore, if we wish to teach God's word as we ought to, let us begin by knowing our own infirmities. And when we have known them, it will lead us to such a modesty and gentleness that we shall have a good-natured spirit to utter the word of God.'[14]

Finally, we come to the heart of what Elihu has to say in this first speech (33:8-30). Elihu answers three arguments put by Job.

Argument no. 1: God is unfair

The first thing Elihu does is to cite (though not verbatim as the words in 33:8 might suggest) what Job has said: **'I am pure and without sin; I am clean and free from guilt'** (33:9). Job had claimed to be 'blameless' (9:21), and 'not guilty' (10:6-7), challenging anyone to find fault with him (13:19), including God himself! (13:23). Furthermore, he had at one point claimed never to have departed from God's commands (23:10-12). Eliphaz, for one, had taken this to mean that Job was claiming sinlessness (15:14-16), but this cannot be the case since we find Job readily conceding that he was a sinner (7:21; 13:26). What Job was claiming for himself was (unknown to him, of course) what God had already pronounced him to be (1:8; 2:3). What Job claimed was not sinlessness, but *integrity*. Already we suspect Elihu has implied that Job was claiming more than he had. Elihu is moving in the direction of the three friends.

When Elihu puts the words, 'I am without sin ... and free from guilt', into Job's mouth, he is imputing to Job something which he did not say. Though the distinction may appear academic, the point is crucial to an understanding of the book of Job. Job never once claims absolute perfection, but there are times when he appears to overestimate his own righteousness. Kline suggests that his conceit becomes 'incredibly bald and bold in Job's final words'.[15]

Job was innocent of any major sin, but this did not give him the right to charge God with injustice (as he had, 27:2). Elihu is quite right in saying to him: **'In this you are not right.'** Why? Because **'God is greater than man'** (33:12); he is 'beyond our understanding' (35:26). In the hope of defending both God's justice and Job's innocence, Elihu wants to suggest that Job is suffering, not because of some past sin (as Job's three friends have been insisting), but because God wants to warn him from committing sin in the future. In other words, God's ways are not our ways. He can never presume to fathom all that God does. God knows best. We must be prepared to come to the point where we say, 'I do not understand why, but I believe that he does and I accept it.' That is the very heart of faith: to believe in God's love, when everything is pointing in a contrary direction.

Argument no. 2: God does not answer prayer

Elihu cites Job as saying that God **'answers none of man's words'** (33:13). Elihu's response is to point out that God uses nightmares to convey a warning to man (33:14-18). These sufferings of the night are effective in warning us against even greater dangers and keeping us from **'wrongdoing', 'pride'** (33:17) and, ultimately, **'the pit'** (33:18,22,24,28,30), that is, the grave (or death). God is speaking to us even when we fail to realize it.

God also speaks through pain:

Or a man may be chastened on a bed of pain
    with constant distress in his bones,
so that his very being finds food repulsive
    and his soul loathes the choicest meal.
His flesh wastes away to nothing,
    and his bones, once hidden, now stick out.
His soul draws near to the pit,
    and his life to the messengers of death

(33:19-22).

This is Elihu's most noble contribution to the argument of the book of Job. Suffering can be remedial (33:19-28). God may well be dealing with Job in such a way as to help him grow in righteousness and faith. God's purposes may well be educational. We who read the book of Job know the real reason for Job's suffering: the challenge issued by Satan to God, but even Job's friends ought to have surmised that other reasons were possible. Not least was the possibility that God allowed Job to suffer to provide us with an example of a man who endured.

Mark Littleton records the following story: 'A missionary in Pakistan went through a difficult time when her six-month-old baby died. An old Punjabi woman came to her and said, "A tragedy like this is similar to being plunged into boiling water. If you are an egg, your affliction will make you hard-boiled and unresponsive. If you are a potato, you will emerge soft and pliable, resilient and adaptable."

'The missionary remarked that it may have sounded funny to God, but often she found herself praying, "O Lord, make me a potato."' [16]

Our suffering produces character. God may use our hurts to transform us to the image of our Saviour (Rom. 5:3-5; James 1:2-4). This is the argument of Hebrews 12:5-11. The experience of griefs and pains in God's children is evidence of the Father's love and God's moral training ground for producing character. 'Endure hardship as discipline' is the key (Heb. 12:7). Ultimately, Job's testing will produce in him 'character' (Rom. 5:4), a state of triumph with God's seal of approval upon him.

It sometimes takes pain to get us to listen. 'God whispers to us in our pleasures, speaks in our conscience, but shouts in our pains: it is his megaphone to rouse a deaf world,' says C. S. Lewis. [17] Elihu is right here. God does use chronic pain and weakness and other afflictions as his chisel to sculpt our lives. We shall return to this contribution in our comments on Elihu's fourth speech.

Argument no 3: No one understands me

Having painted a picture of a man in pain (33:19-21), Elihu conjectures that this experience may yet prove to be a time of rich blessing (33:23-26): **'He sees God's face and shouts for joy'** (33:26). Why? Because pain can refocus our lives to be what they were meant to be. Appreciating this can only result in praise. Praise was the response of Paul and Barnabas as they sat with their feet in the stocks of a Philippian cell (Acts 16:23-25). It seems that Scripture would have us know that, the

fiercer the opposition, the louder the praise should be. And in
the very act of praise there is found the strength to endure. Well
does Richard Baxter, the English Puritan who knew a great
deal about suffering, say:

> Ye saints, who toil below,
> Adore your heavenly King,
> And onward as ye go
> Some joyful anthem sing.
> Take what he gives
> And praise him still,
> Through good and ill,
> Who ever lives!
>
> My soul, bear thou thy part,
> Triumph in God above,
> And with a well-tuned heart
> Sing thou the songs of love!
> Let all thy days
> Till life shall end,
> Whate'er he send,
> Be filled with praise!

How is such praise possible? Because,

> **... there is an angel on his side**
> **as a mediator, one out of a thousand,**
> **to tell a man what is right for him**
>
> (33:23).

Elihu believes that there is a heavenly intercessor who takes up
the sufferer's case. But he is less specific than Job himself has
been! Elihu's mediator seems to be an angel of some sort, and
his statement is less clear than Job's own cries which he had

previously uttered in 16:19 and 19:25.[18] This heavenly intercessor can spare Job from the 'pit', enabling him to say, **'I have found a ransom'** (33:24).

Men live under the shadow of 'the destroyers' (33:22), God's angels of death. Sometimes the deliverance comes at the eleventh hour, when a course of severe chastening has brought a man to the very edge of the pit (33:19-22). Deliverance comes, restoring the blessings of the righteous. And when this is so, it is a time to give thanks and sing God's praise (33:27-28). Job has discovered that God's chastening has in fact kept him from the pit. 'Thus Elihu removes the sting from the suffering of the righteous and the prosperity of the wicked.'[19]

An assessment of Elihu's first speech

Elihu has brought a note that the other three had singularly failed to do. God has not been silent; he has been shouting to Job in his pain. There is a chastening use of suffering that may be independent of some particular sin. Its purpose may be preventative: it can stop a person from sliding down the slippery path of destruction. Elihu is not all that clear, but he is way ahead of Job's three friends. At least, in Elihu's eyes, Job is not suffering for any sin he has committed in the past. He may be suffering to prevent him from falling into sin in the future! This has a great deal of truth in it, but it fails to answer Job's real dilemma. The truth is that Elihu had no more comprehension of the reasons behind Job's suffering than did Job himself. Only God had the key to that knowledge and thus far at least, he had decided to keep that knowledge to himself. Elihu would have been better to have urged Job to trust God, no matter what, than to try to speculate about answers the veracity of which, at the end of the day, he had no means of proving.

A summary of Elihu's first speech

'Since I am younger than all of you I have been quiet up until now. I was sure that your contributions would be helpful. But true wisdom comes from God alone and he may choose a younger person to relate it, so I will speak.

'I've listened to what all three of you have had to say, but not one of you has proved Job to be wrong. I won't bother using your arguments all over again. I'll tell what I think, and I want you to know that I will be completely fair. I will not try to flatter anyone; I'll simply tell the truth.

'Job, I'm not saying that I'm absolutely right, because I'm just a man like you. Don't be afraid, then, of what I have to say to you.

'You have said that you are pure, "without sin". You have even said that God has invented all sorts of sins against you. It isn't right that you should accuse God in this way. His ways are beyond our understanding; you must see that! Why do you complain simply because he does not give you a complete explanation of what he does? God uses all sorts of ways to speak to people, including pain. He uses pain to bring men back to himself.

'Please give me a hearing. You can refute what I'm saying afterwards if you want.'

24.
'God has something to teach you, Job'

Please read Job 34 - 37

Elihu's second speech

Elihu's second speech (34:1-37) is not dissimilar to his first: he begins by asking for attention (34: 2-4), quotes a few things Job has said (34:5-9) and then proceeds to answer them (34:10-28). The speech closes with a challenge (34:29-37). However, Elihu's second speech is very different from his first in content and tone. All compassion has gone. Those promising words about a mediator in the heavenly courts defending the cause of the likes of Job have also disappeared. Here, in the second speech, is the sound of cold, analytical logic. The first speech had closed with a note of joy. This one closes in doom. What is the explanation for the change? The answer appears to lie in Elihu's love of his own rhetoric, and perhaps a little pride that he has managed to gain the attention of the greybeards of wisdom.

Elihu's words become a little fanciful at this point. He claims the skill of a gourmet chef in his presentation of the argument! (34:3). He belongs to the school of wisdom and is in danger of making too much of his skills. Elihu has been angry with Job's three friends, not because their conclusion has been wrong after all, for Elihu comes to the same conclusion; he is angry, it now seems, because of the inadequacy of their arguments. We have to reach the conclusion that Elihu, at the end of the day, sides entirely with Job's companions: he defends God's justice and condemns Job as a sinner.

God is just

Elihu's quotations refer to Job's complaint that God is unjust in punishing one who is innocent:

Job says, 'I am innocent,
but God denies me justice.
Although I am right,
I am considered a liar;
although I am guiltless,
his arrow inflicts an incurable wound'
                                              (34:5-6).

This much, at least, Job has said. But Elihu goes on to cite Job as saying, **'It profits a man nothing when he tries to please God'** (34:5-6,9).[1] Job has not, of course, said this. He *has* said that the wicked seem to prosper without, it seems, reaping any judgement *in this world* (21:7-34). Job has also made the obvious and irrefutable point that trouble seems to fall on both good and bad alike (9:22-24). Elihu is unfair to Job, deeply unfair, for he makes Job out to have fallen to Satan's charge: 'Does Job fear God for nothing?' (1:9). Had Job said this, the test would have been over and Satan would have been vindicated! For all Elihu's cleverness, he has, unwittingly, sided with Satan. According to Elihu, the only reason Job trusts in God is the personal gain he gets out of it. Job has not reached that point and he never will! Despite Job's anger and confusion, he still maintains his trust in God.

Elihu's response is to elucidate the doctrine of the righteousness of God:

So listen to me, you men of understanding.
Far be it from God to do evil,
from the Almighty to do wrong

(34:10).

He is not speaking to Job, but to the **'wise men'** (34:2),
possibly the three friends. His point is simple and forceful: if
God is just (as he undoubtedly is), any criticism of him is
necessarily unjust. Since Job has been criticizing God, he is in
the wrong. The case against Job seems irrefutable.

The problem with this kind of reasoning is that it has failed
to take into account Job's actual predicament. Elihu is arguing
in a manner that seems divorced from the reality of Job's pain.
What he says is true in general, but misses the point that Job
is making. His theology is impeccable: God's right to rule
owes itself to no one except God himself (34:13). He is the
sovereign Sustainer who reveals his grace every moment of
the day by granting life and breath to man (34:14-15). God is
'the just and mighty One' (34:17). He rules without **'partiality'** (34:18-19). The mighty die at God's command (34:20).
They are not in control of it in any way (34:23). He does not
have to give an account for what he does: he may bring down
the mighty suddenly and quickly (34:24-25). Those who have
abused their power will be punished (34:26-28). Even if God
seems slow to act, that is his prerogative: God cannot be
accused of injustice (34:29-30).

For Elihu, then, Job's demand for vindication is constantly
imputing wrong to God. Job has, by this demand, added
'rebellion' to his sins (34:37). Elihu utters an imprecation:
**'Oh, that Job might be tested to the utmost, for answering
like a wicked man'** (34:36). Whatever sin he may have been
guilty of in the first place (this had been the charge of Job's
three friends and Elihu is noncommittal as to whether he
believes them or not), Job is certainly guilty now of adding to

it by the foolish things he has said in response to his sufferings. Job has added unbelief to his sin by complaining so bitterly against God. Job's suffering has something to do with this anger and bitterness that he now expresses. The only thing for Job to do is to accept God's chastening, repent of his sin, and listen to what God is saying to him (34:31-33).

We have heard all this before. Elihu has reached the same conclusion as the other three counsellors. His anger with them is only due to the fact that they had failed to discover the real fault in Job: not anything in his past, but in his current rebellion under the trial itself. 'Elihu is right to defend the justice of God, and he has advanced the discussion by suggesting that Job's greatest sin may not be something he said or did *before* the suffering started, but the rebellion he is displaying *in* the suffering.'[2] The only course left open to Job is to repent (34:31-33). It does not occur to Elihu that Job may be innocent.

Job is stupid

At the close of his second speech, buoyed up by the cleverness of his argument, Elihu turns to those who may be listening and asks them to pay attention: **'Men of understanding declare, wise men who hear me say to me...'** (34:34). And what are they to hear from Elihu? What is his conclusion? Job is a stupid man! **'Job speaks without knowledge; his words lack insight'** (34:35). Job is not only a sinner; he is also foolish. Job is also guilty of sedition, of mutiny against God. According to Elihu, Job **'claps his hands'** (34:37) in defiance. Job is in no position to do any such thing, of course, and it only typifies just how much Elihu has now been carried away with his own rhetoric.

Most commentators think Elihu is too harsh here.[3] Others, however, have been more sympathetic. It is interesting to note that Elihu's contribution is neither commended nor con-demned at the end. It may be that this is so because, as Carson observes, 'If he is not praised, it is because his contribution is eclipsed by what God himself says; if he is not criticized, it is because he says nothing amiss.'[4] At the end of the day, Elihu has said the best that a man can say who does not possess all the truth. He is ignorant of the rôle of Satan in all of this. Taking that ignorance into consideration, and by imputing to Job something he has not said, Elihu has failed to really minister to Job's case.

Elihu's third speech

Elihu's third speech (35:1-16) follows a similar pattern to the two previous ones: he begins by quoting something Job has said (35:2-4) and then proceeds to refute it (35:5-16).

Elihu hasn't finished with his thesis against Job. He still thinks Job is saying that 'It profits a man nothing when he tries to please God' (34:9), for he puts the following words in Job's mouth: **'What profit is it to me, and what do I gain by not sinning?'** (35:3). True, Job had come close to saying this, but Elihu ignores the cries of a man in desperate pain and instead gives him a lecture on how wrong it is to expect to gain from being righteous. The gloves are now off and it has become clear that Elihu does not accept Job's innocence at all.

Elihu further attributes to Job two questions which he then seeks to answer. The questions, 'What is the point in being good?' and 'Why doesn't God answer prayer?', have been considered already (34:9; 33:13) and one gets the impression that Elihu is running out of steam. Perhaps the lesson we are meant to learn is that we should know when to stop talking and start listening.

1. What is the point in being good?

'What profit is it to me, and what do I gain by not sinning?'
(35:3). Elihu's response is to ask Job to consider **'the heavens'**
(34:5). How small he is in comparison to the vastness of God's
creation! Elihu's point is that God is so far removed from us
that what we do cannot affect him one way or another. It is
wrong, Elihu suggests, to expect gain from being righteous: **'If
you are righteous, what do you give to him, or what does he
receive from your hand?'** (35:7). God's character cannot
change because of anything man does. Eliphaz had presented
a similar argument (22:2-4). This is so commonplace an
argument that one is bound to ask why he makes it at all. God
is neither hurt nor helped by our sin; only our fellow men are
affected by it (35:8). This is true, but Elihu is almost at the
point of saying that not only can God not be touched by human
sin, but that he is indifferent to it. Is Elihu really saying that
whatever happens on earth is of little concern to God, even if
it is wickedness? It appears that he is. One gains the impression
that Elihu is almost arguing for the sake of arguing. The pain
and hurt of Job have long since been forgotten. The truth is that
God is grieved by sin and pleased by righteousness. Elihu's
ability as a counsellor is now under severe strain.

The question Job asks deserves a better answer than the one
given by Elihu. Christians in pain do sometimes cry out, 'What
is the point in trying to lead a righteous life?' In our current
climate it is a vital question to answer, for the stress has shifted
away from holiness. Bookshops are filled with books and
videos on how Christians can be healthy, wealthy and happy.
What is currently valued is not holiness but skills, charisma
and personalities. Christian leaders are found guilty of sexual
misdemeanours and consequently fail to acknowledge any
sense of accountability whatsoever. Their reinstatement has
often been hasty, underlining the fact that holiness is held

cheaply, and angry, confused and hurt Christians are tempted
to ask with Job, 'Is there any point at all in living for God?'

What is it that accounts for men like Robert Murray
M'Cheyne declaring: 'My people's greatest need is my personal holiness'? The simple answer is that God demands it,
Christ reinforces it and Scripture, everywhere, requests it.
From Abraham onwards, God has called his people to walk in
his ways and 'be blameless' (Gen.17:1). Job's 'blamelessness' (1:1,8) was an indication that he, too, knew this injunc-
tion even though now, under the severity of his trial, he is
sorely tempted to deny it. Contrary to what Elihu appears to be
saying, being good — obeying God's commandments —
pleases God immensely and, no matter what benefits we may
or may not receive in this life, we are called upon to please him
'through thick and thin'.

2. Why doesn't God answer prayer?

Elihu has touched on this before (33:13; see argument no. 2 of
the previous chapter). Now he takes up the issue once more,
this time considering the case of those who cry out **'under a
load of oppression; they plead for relief from the arm of the
powerful'** (35:9). But they are not always delivered. Why not?
Elihu's answer is simplistic in the extreme: it is because they
have not truly cried out to God (35:10-12). If they had, they
would have been enabled to 'sing in the dark': **'But no one
says, "Where is God my Maker, who gives songs in the
night"'** (35:10). The argument is complicated, but the implication is clear: Job has not been addressing God in his
afflictions. His words have been empty: **'So Job opens his
mouth with empty talk; without knowledge he multiplies
words'** (35:16). According to Elihu, then, Job has not been
addressing God at all, but merely complaining about his

sufferings! And even if Job has been addressing God, he has done so under the assumption that God is essentially unjust and God will not answer him on that basis. According to Elihu, Job's problem lies in his inability to keep his mouth shut under trial (34:16).

So the answer Elihu gives to tormented Christians, wondering why their prayers are unanswered, is that they haven't really prayed! It is at once soul-destroying and wrong. Elihu's response is inadequate and misleading for several reasons. First, it contradicts the experience of godly men like Job, folk who have prayed with confidence for God's deliverance only to be disappointed. Christians have prayed for healing only to know their loved ones die. They have prayed for the salvation of their children only to see them live and die as rebels. They have poured out their hearts for revival only to end their days without seeing it. Are we to believe with Elihu that they haven't *really* prayed? It was Paul's earnest prayer that the thorn in his flesh be removed. Yet, despite seeking the Lord three times for it, he met with disappointment (2 Cor. 12:8). His prayer was passionate, particular and persistent. Yet God did not grant it. The same lesson is taught us by Christ's own prayer in Gethsemane. Throwing himself to the ground in his anguish, he pleaded with the Father that the cup be taken away from him. But it wasn't. We cannot possibly say that the Lord did not believe sufficiently in what he was asking, that he wasn't really praying! Yet this is where Elihu's theology is leading us.

The New Testament does lead us to expect God to grant us whatever we ask of him in prayer, so long as we ask in faith (Matt. 21:22). But there is a caveat: we are to ask for that which is in accordance with God's will. 'What is it to pray in faith?' asked Thomas Watson. 'It is to pray for that which God has promised,' he replied, adding, 'Where there is no promise, we cannot pray in faith.'

There are reasons why God does not give us what we ask of him. One reason lies in the poverty of our judgement when it comes to knowing what is good (or best) for us. Paul's thorn in the flesh was, to him, an inconvenience. He felt sure that he could serve God better without it. But God knew better. The reason for the thorn in his flesh was to keep him from 'becoming conceited' (2 Cor.12:7). The pain was God's means of keeping him humble and malleable.

Amy Carmichael spent all her life in a condition of eminent Christlikeness. As a missionary to South India, she was a living testimony to the grace of God in the transformation of lives into the image of Christ. Yet she ended her days in great pain. Every prayer raised for her healing was ineffective. God said, 'No'. Why? The only answer lies in affirming that though the reason may be withheld from us, it is known to him who is all-wise.

When John L. Girardeau, the Southern Presbyterian theologian, returned from a visit to the Confederate army to a despondent Charleston, many wondered why God had not heard their fervent prayers that he might grant them victory in their struggles for Southern independence. Girardeau's words to his congregation contained the following explanation:

> To him who thus in disappointment and suffering, baffled in his hopes, and tempted to scepticism, yet honours God by a meek and uncomplaining submission due from a sinful, short-sighted creature, to infinite wisdom and absolute sovereignty, it will in time be made conspicuously to appear — as clearly as the flash of a sunbeam through the fissures of a dissolving cloud — that benefits were withheld for the bestowal of greater, that temporary suffering is but the prelude to everlasting blessing, short-lived disappointment to the dawn of unfading honour, and that truth and right go down beneath a horizon of darkness and an ocean of

storms, only to reappear in the morning glory of an eternal triumph.

Jesus as an infirm, dying human being, staggered under the curse of a world, prayed that he might be delivered from suffering the second death. His prayer was unanswered and He died; but His grave was the scene of death's dethronement and the birthplace of unnumbered millions of deathless souls redeemed from Satan, sin, and hell.

Hold, Christian brother! Do not despair because your prayers for certain blessings ... have for a time been unanswered. Where is your faith? Where is your allegiance to your almighty, all-wise, all-merciful Sovereign? Collect yourself. Put on the panoply of God... Look up. God, your Redeemer and Deliverer, reigns.

See He sits on yonder throne, and suns and systems of light are but the sparkling dust beneath His feet. Thousands of thousands of shining seraphs minister before Him. Infinite empire is in His grasp... His eye is upon His afflicted.

See, see, He comes, He comes, riding upon wings of the whirlwind, wielding His glittering sword bathed in the radiance of heaven, driving His foes like chaff before His face, and hastening to the succour of His saints with resources of boundless power and illimitable grace.[5]

Dramatic these words may be, but no less so than Elihu's. But how much more encouraging and helpful!

Elihu's fourth speech

Elihu appears a little more compassionate in tone in this, his concluding speech (36:1 - 37:24). He returns to the theme he has introduced in the first speech: suffering is a discipline. God watches his children and lets them know when they transgress by sending affliction.

The speech begins with a general introduction in which Elihu wants Job to know that **'There is more to be said on God's behalf'** (36:2). But Elihu overshoots himself. His grandiloquence has got the better of him. He now claims perfection for himself: **'One perfect in knowledge is with you'** (36:4). Job need not be afraid! Is it because Elihu is the youngest, and perhaps the least qualified, that he feels the need to claim perfection in what he has to say?[6] Since he uses almost the same expression in 37:16 to refer to God, it appears on the surface at least that Elihu is claiming to be equal to God.[7] Perhaps that is unfair to Elihu, but his language is now rising into the stratosphere.

Still, commentators agree that Elihu has some good contributions to make at this point. 'The harsh tone which Elihu had adopted in his second and third speeches is here softened. Job 36:1-21 is a more mature and engaging statement of orthodox theology than anything found elsewhere in the book.'[8] Orthodox it may be; whether or not it has any relevance to Job's situation is something we shall have to question as we examine Elihu's concluding remarks.

Pain as a discipline

Elihu has already mentioned that suffering can be God's means of disciplining his children (33:15-30; see argument no. 2 of the previous chapter in this book). In his closing speech, Elihu returns to this theme, indeed Job 36:6-9 is about as classic a statement of it as can be found anywhere in Job. He begins with a statement of God's power: **'God is mighty … he is mighty'** (36:4). Next he mentions God's knowledge of what is going on: **'He does not take his eye off the righteous'**

(36:7).⁹ He then moves on to his main point, which is that there is an educational purpose in suffering:

> **But if men are bound in chains,**
> **held fast by chords of affliction,**
> **he tells them what they have done —**
> **that they have sinned arrogantly**
>
> (36:8-9).

Job, who feels in chains, is guilty of arrogant sin according to this and he is being told so by God through his afflictions. **'He makes them listen to correction, and commands them to repent of their evil'** (36:10). Those who listen to God when pain comes are the better for it. As Calvin comments, 'For affliction is the true schoolmistress to bring men to repentance in order that they may learn to hate their faults in which they previously bathed.'¹⁰ Those who **'do not listen'** (36:12) die young and in shameful circumstances (33:14).

There is an element of what Elihu says here that is true. Pain can soften the heart; but it can also harden (Heb. 3:8). Suffering can cause some to question the very character of God (Ps. 73:11). In 1755 an earthquake in Lisbon killed 60,000 people. Goethe, the eighteenth-century German poet, was only six at the time. Later he wrote, 'The boy was not slightly affected. God the creator and ruler of heaven and earth, whom the declaration of the first article of faith [i.e. the *Belgic Confession*] presents as so wise and gracious, did not, when he thus sacrificed the just with the unjust, prove himself to be in any way fatherly.'¹¹ As the Puritan John Flavel put it, 'A cross without Christ never did good to any man.' The wise man rides the wave; the fool is drowned by it.

Elihu's point (at least a part of it) is to suggest that there is more to suffering than just punishment. He gives suffering a *creative* as well as a *destructive* purpose. The pain of childbirth is quickly forgotten because of the outcome: the birth of a child! The pain of kidney stones, on the other hand, tends to be remembered. The absence of any creative purpose tends to make the pain worse. Job is meant to learn something from his pain. He must not look on it simply as chastisement for past sins (though Elihu has not given up on that idea at all). What kind of things are we to learn from our sufferings?

1. Suffering can reveal our true character

Job was not afflicted because he had sinned, but the affliction has, nevertheless, brought out the latent sinfulness of his heart. Pain has revealed his true character: it has in one sense proved his integrity, for he has refused to yield to Satan's suggestion that the only reason he serves God is for the personal gain he gets from it. On the other hand, his protestations have revealed a sinful heart. Suffering can reveal the stuff of which we are made. This knowledge is essential if we are to make any progress in our Christian lives. 'The cross brings a crisis in Job's history, whose final result is, to purge him from the dross of self-righteousness and pride. And this was that root of sin which still kept its seat in his inmost being. Every man has such a root of sin within him, and none dare say of Satan, what the only begotten Son of God said of him, "He hath nothing in me." Even the most intimate disciples of the Lord, even the holy Apostles, were compelled to submit to Satan's request, that he might have them, to sift them like wheat, and to be satisfied if only their faith did not fail them.'[12]

Though it was not true of Job, the psalmist confesses that pain brought him to realize the bankruptcy of his own spiritual condition, a condition of which he was unaware, and would have remained so had not pain brought him up short: 'Before I was afflicted I went astray, but now I obey your word' (Ps. 119:67). When such experiences reveal our need, we should say with George Matheson:

O joy that seekest me through pain
I dare not ask to fly from thee.

2. Suffering can teach us about the character of God

Martin Luther once confessed: 'I never knew the meaning of
God's word until I came into affliction. I have always found it
one of my best schoolmasters.' One gets the firm impression
that after the trial was over, Job would have echoed the words
of the psalmist: 'It was good for me to be afflicted so that I
might learn your decrees' (Ps. 119:71). One of the truths Job
learned in his trial was that of God's incomprehensibility.
When Job failed to understand what God was doing, and when
answers to his questions were not forthcoming, Job ultimately
yielded and refused to curse God. 'It is a right hard thing for
us to submit ourselves to the single will of God, without asking
a reason... It is a perfect and more than Angelical wisdom to
have the skill to yield so much honour unto God, as to rest
merely and simply upon his pleasure, that although we find the
matter strange, and ... utterly contrary to all right and reason:
yet we bow down our heads, and say, "Lord, although thy
judgements be as a deep gulf: yet will not we presume to
encounter them."' [13]

3. Suffering can teach us about the nature of faith

Job found himself questioning why things turned out the way
they did. In doing so his faith was tested. But it is one of the
lessons that 'The general character of faith is not to be based
upon the current appearances of things. Faith is not sight.' [14]
Suffering, when responded to in the right way, can underline
the fact that faith involves trusting God 'in the dark'. This is
where some of the contributions of Elihu are not helpful.
'[God] requires us many times to walk in the dark, trusting him
absolutely, and that for long spells at a time... Now, if God

withholds explanations, it ill behoves men to give them. In such distress, tears of fellowship with suffering are far more profitable than lectures in harsh theology.'[15] Job's pain was teaching him the meaning of trusting in God.

Disciplinary suffering is God's means of training us to keep going. Making the right use of affliction can be to our eternal benefit and we should thank God for it. What Elihu says in this respect is true.

Suffering as punishment

But there is an element of Elihu's teaching which is not right. Once again he lapses into instant retribution theology — a phrase we have used before to describe the counsellors' belief that rewards and punishments are meted out instantly. Elihu believes that those who listen to what God is saying to them through their pain can expect deliverance — here and now! And those who do not can expect an early death (36:14).[16] If Job would only confess and repent, he will be brought to **'a spacious place free from restriction, to the comfort of [his] table laden with choice food'** (36:16). But Elihu does not seem, after all, to believe that Job is among the righteous who can expect this deliverance. According to Elihu, Job is **'laden with the judgement due to the wicked'** (36:17); he prefers **'evil'** to **'affliction'** (36:21). He may or may not have been guilty of some major sin in his past (as the three counsellors had implied), but in his present rebellion and defiance, especially in his calling into question God's justice, Elihu detects the cause of his suffering: God is disciplining him. In this much, at least, Elihu is right. 'The search for an explanation by tracking Job's sufferings to their origin and cause has failed. More light will be gained in the search for their outcome and goal.'[17]

A hymn on the goodness of God (36:26 - 37:24)

Elihu concludes his speech by asking Job to consider God's goodness, incomprehensibility and praiseworthiness:

> **God is exalted in his power.**
> **Who is a teacher like him?**
> **Who has prescribed his ways for him,**
> **or said to him, 'You have done wrong'?**
> **Remember to extol his work,**
> **which men have praised in song**
>
> (36:22-24).

At this point, Elihu breaks into a hymn of praise to the God of creation. Included in this hymn are references to the cycle of evaporation and precipitation which produce rain (36:26-28), to thunderstorms (36:29-37:4) and to the winter frost, ice and snow (37:5-13). The elements unleash their great power in ways we can understand better than Job and his contemporaries did, but still they do so **'at his direction'** (37:12).

It is important to note that each section of this hymn is introduced with a reference to God's incomprehensibility: God is **'beyond our understanding'** (36:26); **'Who can understand how he spreads out the clouds...?'** (36:29); **'God's voice thunders in marvellous ways; he does great things beyond our understanding'** (37:5).

The point which Elihu now wants to make is that if man cannot understand fully what God is doing in the natural world, neither can he understand fully what God is doing in our individual lives. Elihu is on good ground here. What he says in these verses prepares us for what is to come in the concluding chapters when God will speak to Job's situation. Contained within the final 'solution' to Job's questions will be this very point: that it is pointless to ask too many questions, for answers will not be given, cannot be given (for we are in no position to take in all the reasons for them). 'Ours not the reason why, ours but to do and die,' is the final word. Elihu has prepared the ground for it.

Elihu asks a series of humbling questions (37:15-21) designed to underline in Job a sense of how small he is in comparison to God, who **'comes in awesome majesty'** (37:22). Certainly, part of Elihu's point is to underline the foolishness of disputing with God (37:19,20,24). 'The way of wisdom is to fear him who is incomprehensible and excellent in all his attributes (23,24).'[18] But Elihu is also suggesting that it is pointless for Job to seek an audience with God (something Job had insisted on, 31:35). But that is going too far, for God does make a personal appearance to Job in his distress in the very next chapter. At the end of the day, good as Elihu is, his contribution remains inadequate, for the very same reason that he has been instilling into Job: his own knowledge of God and his ways is inadequate. He knows nothing of Satan's charge. Neither has he accepted fully God's own approbation of Job's godliness. Human counsellors have failed to answer Job's questions. It is time to turn to the Lord himself, and hear what he has to say. For it is in these speeches that Job's distress is relieved.

A summary of Elihu's second, third and fourth speeches

'You have said that God has denied you justice even though you are in the right. God has been unfair, you say. And you have come to the conclusion that it's pointless serving God. "It profits a man nothing to serve God," you say.

'Let me say two things to you. First, God is never unjust, never! He is just and righteous. He cannot sin. Could God rule the world as he does and be unfair? Of course not! He always acts in a perfectly just way. If God didn't step in and rule in this way the whole world would disintegrate.

'But second, God chastises. He disciplines us when we go wrong. I have to tell you that I think this is what is happening to you and I hope you learn to take what God gives and that you stop being so arrogant in condemning God in this way. You have accused God of doing wrong and that is a terrible thing and I hope you will repent of it — I urge you to do so.

'You have said that there's no point in being good; that you may as well be evil for all the difference it makes. This is what I say: doing good or doing evil will have no effect upon God. I mean, it will not add to his majesty if you do some good, nor will you take away something from his perfection if you do evil. You are responsible for what you do. If you have prayed and God has not answered, it is because you have been proud, thinking that he is bound to answer you because of your goodness. But it doesn't work like that. That is proud talk and God will not stand for it.

'But I have something more to say: God is powerful, but he will not despise those who are weak. He doesn't have favourites. When God disciplines people he does it in order to help them turn away from their sin. If they do repent, he gives them prosperity. If they don't they will soon perish. Godless people, though, often die in their youth.

'You have to be careful, Job. Recognize that God has something to teach you in your trials. He wants to make you a better person, so don't respond in some silly, selfish way. Try to exalt God's name. Look around you and note how great he is. Think of the weather — storms, lightning, thunder and all that — that's God speaking. He controls everything. Can you control these things? No, of course not. That's why I say that we should fear him. If you want him to look kindly on you, then stop telling us and him that you know everything.'

25.
The Lord speaks

Please read Job 38:1 - 40:5

The Lord breaks the silence. At last what Job has asked for has come about.

Job asked for an encounter with God so that he might put to him his case (31:35). He wanted God to present a 'bill of indictment, with specific charges which he is prepared to answer, or else a verdict from his Judge which he confidently expects to be a declaration of innocence'.[1] The Lord's two replies at first appear not to be a reply to Job's questions or the answers which his friends thought they had supplied. The speeches seem to have little to do with the central issue: why Job suffered so severely when he had done everything humanly possible to maintain a good relationship with God. 'The Lord apparently says nothing about this. Indeed, He makes very few positive statements or affirmations. His speeches are not oracles; He answers Job's questions with a deluge of counter-questions.'[2]

An important point of interpretation needs to be highlighted at this point, crucial if we are to make any sense of the following chapters. Up to this point we have engaged in some fairly critical analysis of the speeches of Job's three friends, together with Elihu's contribution. Sometimes we have noted that whilst the content of their speeches has been orthodox enough, it has been misapplied in Job's case. On other occasions, we have had to point out that the very content of what they were saying was wrong (as in their constant insistence that Job was suffering because of his sin). In the following chapters, which give us God's direct words to Job, we shall not be able to take this position. We shall have to learn from both the form and the content of these two speeches.

In fact, as we shall shortly see, the entire interpretation of the book of Job must be based on the opening two chapters together with these closing five chapters. Bearing this in mind will keep us on the right track.

Does Job fear God for nothing?

The book has come full circle: we are back in the heavenly court. Satan had taunted: 'Does Job fear God for nothing?' (1:9). For a reason that remains a mystery, Satan has been given leave to test Job's faith. Throughout the book, though he never appears in the conversation, and Job himself seems unaware of his presence, Satan has been there fulfilling his rôle as the accuser of God's people (Rev. 12:10). Behind the world that is seen lies an unseen world of spirits, dark and evil powers with strong malignant personalities, planning the destruction of the souls of men and women. If Satan is known as the accuser, he is also known as Apollyon, the destroyer (Rev. 9:11). He works in our lives to destroy and disintegrate. Job has felt Satan's ability to 'tear apart' in his own life. Job, like Christian in Bunyan's *Pilgrim's Progress*, has passed through the Valley of the Shadow, and experienced such spiritual turmoil, oppression and confusion that his mind seemed almost about to be destroyed. Job has, of course, been unaware of Satan's presence and has instead turned his anger upon God. Now, at last, God speaks. But it is not what Job was expecting to hear. Right up to the very end, Job has things to learn about God. And the experience of pain has enforced it.

It is time to listen to what God has to say. He speaks twice to Job (38:1-40:2; 40:6-41:34) and to each, Job gives a brief response (40:3-5; 42:1-6).

The Lord speaks (38:1-3)

A storm is brewing from which God speaks (38:1). This is a favourite way by which God makes himself known in the Old Testament (Ps. 18:7-15; Ezek. 1:4,28; Hab. 3; Zech 9:14). Elihu has already anticipated it (37:1-5,22). More importantly, it is in response to Job's cry, 'Let the Almighty answer me' (31:35). And what strikes us immediately is not so much what God says, but what he does not say. There is no attempt to answer Job's questions with regard to his suffering, and no hint that Job has been caught up in a cosmic struggle with Satan. Instead we are taken on a tour of the created order: the heavens and then the earth. And in what at first seems a gross trivialization of the problem, Job is asked to consider the hippopotamus!

Here is a man who has lost his money, his children, his health, whose marriage is now in serious trouble and his social standing at rock-bottom, and he is told to think about the hippo! Is God serious? Would any of us dare to treat one so needy and in pain with such detachment? But a more careful study reveals a gracious mind at work.

For the first time since the opening prologue, the text of Job includes God's covenant name, Jehovah, or more accurately 'Yahweh' (38:1, 'LORD'). Whatever else may be true, God wants us who read this book to be aware that he has not abandoned Job, nor will he, nor *can* he. And why not? Because he is bound by a covenant which he has made. This was God's name disclosed to Moses in a moment of crisis to reassure him of protection and sustaining power. In a bush that burned without being consumed, God disclosed an aspect of himself to Moses in, we might say, a three-dimensional way. Having already identified himself as the God who had revealed himself to the patriarchs, he further elaborated on it by adding that he was to be known as 'I AM WHO I AM' (or, 'I will be what I will be'), later shortened to 'I AM,' and finally changed to 'the LORD (Yahweh in Hebrew, sounding much the same as the Hebrew for 'I AM'), the God of your fathers' (Exod. 3:6,13-16). Later still, Moses, who had asked to see God's 'glory', heard God's 'name' proclaimed in this way: 'The LORD, the LORD, the compassionate and gracious God, slow to anger, abounding in love and faithfulness' (Exod. 34:6). We are meant to get the idea that God cannot abandon Job, even though he has exposed him to the fires of trial.

So, what is God doing by asking Job to consider the hippopotamus? The answer lies in the imagery found in verse 3 (and repeated again in 40:7): **'Brace yourself like a man.'** This is an image drawn from the world of wrestling.[3] Job is being asked to enter into combat with the Lord! It is what he has been asking for all along. His mind has been seething with anger at what he considers to be his unfair treatment. He is dismissive of God's right to treat him in this way. He wants explanations. If only he could get hold of God, he would... 'If only...!' Job's wish has come to pass: we must be careful what we ask for, because sometimes we get it.

God does not attempt an explanation of Job's suffering, nor does he try to justify himself. Instead he challenges Job. It is reminiscent of Jacob at Peniel (Gen. 32:22-32). No accounting is given of Job's treatment; neither is Job given any opportunity in court to defend himself against the supposed charges made against him. Instead God challenges Job to a dual: a battle of wisdom, for there has been too much talk, too many **'words without knowledge'** (38:2). It is a test of knowledge (Job 38:3; 40:7). The test comes in the form of a series of questions, covering the earth (Job 38:4-21), the heavens (Job 38:22-28) and the animal kingdom (Job 38:39 - 39:30). As a result, Job is speechless! (Job 40:1-5). It is a test in which Job is to learn his lack of wisdom: his own human limitations, his creatureliness. In a daring display of condescension, God agrees to accept 'a handicap'. Instead of continuing to engage Job in combat himself, he commissions one of his creatures to serve as his champion — **'Behemoth'** (Job 40:15). Job has met his match. When asked to explain the meaning of the hippopotamus, Job can find no explanation. 'Innocent suffering is a hippopotamus. The only sense it makes, it makes to God, for it is not amenable to human rationality.'[4]

The mystery of God

What is to the fore in this contest is that ultimately God and his ways are incomprehensible to us. Mystery is the vital element of all our theologizing. Ultimately, God dwells in unapproachable light (1 Tim. 6:16). God is great, Scripture says (Deut. 7:21; Neh. 4:14; Ps. 48:1; 86:10; 95:3; 145:3; Dan. 9:4), by which it means that he is greater than we can ever fathom. We lack the capacity to fully understand God. Though we insist that what we do know of God, we know truly, it remains true that what we know of him, we know only a little. Calvin spoke of God having 'accommodated' himself to our capacity in his self-revelation. 'The faithful must content themselves with that which is revealed unto them: and it is far greater and better wisdom, than to be inquisitive of all things without exception ... it is not that [God] is niggardly to show us his will any further, but because he knows what is convenient for us.'[5] 'Let us always bear in mind that even in the basest things, there is an incomprehensible wisdom of God.'[6] 'And when man has debated the matter thoroughly to and fro, he must needs come to the said conclusion, namely that we comprehend not the greatness and height of God's doings, further than it please him to give us some taste of them, at least wise according to our capacity: which is oversmall.'[7]

So much is this issue to the foreground in Calvin's thinking that he begins one sermon with the words: 'We have to go forward with the matter that we began yesterday: which is, that the Scripture shows us many things which our understanding cannot brook.'[8] It is interesting to note that in discussing 'The Knowledge of God the Creator' in the *Institutes*, Calvin speaks of God's essence as 'incomprehensible ... his divineness far escapes all human perception'.[9] Similarly in Calvin's catechism of 1542 he wrote, 'Our understanding is not capable of comprehending his essence.'[10] For Calvin, the best help to offer those in trouble is that they should patiently yield themselves to the purposes of a sovereign God. This is Job's patience! It is his willingness, in the end, to submit to God's ways, *despite his lack of understanding.*

The story is told of the British general Bernard (Monty) Montgomery, a man notorious for a large ego. In a speech he related a conversation between God and Moses. Montgomery said, 'As God pointed out to Moses — and I think rightly so...' Such arrogance is something God wishes to deflate and it is a part of what this book is about. Job's efforts to understand the ways of God in the world had come to nothing. Like Asaph in Psalm 73, Job has discovered that the very attempt to comprehend them has given him a headache. Asaph describes his own behaviour as being like that of a brute beast (Ps. 73:22). Job, too, has been questioning God — yes, questioning God! The Lord then sets before Job a magnificent vision of the wonders of his creation. It is a theatre in which he shows the ingenuousness of his wisdom. It is something which eventually humbles Job's pride:

Then Job replied to the Lord:
'I know that you can do all things;
    no plan of yours can be thwarted.
[You asked,] "Who is this that obscures my counsel
    without knowledge?"

Surely I spoke of things I did not understand,
**   things too wonderful for me to know.**
[You said,] "Listen now, and I will speak;
**   I will question you,**
**   and you shall answer me."**
My ears had heard of you
**   but now my eyes have seen you.**
Therefore I despise myself
**   and repent in dust and ashes'**

(Job 42:1-6).

Job had forgotten who he was. As a child of God he was to learn that God was more concerned with his Christlikeness than his material prosperity or health.

'Where were you...?' (38:4-38)

Watching our children grow can be exciting. My mother's kitchen door is etched with years of pencil markings recording the spurts of growth made by her seven grandchildren. It is often fiercely guarded and needs strict supervision lest one errant youngster bends the rules to record a height in excess of the truth. Growing up is a natural process in which we take great pleasure. But there is a rule in the kingdom of God which runs counter to natural law: in order to grow up spiritually, we shall need to grow downwards, to grow *up* into Christ we shall need to grow *down* into lowliness, or humility. As Packer puts it: 'Christians ... grow greater, by getting smaller.'[11]

Job's demeanour, it has to be said, has exhibited a certain amount of pride in the later chapters of the book, and pride blows us up like balloons. Grace, on the other hand, punctures our arrogance, letting out the hot air of pride from our system. The result is that we shrink, becoming in our estimation less important. Think of these closing chapters recording God's encounter with Job as a shrinking process. Job must see that he is small, even insignificant. It is not a theology of building up one's self-esteem that God engages in here, whatever the value of that may be in another context; Job is made to crawl!

Joni Earecksen Tada records a fishing trip she made with her husband in scenery 'that was enough to suck the breath out of your lungs'. Commenting on the effect of this experience, she added: 'It made me feel so small, drifting around in that little rowboat, surrounded by soaring mountain peaks, wide blue water, and blustery winds. Like being in some vast cathedral. I felt like whispering.'[12]

'**Where were you,**' God asks Job, '**when I laid the earth's foundation?**' (38:4). And in a searing line of irony, God adds: '**Surely you know, for you were already born! You have lived so many years!**' (38:21). Job, of course, was not around when God made the world. He knew nothing of how the earth was made (38:4-7), or how the sea was formed (38:8-11), or how the planetary rotations constitute day and night (38:12-15,19-21). Job had neither measured the sea's depth nor the breadth of the land (38:16-18).

The point is that Job cannot expect to understand everything that God is doing with this world. Job, like the rest of creation, has a finite and limited understanding. Hence the question: '**Who endowed the heart with wisdom or gave understanding to the mind?**' (Job 38:36). Today, great advances have been made in understanding some of these questions: the earth's rotation (38:12-15), oceanic currents (38:16), cartography (38:18), the origin and dispersal of light (38:19,24) and meteorology (38:28-30,35). These questions anticipate the great scientific advances made by such men as Newton, Maury, Faraday and Morse as they endeavoured to carry out God's creation (dominion) mandate: to think God's thoughts after him by scientific enquiry and discovery (cf.

Gen. 1:28). Some issues remain relatively unexplored, including astronomical research into the **'Bear'**, **'Pleiades'**, and **'Orion'** (38:31-32; cf. 9:9), and more significantly, the study of the nature and meaning of death (38:17).

Job must have said to himself, as he listened to God speaking to him, 'All these things are bigger than I am; I will never comprehend all these things. I am so small. I cannot begin to fathom the mind that made all these and set them on their course.'

And yet, despite our smallness and insignificance, God himself became just like us when in Jesus Christ he became incarnate and dwelt among us. As Paul wrote:

> Christ Jesus:
> who, being in very nature God,
>> did not consider equality with God something to be grasped,
> but made himself nothing,
>> taking the very nature of a servant,
>> being made in human likeness.
> And being found in appearance as a man,
>> he humbled himself
>> and became obedient to death — even death on a cross!
>
>   (Phil 2:5-9).

Jesus Christ became small and insignificant in the eyes of the world. He dwelt in a finite frame in order to raise sinners like us to heaven. When we read of the Creator of the universe taking time to talk to little children, we discover that there really is nothing too small in his eyes (Matt. 19:13-14).

What is this chapter all about? God is systematically reducing Job to size, deflating all the excess pride inside him by removing from Job's mind every thought that makes God out to be small. It is an outworking of something Elihu has said: 'God comes in awesome majesty' (37:22). Job has been shown a little of that majesty in a tremendous display of God's wisdom and power in nature. Since Job is unable to match it, indeed he is ridiculously puny in comparison, he is not in a position to question what God is doing.

'Talk to the animals' (38:39 - 39:30)

The original intention of God in the creation appears to have had in mind a harmony between man and the animals. Most of the animal kingdom fear and dread man, and some have been pursued to the point of extinction. The point being made is that God, and not man, provides for the animal kingdom, one which includes carnivorous animals (e.g., **'lions'**, 38:39-40), herbivorous animals (e.g., **'the horse'**, 39:19-25), birds of prey (e.g., **'the raven'**, 38:41) and scavenger birds (e.g., **'the eagle'**, 39:27-30).

Other animals mentioned in this section include some which are now extinct (e.g., **'the wild ox'**, 39:9-12). The Hebrew word (translated 'unicorn' in the AV) is thought to refer to the huge and ferocious aurochs (or bison) which inhabited the Middle East but is now extinct. The bull was said to be huge, over six feet wide at the shoulders, with long horns pointing forward. The psalmist asked in ᵔsalm 22 that he might be delivered from these horns (v. 2ᵢ). The Egyptian Pharaoh Thutmose III boasted of killing seventy-five aurochs in a single hunt. Other creatures of note are: **'the mountain goats'** (or Nubian ibex, 39:1), the **'doe'** (or fallow deer, 39:1-4), **'the wild donkey'** (or onager, 39:5-8), **'the ostrich'** (39:13), **'the hawk'** (possibly a falcon or kestrel, 39:26) and even **'the locust'** (39:20).

Job had noted earlier that the natural world in its entirety is a product of God's creation. He had even expressed a desire to learn to appreciate more of God as the Creator (12:7-10). It is not without importance that when Jesus Christ came into the world he was surrounded by the animals he had created. Later he would say, 'Are not five sparrows sold for two pennies? Yet not one of them is forgotten by God' (Luke 12:6).

The mistake made by Job's three friends was that they reduced God to workable definitions. But Job has slowly realized that God is greater than we imagine. Already he has given expression to God's transcendent power over mountains, the earth and the sun (9:5-7). He is also sovereign over the monsters of chaos (26:13). Job may have no answers to the problem of his suffering, but that is just the point: he is being moulded into shape so that, come what may, trust will be uppermost in his heart. There is a similarity here in Job with the book of Ecclesiastes. Everything, says the disillusioned Preacher, has a time and a way set for it by God (Eccles. 3:1-8,17; 8:6). 'The book,' comments Stafford Wright, 'is a record of a search for the key of life. It is an endeavour to give a meaning to life, to see it as a whole. And there is no key under the sun. Life has lost the key to itself. "Vanity of vanities, all is vanity." If you want the key you must go to the locksmith who made the lock. God holds the key to all unknown. *And He will not give it to you.* Since then you cannot get the key, you must trust the locksmith to open the doors.'[13] Life is unknowable without the Creator. Job's trials make no sense to Job or anyone else. He can only look to God, the Creator and Sustainer of all that is, and trust him. He has the key to the riddle and we must trust him to open the door for us.

God made the world according to a perfect blueprint. And despite the coming of sin, and its consequences for the world, God continues to rule over the entire world — animate and inanimate. There is not a single part of the entire universe where God's rule does not extend. And he governs it wisely. Things may appear to be out of control at times, but they are not. He sets limits beyond which sin, and the kingdom of evil, cannot transgress. Just as he restricts the activity of the sea —

'**Who shut up the sea behind doors?**' (38:8) — so he restricts the progress of evil. It may appear as though injustice rules, but this is false. God rules, even though he may wait a while before he executes his justice upon transgressors.

I am reminded of a colleague in the ministry, an older and much wiser man, not given to suffering foolishness gladly. At a prayer meeting one night the subject for prayer was the forthcoming Sunday School outing. Unfortunately, the weather forecast for the next day was full of bad news: rain and gale-force winds. Several had interceded that God might overrule, but with little by way of zeal, given their trust in the reliability of the well-known weather forecaster. The minister finally rose to his feet and began an earnest intercession: 'Lord grant us favourable weather...', and added, 'Who do these weather forecasters think they are anyway?' The story is amusing, but contains an important point. Whether or not God gives us insight into his intentions as far as the weather is concerned through the science of meteorology (and no doubt he does), ultimately the weather is from the Lord. As I write these lines, a gale-force wind is blowing and it is snowing. The very birds have gathered on the windowsill for shelter — a sight which I have not seen before. And I am reminded of what Job was being taught:

> **Can you raise your voice to the clouds**
> **and cover yourself with a flood of water?**
> **Do you send the lightning bolts on their way?**
> **Do they report to you, 'Here we are'?**
> **Who endowed the heart with wisdom**
> **or gave understanding to the mind?**
> **Who has the wisdom to count the clouds?**
> **Who can tip over the water jars of the heavens**
> **when the dust becomes hard**
> **and the clods of earth stick together?**
>
> (38:34-38).

If I had my way, I would have the warmth of a Spanish summer shifted northwards to cover the British Isles! But that would seriously upset some other part of the world, and I must trust that in his wisdom God has made it this way — that in Belfast it seems as though we get more rain than most others in the world! There must be some purpose in it. And I must simply trust him, or emigrate!

God is equally in control of wild animals and birds. And the point is again a simple one: that if God knows about the needs of these creatures who occupy the lonely, inaccessible parts of the world, how much more does he care for human beings whom he has made in his own image — particularly those, like Job, who are in covenant with him. Job's trials have not in any way called into question God's sovereign rule. Whatever the explanation is for Job's suffering, it is not that God has lost control.

Nor is this a theme peculiar to the book of Job. The Son of God upholds all things by the word of his power (Heb. 1:3). Nor is the slightest thing that occurs outside of his will (Matt. 10:29). This theme is the subject of the worship of God's saints throughout the Scriptures:

> You alone are the Lord. You made the heavens, even the highest heavens, and all their starry host, the earth and all that is on it, the seas and all that is in them. You give life to everything, and the multitudes of heaven worship you (Neh. 9:6).

> You open your hand
>   and satisfy the desires of every living thing
>   (Ps. 145:16).

> He determines the number of the stars
>   and calls them each by name
>   (Ps. 147:4).

Lift your eyes and look to the heavens:
   Who created all these?
He who brings out the starry host one by one,
   and calls them each by name.
Because of his great power and mighty strength,
   not one of them is missing

                        (Isa. 40:26).

'Will you now submit?' (40:1-2)

Continuing the imagery which we have already noticed, of a challenge to engage in a wrestling match, this section concludes with a request that Job yield to the Lord's greater strength and wisdom. It is, basically, an appeal for Job's submission.[14]

God has questioned Job about the earth (38:4-21), heaven (38:22-38) and the animal kingdom (38:39-39:30), spanning the entire course of time from creation to the shouts of captains in the very latest military conquests (39:25). Job has not been able to stop the barrage of questions. Each one has increasingly revealed his impotence. He has not been able to gain a decision in his favour. When, at last, he is given an opportunity to respond, all he can do is to lay his hand upon his mouth (40:4).

'I am unworthy' (40:4), Job replied. The word Job uses is the exact opposite of the one he had used earlier when he spoke of his 'glory' (29:20; cf. 19:9). He had suggested that he would approach God as a 'prince' (31:37). Once God has spoken, Job's ego has burst. He is reduced to saying that he is without intrinsic honour and worth.[15] In placing his hand over his mouth — a gesture of awed silence — Job is expressing the truth of God's accusations against him and acknowledging that he is suitably shamed by them. Job is guilty of having spoken out of turn, something for which he is profoundly sorry. He is guilty and makes an attempt, now, to justify himself.

There comes a time in God's dealings with us when it is as well to acknowledge that what he is says about us is right. We need to learn to take the trouble he sends our way in order that we might learn to be subject to him in all things. Job's response here is one worth noting for several reasons.

1. We neeed to grow smaller in our own eyes

As we have already noted, shrinking in self-importance before God's greatness is an essential part of growing *up* in the Christian life. Growing *downwards* into humility (from the Latin word *humilis*, meaning 'low') is the point to which God wants to bring each one of us. Bursting the bubble of self-importance is what we need. Job is reflecting here what John the Baptist would say of his Lord: 'He must become greater; I must become less' (John 3:30). We are to settle for being insignificant and dispensable. Job, whose trust in God's ways had been wavering, is now expressing his complete obedience, dependence, patience and willingness to comply with whatever God sends his way in their ongoing relationship with each other. His dreams have been shattered. It is impossible for us to entertain the notion that we are great Christians whilst at the same time insisting that Jesus Christ is a great Saviour.

2. We need to repent

Job's downward growth involved an expression of repentance. When challenged that he made too much of repentance, the Puritan Philip Henry (father of the more famous Matthew Henry) expressed the desire to carry his repentance with him to the very gates of heaven. What is repentance? Job's response traces two of its essential features.

The first was a recognition that he had failed God, that he had said things which were wrong. Job had been deceiving himself—for all sin is at base deceitful (cf. 1 John 1:8). He had been guilty of what modern counsellors call 'denial'. And Job has been convicted of his error—his sin! Job has been silenced (cf. Rom. 3:19).

Secondly, Job is filled with remorse. God's honour has been impugned by some of his remarks and Job is filled with regret. Discouragement has caused Job to argue his good case badly. He has gone too far. And now he is sorry.

3. We must stand in awe of God

Job also teaches us here that the right response to a sight of God's majesty is one of awe. God, who has revealed himself to Job from the midst of a whirlwind, is not to be trifled with. Majestic power ought to cultivate a sense of impotence and awe in us. This phenomenon in Job is replicated in the experiences of many others in the Bible, including Isaiah (Isa. 6:5), Habakkuk (Hab. 3:16), Peter (Luke 5:8) and John (Rev. 1:17).

Round one is God's by a submission on Job's part.

26.
The storm subsides

Please read Job 40-42

The wrestling match continues: **'Brace yourself like a man...'** (40:7; see comments on 38:3 in the previous chapter). Job has already yielded to a 'fall' as a result of the first round in the contest:

> **I am unworthy — how can I reply to you?**
> **I put my hand over my mouth.**
> **I spoke once, but I have no answer—**
> **twice, but I will say no more**
>
> (40:4).

Technically, then, according to the rules of wrestling, the match is over. God has won! But Job is given a second chance and is asked, in effect, to take hold of the belt once again. 'His initial submission was good but only the beginning of his repentance. He must recognize not only the unreasonableness but also the sinfulness of criticizing the Almighty.'[1]

In protesting his innocence, Job had gone too far. He had lashed out against God and called into question his justice. In justifying himself, Job had, in effect, condemned God (40:8). But can Job do any better? After all, judges who pass sentences are obliged to see that the penalty is carried out. Is Job powerful enough to change things in his favour? (40:9). Is he godlike enough to execute the punishment that he thinks his enemies deserve? (40:10-13).

What is God getting at? Simply this: that Job is in no position to pass judgement on God's government of the world. If the world has treated him badly, it is for a reason that is beyond Job's ability to do anything about. And in an amazing display of condescension, God offers to bow down in deference to Job's godlike powers if he can demonstrate his ability to do something about the wickedness in the world: **'I myself will admit to you that your own right hand can save you'** (40:14). Job has been usurping God's rôle as governor of the world. He has been 'lusting after god-like knowledge of good and evil (cf. Gen. 3:5)'.[2]

Whenever we complain at what is happening to us in our lives we are doing the same as Job: suggesting that we could run things better than Almighty God. It is worth a moment's reflection: how would *we* deal with those who treat us badly, if we only had the power? The history of the world is a catalogue of man's inhumanity and brutality when given positions of authority and power. God has the power so to manipulate events that even the evil things turn out for our good. Paul insists, 'And we know that in all things God works for the good of those who love him' (Rom. 8:28). Job can never hope to attain to this level. Job is not only impotent, he is also ignorant! Behind these events lie the schemes of Satan — a malevolence of which Job seems totally unaware. God is actually ordering all of what Satan is doing in order to bring good into Job's life.

Behemoth and leviathan (40:15 - 41:34)

Since Job cannot ascend to heaven and try his hand at judging the wicked, God proposes an easier test for him to demonstrate his greatness. God is prepared, or so it seems, to accept a handicap: instead of engaging Job himself, he will allow two of his created beings to do it instead. Maybe it will prove a 'fairer' match — particularly since the creatures in mind are of a lower order than man! **'Look at the behemoth which I made along with you'** (40:15); **'Can you pull in the leviathan with a fishhook?'** (41:1). Behemoth and leviathan — are Job's strength and wisdom equal to these creatures?

This may seem to be the answer to Job's prayer. Had he not prayed for a trial in which his case might be justly heard? Had he not asked for a fair contest? (9:34-35; 13:21). What could be fairer than a contest with one of the animals of God's creation? Surely it was going to be easier to do battle with the king of beasts than the King of kings! But who (or what) *are* 'behemoth' and 'leviathan'?

'Behemoth' seems to mean 'beast *par excellence*' and the generally accepted identification is that of a hippopotamus or an elephant. 'Leviathan', on the other hand, refers to a creature of the water, and has usually been thought to refer to the crocodile. But these identifications are not without their difficulties. To begin with, it is difficult to see how the **'tail'** of a hippopotamus **'sways like a cedar'** (40:17), since its tail is fairly insignificant! Some have identified 'behemoth' with the crocodile and 'leviathan' with the whale. One possible explanation is that both names refer to the one creature (crocodile), and that 'behemoth' ('chief *par excellence*') is just a more vivid way of describing it.[3] Some have been unwilling to accept an identification with either the hippopotamus, elephant or crocodile and have suggested instead that the characteristics listed in these chapters do not fit any known animals. The creatures could be extinct.[4] On the other hand, it is possible that a purely figurative or symbolic portrait is being given in these verses, along the same lines as that of the book of Revelation when it refers to Satan as a 'dragon' (Rev. 12:7; 13:2; 20:2).[5] But this last interpretation seems unlikely since 'behemoth' is said to have been created in the same way as Job: 'Look at behemoth, *which I made along with you...*' (40:15). And this is crucial, for Job is shown how unable he is to do battle with a *fellow creature*! Mythological interpretations seem, then, to detract from the point being made.

Though it may appear an unsatisfactory conclusion, an exact identification seems irrelevant; it is to miss the point. Job is asked to engage in a battle with a powerful creature, or possibly with two. It is an unequal contest, for Job is wiser than either 'behemoth' or 'leviathan'. It ought to be easy, a walkover. But as we shall see, Job is going to lose this contest, too. What possible hope does he have in a contest with the Creator? Job is no match for the transcendent God of creation:

Who then is able to stand against me?
Who has a claim against me that I must pay?
Everything under heaven belongs to me
(41:10-11).

'If we tremble at the sight of a beast, should we play the bold fellows against God, to contend with him against God, to contend with him when he chastises us...?'[6]

Job is discovering that God is just after all. Though he has not been supplied with all the answers to his questions — in that sense the book of Job has proved a disappointment — the essential question has been: 'Is God just in what he does?' It is to this that God now directs Job's attention in the closing verses of the book: **'Would you discredit my justice? Would you condemn me to justify yourself?'** (Job 40:8). God has no need to spell out the justice of his ways to Job, or to anyone else. It is enough that he *is* God. God *is* God and there is no other! He is the sovereign Lord of all creation and the lesson Job is being asked to learn is that submission is the better way of discipleship. He is the God who exists: infinite, eternal and unchangeable in his being, and wise, powerful, holy, just, good and true. The Christian life is covenantal in nature and at the heart of it is the demand for consecration on our part.

Consider the crocodile!

Assuming 'leviathan' refers to a crocodile, Job is given a detailed summary of its essential characteristics, as Mckenna puts it, in the style of a book entitled 'Everything you always wanted to know about crocodiles but were afraid to ask'![7] It is uncatchable (41:1-2), unfeeling (41:3), untrustworthy (41:3-4), unmanageable (41:5), undesirable (41:6) and totally un-ethical (41:8-9). Further biological details are given (41:12-24), ending with yet another description of how untameable a crocodile is (41:26-32).

What is the point of all this? Why has God introduced Job to a hippopotamus and/or a crocodile? As we saw in the previous chapter, the principal lesson here is that ultimately God and his ways are incomprehensible to us. There are so many issues in this life which call from us the response of modesty. As Calvin said, 'The Scripture shows us many things which our understanding cannot brook.'[8]

Beasts of the imagination

But there may well be a second lesson in these pages, one that lies behind the choice of 'leviathan' in particular. The name 'Leviathan' was associated with a seven-headed sea dragon in ancient mythology. We need not assume that in choosing this name, we are meant to infer that such a creature was thought to exist. It is perfectly possible that Job understood the word to mean a crocodile, but lurking in the back of his mind were fears associated with mythological descriptions of a superbeast of the sea. As I write these lines news has just broken that famous photographs of the Loch Ness monster are fakes. Some of the most eminent scientists of our age have told us of their genuineness and reliability. Even to those of us who were sceptical, it would have made us think twice as to whether or not to swim in Loch Ness. No doubt, even after this news, there are many who fear the possible dangers associated with this great dragon of the Scottish lochs.

We are all subject to fears, some of which are based on what are known to be myths. To this day I find that so-called haunted houses and graveyards give me cause for concern, even with all I now know about what is true and false. So, too, Job was being tested at the level of his greatest fears. It was a psychological test. Leviathan was associated with evil and what better way to convey to Job that the real contest in which he was engaged was against forces of evil beyond his imagination? In showing to Job this leviathan-creature, God was calling upon Job to think through the complexities of the providence that had formed his life so far, and realize that the universe is much more complicated than we imagine. There is a cosmic battle taking place between the forces of darkness and the forces of good, one in which Jesus Christ has proved altogether victorious. On the cross he 'disarmed the powers and authorities, [making] a public spectacle of them, triumphing over them by the cross' (Col. 2:15). 'The reason the Son of God appeared was to destroy the devil's works' (1 John 3:8). And again, 'Since the children have flesh and blood, [Christ] too shared in their humanity so that by his death he might destroy [or render powerless, disarm] him who holds the power of death — that is, the devil — and free those who all their lives were held in slavery by their fear of death' (Heb. 2:14-15).

Confession — the way of wisdom (42:1-6)

It might be helpful at this point to remind ourselves of the structure of the book of Job and point out one or two things that help us understand more of its contents. The book opened with a description of Job's wisdom, a wisdom which Satan intends to try (1:1 - 2:10). There follows an immediate complaint on Job's part in which he descends from patience to deep despondency as it becomes increasingly clear that his trials are not over (2:11 - 3:26). Then follows the lengthiest section of the book in which the contributions of Job's three friends are taken into consideration, followed by that of Elihu (4:1 - 37:24). Then the Lord himself speaks (38:1 - 41:34). Two final short sections are recorded in the closing chapter, the first of which records Job's confession of his sin (42:1-6), and the second in which Job is restored and his wisdom once more vindicated in the eyes of the people (42:7-17).

The sin which he confesses here in chapter 42 is evidenced in Job's complaint in the opening chapters. In other words, Job's response to his trial has borne the marks of sin from the very beginning. Job's protestations of innocence had a ring of truth about them, as we have seen. He was not guilty of any observable crime. But Job had protested a little too much; if he wasn't as sinful as others around him — and God himself had testified to his blameless and upright character (1:1,8) — it did not follow that Job was *without* sin. The trial had brought to the surface latent (besetting) sins that were otherwise hidden from view — hidden from our view, that is, but not from God's, for he sees and knows all things. '[Jesus] said to them, "You are the ones who justify yourselves in the eyes of men, but God knows your hearts"' (Luke 16:15). Job's trial has, amongst other things, brought to the surface his latent tendency to sin — something for which Job is now repentant. In fact, in both responses (40:4-5; 42:2-6), Job has shown that he is penitent.[9]

John Calvin made the point, in the opening sentence of his *Institutes of the Christian Religion*, that all the wisdom we ever need to know is to be found in knowing God and knowing ourselves. That just about sums up what Job has learned in trial.

Earlier, God had solicited a response from Job (42:4 citing 38:3 and 40:7), a response that at the time was not forthcoming. Job has been plied with questions, to which he has given no answer. They are unanswerable. God has said nothing at all about Job's suffering, nor has he addressed the issue of the justice of it all. Job does not receive a bill of indictment, or a verdict of innocence. More importantly, God does not humiliate Job or condemn him — something we might expect him to do had the counsellors been right all along. By implication, therefore, Job has been vindicated. This will be evident in the final section of the book where Job is restored and his position directly affirmed. Even now, however, Job is ready to respond because he has come to appreciate two things: a truth about God and a truth about himself (40:5-6).

Back in 19:24-27 Job had longed that he might see God in order that he might receive some kind of vindication of his position. That vision has been partly fulfilled in the visions of God that Job has now seen in the storm (though it awaits the resurrection of Job for it to be fully realized). Already, Job has come to appreciate something about God that he had not known before. Through this trial Job has come in some way face to face with God. What Job had known of God in the past was 'second-hand'. Even so, Job had believed in God and lived for him. Now Job has received a personal experience of God. What Job saw physically is not important. Perhaps the storm had conveyed to Job some impression of God's presence. But Job's knowledge of God owed more to the fact that God had spoken to him. He knew God better now than he did before.

In response, then, to God's earlier challenges (38:2-3; 40:7), Job now concedes that he is in no position to question God's plan for the universe since he was in no position to fully understand it. **'Surely I spoke of things I did not understand, things too wonderful for me to know'** (42:3). If Job's suffering had made no sense to him, it had made sense to God, even if God had chosen not to disclose that information to Job. To demand an answer to the problem of suffering was, Job admits, to trespass into an area that was beyond his understanding. Job's response had been one of *rebellion* against the sovereignty of God, a rebellion which he now concedes to have been sheer folly.

Job has learnt something about himself. **'Therefore I despise myself and repent in dust and ashes,'** Job says (42:6). If Job had been guilty of rebellion, that rebellion was itself an indication of his sinful heart.[10] In some of Job's responses, there is evidence that he had sinned against God. In particular, this section of Job corresponds to chapters 2 and 3 of Job, in which Job's initial response is highlighted. From the very start, Job had erred in his response to his trial. This sin which he now confesses was not committed *prior to* his suffering: it was not the cause of his suffering. He sinned in the words and the attitude that he adopted towards God. On more than one occasion Job had set himself up as a rival god! This is something he now bitterly regrets. He repents of his arrogance in impugning God's justice. He repents of the attitude whereby he simply demands an answer, as if such were owed him. He repents of not having known God better.

Such is Job's awareness of his wrongdoing that he despises himself. Strictly speaking, it is not himself that he despises so much as his words.[11]

He repents **'in dust and ashes'** (42:6), probably implying that he sprinkled ashes on his head as an indication of humility (cf. Job 2:12). 'I have been driven many times to my knees by the overwhelming conviction that I had nowhere else to go,' said Abraham Lincoln. But behind even these words of contrition there lies an insistence as to his original integrity and innocence. Job is not conceding one inch to the demands of his friends that his suffering is due to his sin. Not at all! The cause of his suffering is as much a mystery to him at the end as it was in the beginning. The thing that has changed is his attitude to it. Instead of demanding an explanation, Job now quietly resolves to let it be known to God. It is the practical outworking of what Paul meant when he said that 'In all things God works for the good of those who love him, who have been called according to his purpose' (Rom. 8:28).

There had been a moment when Job could not imagine that his life would ever be happy again. His thoughts had turned to springtime, when lifeless twigs burst forth with new life. It was something Job believed he would never see.

> At least there is hope for a tree:
>> If it is cut down, it will sprout again,
>> and its new shoots will not fail.
> Its roots may grow old in the ground
>> and its stump die in the soil,
> yet at the scent of water it will bud
>> and put forth shoots like a plant
>
> (14:7-9).

God's pruning shears had clipped his life so close to the roots he despaired of ever seeing growth again.

> Only a few years will pass
>> before I go on the journey of no return.
> My spirit is broken,
>> my days are cut short,
>> the grave awaits me
>
> (16:22-17:1).

God's actions seemed to have been merciless. There had seemed no point to it. Job's descent into anger and bitterness seems understandable. But spring does arrive in Job's life

again. It is a spring of beauty and fragrance. Hope returns.
Faith is revived. Trust blossoms. Fresh signs of grace appear.

The opening words of Isaiah 61 promise, amongst other
things, that God will bring beauty into broken lives. He will
give beauty in exchange for ashes (Isa. 61:3). He will do this
so that these very people might be called 'oaks of righteousness, a planting of the Lord for the display of his splendour'.
Job is about to be displayed as an oak tree! From the broken,
distorted shape that was Job arises a confession of trust in God
that can only be described as beautiful. Through pain, Job had
grown in his appreciation of God's character. Trials had had
an educational effect on Job. They had taught him things that
otherwise he would never have known. What are they? Four
words spell them out.

1. Power

Job, like other Bible characters, caught a glimpse of God's
lordship or sovereignty. Isaiah caught sight of it during worship in the temple (Isa. 6) and Ezekiel saw God's greatness in
a storm cloud during his exile in Babylon (Ezek. 1). Others
expressed it too: the psalmist proclaiming in psalm after psalm
that 'God is King'; the apostle John during a lonely banishment to a prison island when he was confronted by a vision of
a throne in heaven and someone sitting on it (Rev. 4:2). To
know that God is sovereign in providence is enormously
strengthening. It gave muscle to Job when he needed it most.
To know that nothing happens in this world without God's
consent only terrifies those who are sceptical of God's intent.
To those, like Job, who have come to be assured that God will
not ultimately abandon his own, even though for the present he
may ask them to pass through fiery trials, it is a stabilizing
truth. Everything has been worked out. Everything has a
meaning. Everything is in God's hands, even if we cannot see
the sense of it.

This is a truth that applies not just to matters concerning ourselves but to the cross itself. On one level the crucifixion of Jesus Christ was an act of brutality and hatred on behalf of the Jews in Jerusalem. It was also part of God's plan: 'This man was handed over to you *by God's set purpose and foreknowledge*; and you, with the help of wicked men, put him to death by nailing him to the cross...' (Acts 2:23, emphasis added). Knowing that God is in control, even when things appear out of control, keeps us from falling apart under the strain of events. It now proved a wonderfully supportive truth for Job.

2. Greatness

Another feature is apparent: God is not only sovereign; he is also *great*. The physical demonstration of Job's humility, either sitting on dust and ashes, or else pouring them over his head, is meant to convey how small and insignificant he is in comparison to God. In terms of Isaiah's vision, God is 'high and exalted' (Isa. 6:1). Job had come to realize the pointlessness of trying to pry into God's secrets. He was now content to live with what God had revealed to him. He had wanted to know more, but the desire was futile and brought out the worst in Job. Augustine was once asked, 'What was God doing before he made the world?', to which he replied, 'Making hell for people who ask questions like that!' It was a reply calculated to underline the irreverence in the questioner. The point we are to learn, Calvin comments on an earlier passage in Job, is 'to keep our mouths shut' even in the face of intense provocation.[12] God is not like the genie in Aladdin's lamp — to be controlled at our whim. This is the lesson Jesus taught so profoundly in the garden of Gethsemane when he was heard to cry: 'Not my will, but yours be done!' (Luke 22:42).

Job's confidence is not in himself but in God. It is the confidence of the apostle Paul, who praised God even though he did not know why things were happening the way they were. He often found himself in situations in which he did not know what lay around the next bend. He didn't know *why* things were happening, or *what* lay ahead, or *how* difficult they would be, but he knew *whom* he believed: 'That is why I am suffering as I am. Yet I am not ashamed, because I know whom I have believed, and am convinced that he is able to guard what I have entrusted to him for that day' (2 Tim. 1:12). Knowing Jesus Christ is all we need to know.

3. Purity

Another feature of Job's response is his appreciation of God's purity. In comparison Job belongs on the ash-heap. To underline the point he sprinkles the ashes over himself. There is more to sin than rebellion. It is a condition of being unclean. Job now demonstrates that things have happened during this encounter that have rendered him soiled. Nor is there anything neurotic about Job's response. It is the way of biblical wisdom to acknowledge that God's purity shows up our grubby natures. Job has sinned in what he has said and the Bible has much to say about such sins, for they reflect what is in a person's heart. 'Out of the overflow of [a person's] heart his mouth speaks' (Luke 6:45). Words can convey the worst aspects of our natures. Obscene talk cheapens our lives; irresponsible chatter ruins relationships.

Job has been confronted by the God whose 'eyes are too pure to look on evil' (Hab.1:13).

4. Grace

Yet another element now firmly etched on Job's knowledge of God is his mercy and grace. When Job bows in humble self-diffidence before the Almighty it is not only the sheer power and greatness of God that have over-awed him. That is only a part of it, even though a great part of it. Job has come to glimpse God's love, his mercy, his grace for sinners. True repentance involves not only a 'true sense of sin' but also an 'apprehension of the mercy of God in Christ' (*Shorter Catechism,* Answer 87). The full extent of God's mercy is revealed in Job's restoration (42:7-17). By speaking to Job, and now in coming to Job in the form of a theophanic appearance, God had revealed his gracious concern. He had not, after all, abandoned his servant.

Job's friends had made the point over and again that God's favour was dependent upon Job's righteousness. Had that been true, it would have brought nothing but despair. Job's final plea to God is one in which he acknowledges his unrighteousness. He may not understand why the suffering had come: there was no obvious sin in Job's life that beckoned God's anger. Nevertheless, Job was not as righteous as perhaps he had thought himself to be. The suffering had called forth from Job words of anger, arrogance and abhorrence towards God. Nevertheless Job finds that there is a way to know God's favour. It is the way of confession and contrition.

Job had questioned the goodness of God in his trial and said that God denied him justice. This was a serious allegation. As Philip Hughes has said, 'To question the goodness of God is, in essence, to imply that man is more concerned about goodness than is God ... [it is] to suggest that man is kinder than God ... [it is] to subvert ... the very nature of God... It is to deny God.'[13] It is the allegation Satan made in Eden.

The education of pain

If there is one lesson in the book of Job that is obvious, it is that the sovereignty of God and the constancy of his love towards his own do not mean that we should not expect adversity. As the author of Hebrews points out, pain is an evidence of a father's love: 'And you have forgotten that word of encouragement that addresses you as sons: "My son, do not make light of the Lord's discipline, and do not lose heart when he rebukes you, because the Lord disciplines those he loves, and he punishes everyone he accepts as a son"' (Heb. 12:5-6). Discipline is the mark of a father who cares enough to reprimand. Nor is our adversity evidence of *specific* sin. The issue is not what Job has *done*, so much as what Job *is*. All of us underestimate the remaining corruption of our hearts. We fail to see the extent of pride and prejudice in our hearts, and affliction has a way of bringing these to the surface just as the refiner's fire brings hidden impurities to the surface of molten metals. Like it or not, Job is not as pure as he thinks he is and this trial has made it abundantly clear.

Eating raw flour and yeast is not our idea of a good meal, not even when they have been mixed with salt and water. Only when the ingredients have been baked in the oven does the aroma of fresh bread induce the saliva glands to flow. And only after God has blended the ingredients of life together in the fires of affliction is the 'good' of the apostle's 'All things work together for good' apparent. Trusting God even when everything appears to be falling apart is something Job has come to acknowledge as the way of wisdom.

Job seems, even now, before his full and complete restoration, to be at peace.[14]

Restoration — the triumph of wisdom (42:7-17)

The story of Job is not finished yet. True, his relationship with God has been healed. Though he has progressed little in his understanding of God's ways or the cosmic purposes that lay behind his suffering (nothing has been told Job of Satan's involvement, for example), Job nevertheless has resigned himself to God's sovereignty. He has repented of his reactions which displayed the sinfulness of his heart. He has despised himself, 'melted into nothingness' — a possible translation of the word 'despise'. Job may still be on the ash-heap, but his meeting with God has removed the bitterness. But the story could hardly finish here. Job had wanted vindication, that is, some kind of public demonstration that he did not deserve this punishment. Job had been willing to accept it in any case, deserving or not, but the underlying sense of injustice remained. It now appears as though Job would have been prepared to live with the sense of injustice for the rest of his life in the knowledge that all would be resolved in the righteousness of the world to come. But God has other ideas in mind.

Job's vindication is public and full. God reminds Job's friends *four* times that Job alone is **'my servant'** (42:7-8). Seven things are highlighted by this reference.

1. Job's saving relationship with God

Job has affirmed his faith several times, alluding to God as 'my Redeemer' (19:25). Now it seems that an echo rebounds from heaven, confirming to Job that God holds him in a special relationship too. Job, and not Job's friends, knows God in this way. Whatever the outward circumstances indicate, Job and God are intimately related to each other in a bond that is evidently inseparable. And the personal prepositions only further add to the reality of the redeemed relationship.

2. Job's wisdom

The expression serves to remind us that Job, and not Job's friends, has **'spoken of me what is right'** (Job 42:7). The counsellors had been convinced of their own rightness, but their contribution has been **'folly'** (42:8). The contrast is between wisdom and foolishness. Job has been the wise one throughout; his friends have been fools. They learn to their amazement that God is **'angry'** with them (42:7). Furthermore, Job's counsellors, who have been scornful of Job from the very beginning, now discover at last that the only means of delivery from God's anger is through Job's prayerful intervention on their behalf. What fools they have been!

If there is one piece of advice that the Wisdom School of the Old Testament wished to convey more than any other in regard to the use of words it is this: the fewer the better! 'When words are many, sin is not absent, but he who holds his tongue is wise' (Prov. 10:19). Listening is a sign of wisdom; prattle a sign of folly. As Solomon could well recall, idle chatter brings ruination (cf. Prov. 10:8,10). If only Eliphaz and his friends had heeded the advice!

3. The need for a sacrifice

As God's servant, Job is asked to offer a sacrifice to God on behalf of his friends to gain forgiveness for them. The sacrifice is costly: seven bulls and seven rams (42:8). Only royalty could afford such an offering. The sacrifice is referred to as a **'burnt offering'**, the commonest offering in the Old Testament. As part of the ritual, hands were laid on the animal's head, firstly to identify the victim with the worshipper, but also, and more importantly, to signify a representative and substitutionary significance in the act that followed. Of all the sacrifices offered, the burnt offering demonstrated most clearly God's anger poured out against sin in that the victim of the sacrifice was totally consumed. The offering, which represented and was a substitute for the offerer, quite literally went up in smoke! It underlines several things all at once, including the reality of God's anger and the seriousness with which God treats their offending words. Words spoken out of place are the weapons of murder (Matt. 5:21-26; James 1:19-20; 3:1-6).

4. *The defeat of Satan*

This phrase 'my servant' stands as a warning to Satan of a boast that God had originally made with respect to Job: 'Then the Lord said to Satan, "Have you considered my servant Job?"' (1:8; cf. 2:3). Job's suffering has been due to the struggle between good and evil on a cosmic scale. Satan's aggrandizement is now over. He has been defeated. God has triumphed.

It is a vital element of our understanding of the nature of God's redemptive work, that Jesus Christ came into the world to overthrow Satan's proud boasts. 'The reason the Son of God appeared was to destroy the devil's work' (1 John 3:8). 'Since the children have flesh and blood, he too shared in their humanity so that by his death he might destroy him who holds the power of death — that is, the devil — and free those who all their lives were held in slavery by their fear of death' (Heb 2:14-15; cf. Col 2:14-15). Commenting on Colossians 2:14-15, Calvin writes, 'Paul with good reason, therefore, magnificently proclaims the triumph that Christ obtained for himself on the cross, as if the cross, which was full of shame, had been changed into a triumphal chariot.' Similarly in Job's life, God has displayed his victory over Satan's unfounded allegations. God, and not Satan, has been triumphant.

5. *The coming kingdom of God*

The expression 'my servant' is an anticipation of words that Job, together with all of God's faithful children, will hear in the coming kingdom: 'His master replied, "Well done, good and faithful servant!"' (Matt. 25:21). God's relationship to his children now is confirmation of a relationship that cannot be broken. The pain has not managed to sever the relationship, only confirm it.

6. The believer's relationship to his Master

It is a reminder that our most basic of relationships to God is that of a servant to a Master. R. A. Torrey once wrote, 'If you wish to be a happy Christian, if you wish to be a strong Christian, if you wish to be a Christian who is mighty in prayer, begin at once to work for the Master and never let a day pass without doing some definite work for him.'[15]

7. Job's intercession for his friends

Job's friends complied with God's request to offer a 'burnt offering', an offering supervised by Job acting in a priestly capacity (in much the same way as the patriarchs did), superintending the mechanics of the sacrifice, but also interceding for them in a prayer for forgiveness and reconciliation (42:9).

Several strands of Job's life and testimony at this point allude to a typological reference to Jesus Christ. Job is God's suffering servant, who offers a prayer on behalf of his friends, by which God's wrath is appeased and they in turn are reconciled to God. As God's priestly representative, Job supervises in the atonement of his friends. The analogy of this scene with that portrayed by Isaiah concerning Christ can hardly be avoided.[16] Isaiah also draws attention to a 'Servant' who stands in the place of God's people, interceding on their behalf and offering atonement for their sins (Isa. 42:1-4; 49:16; 50:4-9; 52:13 - 53:12). As Atkinson so rightly puts it: 'Once again, the book of Job is pointing beyond itself to the Mediator between God and human beings, the man Christ

Jesus who gave himself as an offering for sins and now ever lives to make intercession for us.'[17] In the unfolding revelation of God's dealings with his people, Job's friends were given a glimpse of the Saviour to come.

In a lengthy section in his very last sermon on Job, Calvin draws a comparison between Job's suffering and consummate patience and that of Christ: '... in all our adversities we be shaped like to the image of our Lord Jesus Christ, who is the eldest Son in the house of God. And truly if we look but only on the cross of Jesus Christ, it is cursed by God's own mouth: we shall see nothing there but shame and terror: and to be short, it will seem that the very gulf of hell is open to swallow up Jesus Christ. But when we join his resurrection to his death, behold wherewith to comfort us, behold wherewith to assuage all our sorrows, to the end we be not over sorrowful whenever it shall please God to afflict us. And this was purposely fulfilled in our Lord Jesus Christ, to the intent we should know that this was not written for any one person only: but to the intent that all of us should understand, that the Son of God will make us partakers of his life if we die with him, and partakers of his glory, if we bear all the shames and adversities which it shall please God to lay upon our shoulders ... we should always have an eye to the end which God hath promised to his children, according as he hath showed by effect, as well in Job, as also in David, and others, but chiefly in our Lord Jesus Christ, who is the true and chief pattern of all the faithful.'[18]

Public vindication (42:10-17)

Having been vindicated in the sight of his friends, Job is now further vindicated in the sight of his family and fellow-citizens. His fortune is restored in double measure. Nowhere is it suggested that Job receives this bounty *as a reward* for his faithfulness. Christianity is not a means to prosperity, despite what some have advocated and continue to do so. The double blessing extends both to his property (42:12) and his family (42:13-15). Something of a father's pleasure in his daughters is evident in some of the names: **'Jemimah'** meaning 'dove'; **'Keziah'** meaning 'cinnamon'; and **Keren-Happuch'** meaning 'container of antimony', a highly prized black eyeshadow! It is also seen in that, contrary to the norm, his daughters received a share in his wealth, a share normally given only to male issue (Num. 27).

The double favour also extended to his life, living as he did for twice the given age (42:16-17; cf. Ps. 90:10).

As we have already seen, there had been a time when Job failed to imagine God ever being good to him again or any renewal of his own life. Everything that was dear to him had been taken away. There only remained the certainty of death. God's pruning shears had seemed devoid of mercy and, unlike the tree which had been cut down, there was no hope for him.

But spring came again to Job's life. It was a spring of such beauty and fragrance that the bitterness of the past seemed almost forgotten. Hope and life and joy returned in abundance. In God's way of doing things, winter is followed by springtime. For some it may be in just the very terms given to Job. But for others, the blessing will be even greater. It will not be a blessing of life in this world but a fuller and better life in the world to come.

Calvin had a theory about why the patriarchs were allowed to live as long as they did. It was because they lived so far away from the full revelation of Jesus Christ. They needed more time to confirm to them God's goodness: 'The fathers of old time were wont to confirm their faith by the length of the life God gave them ... [but we] must not look to live long to take knowledge of God's fatherly love: for if we lived but three days in this world it were enough to give us a taste of God's goodness and mercy, and to confirm our faith... Therefore as soon as he gives us knowledge of the truth of his gospel, let us always be ready to die, assuring ourselves that he has adopted us for his children, and that he will show himself our Father both in life and in death... Wherefore let us continually pray him, that having guided us continually with his Holy Spirit, he will draw us hence to himself: and that we may come thither fully satisfied, because he has nourished us, maintained us, and showed us that our life and everlasting happiness is prepared for us above.'[19]

In this way the book of Job ends, as it had begun, in a scene of great blessing and favour. Job, having received grace, now demonstrates it in forgiving his friends' duplicity, in bearing no grudges, in giving to those who legally were entitled to nothing. Job **'died, old and full of years'** (42:17).

John Calvin's coat of arms was a hand holding a heart and encircled by a motto: *Cor meum tibi offero Domine prompte et sincere* ('My heart for thy cause I offer thee, Lord, promptly and sincerely'). It could well have been Job's motto also, for he too testified that life is lived best when offered, humbly and submissively, to God through whatever pains he is pleased to send our way.

Notes

Introduction

1. The full quotation is cited by David J. A. Clines in Job 1-20: *Word Biblical Commentary,* (Word, 1989), vol. 17, p.xiv.
2. John Calvin, *Sermons on Job* (Facsimile edition of the 1574 edition: Banner of Truth, 1993).
3. Timothy George, *Theology of the Reformers* (Apollos, 1988), p.234.
4. Cited by Ronald S. Wallace, *Calvin, Geneva and the Reformation* (Baker, 1988), p.82. Calvin had been involved in the distressing execution of Michael Servetus in the previous year.
5. His sufferings were to increase over the years that immediately followed these sermons. In 1558 he reports himself in a letter as reaching 'the acme of suffering'. In 1563 he describes his experience of excruciating torture when his physician cured him of the pain from 'a very painful and large stone' by making him ride a horse, lacerating himself internally in the process.
6. Calvin, *Sermons on Job,* Sermon 1 (on Job 1:1), p.1

Chapter 1

1. The exact location of Uz is uncertain. Two men named Uz appear in the Bible: the son of Aram (founder of the Arameans and grandson of Noah); and a grandson of Seir the Horite who first settled in the area known as Mount Seir which eventually fell into Saul's hands and became part of Edomite territory (Gen. 36:8,20,21,28). Uz was in or near the region known as Edom. Today it is desert, but in Abraham's time it was fertile and well-populated.
2. Boston's sermons on the sovereignty and wisdom of God as displayed in the afflictions of men are published under the title, *The Crook in the Lot* (Silver Trumpet Publications, 1989).

3. John E. Hartley, *The New International Commentary on the Old Testament, Job* (Eerdmans, 1988), p.67.
4. Boston, *The Crook in the Lot*, p.64.
5. Thomas Watson, *The Nature of Repentance* (Banner of Truth, 1992), p.7.
6. John Calvin, *The Institutes of the Christian Religion*, trans. F. L. Battles, ed. John T. McNeill (Westminster Press, 1975), I.I.i.
7. Cited by Richard J. Foster, *Money, Sex and Power* (Hodder & Stoughton, 1985), p.51.
8. The Hebrew has 'sons of God'. They are members of his (Christ's) family and therefore intimately concerned about his welfare. A summary of the nature and rôle of angels may be useful here.

The Bible's words for angels are *Malak* (Hebrew) and *Angelos* (Greek) — both of which mean 'messengers'. Psalm 148 tells us that they were created by God (v. 5). And various passages allude to their great number: Jesus suggested that he could call upon the aid of twelve legions (3-6,000 in a legion; Matt. 26:53 cf. Deut. 33:2); the book of Revelation seems to indicate the number of angels to be immense (Rev. 5:11, which speaks of 'thousands upon thousands, and ten thousand times ten thousand'). There are two groups of angels:

> *Fallen angels.* Jesus speaks of hell as the residence of the devil and 'his angels' (Matt. 25:41). Satan, we are told, did not keep his place (John 8:44; 1 John 3:8-10). Of particular note here is 2 Peter 2:4: 'For if God did not spare the angels who sinned, but cast them down to hell and delivered them into chains of darkness, to be reserved for judgement...'
> *Faithful angels.* These are the 'elect angels' (1 Tim. 5:21). They are God's 'watchers' (Dan. 4:13,17,23) and 'protectors' (Zech. 1:10-11; 6:5-8).

There appears to be a difference in *rank* amongst the angels. There are thrones, powers, rulers and authorities (Col. 1:16), and different ranks within these orders: we know of at least one archangel (1 Thess 4:16) called Michael (Jude 9) who is the protector of the people of God (Dan 10:13,21; 12:1). Also Gabriel, who announces to Zechariah and Mary the births of John and the Lord Jesus, may be an archangel.

There are also different kinds of angels: *cherubim* (Gen. 3:24), who appear to be guardians of the glory-presence of God; *seraphim* (Isa. 6) who appear to be servants of the holiness of God and agents of reconciliation with God.

Angels appear at important points in biblical history: creation (Job 38:4-7); the Fall (cherubim guarded the way back to Eden, Gen. 3:24); in the establishment of the covenant line — Abraham (Gen. 19), Isaac (Gen. 24:7,40, in relation to Rebekah) and Jacob (Gen. 32); at the time of the exodus from Egypt (Exod. 23:20,23); the giving of the law (Acts 7:53; Gal. 3:19; Heb. 2:2); the settlement in Canaan (cf. the stories of Gideon and Samson); in the era of the prophets (1 Kings 19:5,7) and the exile (Daniel 10). Angels appear prominently in the ministry of the apostles (the release of Peter and John, Acts 5:19; 12:7-10). They are especially active *in the life and ministry of Christ.* 1 Peter 1:12 tells us that the angels long to look into what Christ has done for his people in the work of atonement. Thus angels figure in Christ's ministry: at his incarnation — to Zechariah, Mary, Joseph and the shepherds (Luke 1:11-38; 2:8-20); at the temptation (Mark 1:13); in Gethsemane (Luke 22:43); at his arrest, when twelve legions were ready to help him (Matt. 26:53); at the resurrection (Matt. 28:2); after the ascension (Acts 1:10-11) and during the 'session', where 'many angels numbering thousands upon thousands and ten thousand times ten thousand' sing the praises of the exalted Christ sitting upon his throne (Rev. 5:11-12). Finally, at his return in glory he will come with his holy angels (Matt. 25:31; Luke 9:26).

Of importance for our present study is the fact that angels are *agents in the spiritual conflict between good and evil.* This is particularly important for Job. The best illustration is found in Daniel 10. Daniel is ministered to by Michael who had come to help another angelic figure (probably an Old Testament description of Chist — i.e. a Christophany, Dan. 10:5-6) who had been battling with the prince of darkness. Though it took him three weeks to come to Daniel's side, he had been sent whilst Daniel was still praying! The reason for the delay lies in his doing battle with Satan and his forces.

Paul exhorts Christians to be fully equipped for Satan's onslaughts (Eph. 6:10-18). As Christians we are involved in a battle, much of which is unseen. Angels rejoice when someone is snatched from Satan's grasp and added to the number of the elect (Luke 15:7,10). They therefore have a special rôle to play in the final judgement (Matt. 13:39-42).

9. Mark R. Littleton, *When God seems far away — Biblical insight for common depression* (NavPress, 1987), p.26.
10. J. I. Packer, *God's Words* (IVP, 1981), p.88.
11. Francis I. Andersen, *Job: Tyndale Old Testament Commentaries* (IVP, 1976), p.82.

12. Calvin, *Sermons on Job*, Facsimile edition (Banner of Truth, 1994), Sermon Number 4 (on Job 1:6-8), p.15.

13. J. H. Green, *The Argument of the Book of Job Unfolded* (Klock & Klock, 1977), p.74.

14. Packer, *God's Words*, pp.91-2.

15. David L. McKenna, *Job: The Communicator's Commentary* (Word, 1987), p.38.

16. Joseph Caryl, *Exposition of Job*, 6, Sovereign Grace Publishers, 1959. Caryl began his expositions of Job in May 1643 and finished them some twenty-four years later in 1666. The twelve volumes were published by the express order of a committee of the House of Commons.

17. This is F. F. Bruce's phrase in a comment on Hebrews 2:14 (F. F. Bruce, *The Epistle to the Hebrews*, Eerdmans, 1964, p.50, n.80). This is misleading, for the writer to the Hebrews is thinking of the tyranny which Satan exercises over the sinner through death. Men are delivered from the bondage of this fear by Christ's death which conquered 'the last enemy' (1 Cor. 15:26).

18. H. L. Ellison, *From Tragedy to Triumph* (Paternoster Press, 1958), p.25.

19. F. Leahy, *Satan Cast Out* (Banner of Truth, 1975), p.36.

20. Packer, *God's Words*, p.89

21. Frederick K. Price, *Is Healing For All?* (Harrison House, 1976), p.10.

22. *Heidelberg Catechism*, Answer to Question 27, 'What do you mean by the providence of God?'

23. Caryl, *Exposition of Job, 6.*

24. Calvin, *Institutes*, I:xvii.1.

25. J. I. Packer, *A Passion for Holiness* (Crossway, 1992), p.263.

26. *Ibid.*

27. Calvin, *Sermons on Job,* Sermon 1 (on Job 1:1), p.1.

28. *Ibid.*

29. *Sermons From Job:* Introduction by Harold Decker (Baker, 1979), p.xxxvi.

30. Price, *Is Healing For All?* p.10. Cited by Samuel Storms in *Healing & Holiness* (Presbyterian & Reformed,1990), p.49.

31. Cited by G. C. Berkouwer, *A Half-Century of Theology: Movements and Motives,* trans. and ed. Lewis B. Smedes (Eerdmans, 1977), p.196.

32. Dualism is the belief that there are two ultimate sources of power in the universe. C. S. Lewis has written of the inadequacy of this system. If one power really is good and the other really is bad, then we are introducing into the universe a third thing, 'some law or standard or rule of good which one

of the powers conforms to and the other fails to conform to'. Lewis concludes: 'Since the two powers are judged by this standard, then this standard, or the Being who made this standard, is farther back and higher up than either of them, and he will be the real God. In fact, what we meant by calling them good and bad turns out to be that one of them is in a right relation to the real ultimate God and the other in a wrong relation to him' (*Mere Christianity*, MacMillan, 1954, p.34).

Chapter 2
1. Green, *Argument of the Book of Job Unfolded*, p.73.
2. Calvin, *Sermons on Job*, Sermon 7 (on Job 1:20-22), p.28.
3. *Ibid.*, Sermon 5 (on Job 1:13-19), p.26.
4. *Ibid.*, Sermon 7 (on Job 1:20-22), p.30.
5. Packer, *God's Words*, p.213.
6. Green, *Argument of the Book of Job Unfolded*, p.80.
7. Cited by George, *Theology of the Reformation*, p.25.
8. David Watson, *Fear No Evil: One Man Deals With Terminal Illness* (Harold Shaw, 1984), p.119.
9. *Ibid.*, Sermon 159 (on Job 42:9-17), p.749.
10. C. Urqhart, *Receive Your Healing* (Hodder & Stoughton, 1986), p.38.
11. K. Hagin, *Healing Belongs To Us* (Faith Library, 1969), p.16. i.e. sickness is a sin to be atoned for. We should pray: 'Forgive us for our cold, headache...'
12. Job accused God of a number of things:

oppressing him while he smiled on the schemes of the wicked (10:3);
attacking him in anger and shattering him (16:9,12);
wronging him and counting him an enemy (19:6-11);
denying him justice (27:1);
maltreating him ruthlessly (30:19-21).

Alongside these are statements that reveal Job's continued faith in God and in his righteousness and justice (e.g. 12:13; 13:15; 14:15-17; 17:3; 19:25; 23:6,7,10-12).

As Lynne Newell comments, 'In all that he said, Job does not appear to be spurning God but rather Job is seeking God and his answers' ('Job: Repentant or Rebellious?', *Westminster Theological Journal*, vol. XLVI, Number 2, Fall 1984, p.303).
13. Calvin, *Sermons on Job*, Sermon 63 (on Job 16:10-17), p.295.

14. *Ibid.,* Sermon 69 (on Job 19:1-12), p.325.
15. Meredith Kline, *The Wycliffe Bible Commentary,* Editors: Charles F. Pfeiffer and Everett F. Harrison (Moody Press, 1962), p.463.
16. Readers should note that some have been more sympathetic to Job's wife than the interpretation followed here. W. H. Green, for example, points out that following the first trial, Job's wife said nothing at all. There is no evidence that their marriage was an unhappy one. She had borne the loss of her children and wealth with meekness and submissive resignation. She offered no word of protest. Yes, she says to Job, 'Curse God and die', but only because she cannot bear to see him suffer in this way. 'For her, in her grief, a God so pitiless and cruel, it were better to take leave of than to worship' (*The Argument of the Book of Job Unfolded,* p.97).
17. The full account of Andrew Cardy's testimony can be read in the July/ August 1994 edition of the *Evangelical Presbyterian.*
18. Cited by McKenna, *Job,* p.41.
19. Joni Earecksen Tada, *Secret Strength* (Multnomah Press, 1989), p.105.

Chapter 3
1. Teman was a village in Edom, south of the Dead Sea (Jer. 49:7,20; Ezek. 25:13; Amos 1:12; Obad. 8-9); *Eliphaz* is an Edomite name (Gen. 36:11,15). Uncertainty exists over *Bildad's* place of origin, though a link with 'the middle Euphrates' has been suggested. Bildad may have been a descendant of Shuah, the youngest son of Abraham and Keturah (Gen. 25:2). Naaman, the place from where *Zophar* came, is unknown outside Job.
2. This is part of the reason why the events described in the book of Job are thought to predate the patriarchs. 'There is no hint of pantheism, polytheism, idolatry, or evolutionism anywhere in the book, and such a situation is inconceivable anywhere in any nation much after the time of Abraham' (Henry M. Morris, *The Remarkable Record of Job,* Baker, 1988, p.13). Morris places Job at around 2000 B.C.
3. Cf. 1 Sam 18:4; 24:5,11; Ezek. 26:16; Ezra 9:3,5. Tearing one's garments could symbolize many things: that the pain had reached one's heart, or that one was identifying with the destruction of the dead person, or even that a significant part of one's life had now been ended by the person's death.
4. Shaving the head as a mourning ritual was common (Isa. 15:2; 22:12; Jer. 7:29; 16:6; 41:5; 47:5; 48:37; Ezek. 7:18). Later, this practice was forbidden to priests (Lev. 21:5), and any association of shaving with laceration

of the head (mimicking Ancient Near-Eastern mourning rituals) was strictly forbidden (Deut. 14:1). Shaving the head was a common means of showing mourning because loss of one's hair and beard was considered humiliating and self-abnegating (2 Sam. 10:4-5).

5. Caryl, *Exposition of Job*, p.11.

6. Calvin's comment here is helpful: 'Now there is a mixture, so as the frailty of his flesh maketh him to ... fall out with God. Howbeit that his intent is not to fall out with God. Nevertheless words escape him which are evil, and proceed from a faulty mind, and cannot be justified... Job showeth himself not so steadfast as he did afore, but encountered with such a battle, as doth well show him to be a frail man, and not able to bear out his temptations as he would, nor to submit himself to God with so peaceable a mind as were requisite, and as he had been wont to do. And here we have a very profitable warning. For first we see, that men are able to do no more than is given them from above. Therefore let us learn, not to brag of our own strength... We must not be deceived with such imaginations, but must assure ourselves, that as long as God upholdeth us, we may well stand, but if he loosen his hand from us, we shall by and by be cast down. Then is there not anything whereof men can boast, but they must altogether depend from above, and resort always thither when they will be well strengthened' (*Sermons on Job,* Sermon 11, on Job 3:2-10, p.47).

7. Andersen, *Job,* p.101.

8. Morris, *Remarkable Record of Job*, pp.115-22.

9. A fuller description of these beasts will be given later in our study of chapters 40 and 41.

10. Eareckson Tada, *Secret Strength*, p.169.

11. *Ibid.,* p.171.

12. Cited by Cornelius Plantinga, Jr, in *Assurances of the Heart* (Zondervan, 1993), pp.38-9.

13. David J. A. Clines, *Job*, *New Bible Commentary,* 21st Century Edition (IVP, 1994), pp.463-4.

14. Albert Barnes, *The Book of Job* (Routledge, Warne and Routledge, 1860), p.166.

15. Caryl, *Exposition of Job,* p.11.

16. Andersen, *Job,* p.101.

17. Hartley, *The Book of Job*, p.101.

18. Samuel Rutherford, *Letters of Samuel Rutherford* (Banner of Truth, 1984), Letter 35, 'To Lady Kenmure', pp.97-8.

Chapter 4

1. The verse is capable of being translated: 'Can a mortal be righteous [that is, absolutely without sin] in the sight of God?'

2. Andersen, *Job*, p.116.

3. The translation of 4:17 is difficult. The NIV and NKJV both translate it: 'Can a mortal be more righteous than God? Can a man be more pure than his Maker?' Most commentaries argue that this translation is incorrect (see, for example, Elmer B. Smick in *Expository Bible Commentary*, vol. 4, edited by Frank E. Gaebelein, 'Job', Zondervan, 1988, p.895). This would be unfair, since Job has not questioned God in any way so far, only cursed the day he was born — let alone claimed to be purer than God. Hence the translation.

4. Packer, *A Passion for Holiness*, p.255.

5. David Atkinson, *The Message of Job, The Bible Speaks Today* (IVP, 1991), p.40.

6. Jay Adams, *Coping With Counselling Crises* (Baker, 1976), p.9 (emphasis his).

7. Andersen, *Job,* p.123.

Chapter 5

1. Clines, *Job* (NBC), p.465.

2. Job's reaction is one of seething anger. The word he himself uses (though translated 'anguish' in 6:2) is wrath, as foreseen by Eliphaz, in 5:2 (and there translated 'resentment').

3. These mythological creatures were known as *Yam* and *Tannin.* Along with Leviathan and Behemoth, Job is drawing upon as many creatures as he can think of, real or imaginary, to make his point that, in contrast to them, he poses no threat to anyone at all.

4. Clines, *Job* (NBC), p.466.

5. Kline, *WBC,* p.468.

6. George Philip, *Lord, from the Depths I cry: A Study of the Book of Job* (Gray Publications, 1986), p.34.

7. Matthew Henry, *Commentary on the Whole Bible* (Ward, Lock and Tyler), vol. 2, p.19.

Chapter 6

1. McKenna, *Job,* pp.78,84

2. *Ibid.,* p.82.

3. Smick, *Expository Bible Commentary,* vol. 4, p.907

Chapter 7

1. Calvin, *Sermons on Job,* Sermon 33 (on Job 9:1-6), p.151.

'There is nothing better than to submit all things to God's majesty and to acknowledge that if he should let us follow our own sway, there were no way with us but confusion; and that if he governs us according to his will, all will be to our profit and welfare' (*Ibid.,* Sermon 7, on Job 1:20-22, p.32).

And nowhere is this clearer than in the very opening sentence of Calvin's expositions on Job: 'The better to profit ourselves by that which is contained in this present book, first and foremost it behoves us to understand the sum of it. For the story here written, shows us how we be in God's hand, and that it lies in him to determine of our life, and to dispose of the same according to his good pleasure: and that it is our duty to submit ourselves to him with all humbleness and obedience...' (*Ibid.,* Sermon 1, on Job 1:1, p.1).

The principal issue is, therefore, a revelation of God's sovereignty.
2. *Ibid.* p.152.
3. Clines, *Job* (WBC), p.248.
4. Calvin, *Sermons on Job,* Sermon 34 (on Job 9:7-15), p.159.
5. Other references to Rahab are in Ps 89:10; Isa. 51:9.
6. Christian Science teaches that pain is an illusion.

Chapter 8

1. Calvin, *Sermons on Job,* Sermon 62 (on Job 16:1-9), p.290.
2. Used elsewhere of proud boasting (Isa. 16:6; Jer. 48:30).
3. McKenna, *Job,* p.100.
4. Clines, *Job* (WBC), p.261
5. Philip, *Lord, From the Depths I Cry,* p.45
6. Kline, *WBC,* p.471.
7. Watson, *Nature of Repentance,* p.21.
8. Hartley, *Book of Job,* p.201.
9. For those wishing to trace this idea further in Chronicles, see Ray Dillard on *1 & 2 Chronicles,* (Word) pp.70ff.
10. When such ministers are themselves ill, it is strangely enough always a matter of 'God's sovereignty', but when 'ordinary' Christians are ill it is a matter of unconfessed sin!
11. J. I. Packer, *Laid Back Religion* (IVP, 1987), pp.128-9.

Chapter 9

1. Calvin, *Sermons on Job,* Sermon 50 (on Job 13:11-15), pp.235-6.

2. Further notes on Job's insistent plea for a day in court with God can be found in the chapter dealing with Job 31.

3. J. I. Packer, *Concise Theology* (Tyndale, 1993), p.259.

Chapter 10

1. Andersen on Job 15:2

2. Some have thought that Eliphaz's point here is to 'encourage Job by displaying a negative image of what he foresees as Job's own destiny' (Clines, *Job* (WBC), p.354). Clines insists that Eliphaz's aim is always to 'encourage' Job (4:6); thus, this detailed account of the fate of the wicked is 'an account of what the life-history of Job will *not* be' (p.354). Most commentators believe, however, that there is more than an element of duplicity in Eliphaz's words: that there are occasions when Eliphaz is personally hurt and reacts stormily. Clines suggests that when he accuses Job of lacking in wisdom, 'Eliphaz has little, if any, personal animus against Job; he is affronted rather by the threat Job poses to the intellectual values of his day' (p.351). This smacks too much of the theoretical philosopher rather than the real-life situation in which these two were involved. This is not just an intellectual debate about the values of life; there are moments of heat and real anger in the flow of words between Job and his friends — moments when their emotions get the better of them.

3. Clines, *Job* (WBC), p.356.

Chapter 11

1. Clines calls it 'disjointed' (*Job,* NBC, p.471). Kline speaks of Job 'musing aloud' (*WBC,* p.474).

2. The AV has 'My record is on high,' which is inadequate.

3. John Murray, *Redemption Accomplished and Applied* (Banner of Truth, 1961), p.161.

4. Calvin, Commentary on 1 Peter 1:11.

5. Dietrich Bonhoeffer, *The Cost of Discipleship* (SCM, 1959), p.79

6. There is a suggestion that the words of 16:3 are in fact those of his counsellors. Thus Job is citing what they were saying about Job, namely that his (Job's) speeches were lengthy and 'windy'. The fact that Job follows this by saying, 'I also could speak like you' (15:4) would seem to add weight to this view.

7. Andersen, *Job,* p.182.

8. Clines, it should be noted, thinks that Job's witness in heaven is 'the truth about his innocence ... placed on record in the heavenly court' (*Job*, WBC, p.390). But this seems far too reticent an interpretation of Job's belief in a

heavenly being who will vindicate him. We must be careful not to read the revelation of the New Testament into Job's words; but this interpretation by Clines is far too careful! Later we shall see that Job maintained a belief in a Redeemer in heaven, despite having said that God was his enemy in this chapter (16:7-14).

9. Hartley, *Book of Job,* p.264.

Chapter 12

1. Clines, *Job* (NBC), vol.1, p.410.

2. McKenna, *Job,* p.135.

3. Andersen, *Job,* p.188.

4. Clines is more sympathetic to Bildad, seeing Eliphaz in a darker light. 'Bildad never directly says that Job is a sinner, and ... his dearest wish for Job is that he will come to his senses, give up his controversy with God, amend his life and live happily ever after' (*Job,* WBC, p.425). Earlier, Clines writes, 'The few words that Job has spoken, unwise and hostile against heaven though they may have been, cannot outweigh the simple fact that Job is still alive; and that for Bildad is the difference between a rescuable sinner and a doomed one' (*ibid.,* p.409). The problem with this view is that Job, in his response in chapter 19, sees Bildad's contribution as 'tormenting' and 'crushing' (19:1).

5. Clines comments: 'We should read Bildad's second speech in the light of his first and see him as describing the kind of person that Job is *not*' (*Job,* NBC, p.471, emphasis his).

6. The NIV thinks of it as a table lamp ('beside him', v. 6), but it can also be taken as 'above him' and imply a hanging lamp. Ecclesiastes alludes to the same picture when it refers to a silver cord and a golden bowl (Eccles. 12:6).

7. Andersen, *Job,* p.189.

Chapter 13

1. Note the use of the word 'strike' or 'struck' in 1:11,19; 2:5; 4:5; 5:19 etc. And for its use as the cause of illness, see 1 Sam. 5:6; 6:3-5; Ps. 32:4; 39:10.

2. 'The only way to handle Job's words in 19:6 is ... that it was Job's faulty perception or, better, his lack of full perception' (Smick, *Expository Bilbe Commntary,* vol. 4, p.939).

3. The rock of Masada, at the eastern edge of the Judean desert, with its sheer drop of 1300 feet to the western shore of the Dead Sea, provides the site of one of the most dramatic episodes in Jewish history.

Following an attempted Jewish rebellion against the occupying Roman forces, the Roman general Titus conquered Jerusalem (as prophesied in the Gospels). The city was sacked, the temple destroyed and Jewish survivors were largely evicted from the country. One outpost alone remained — Masada. In A.D. 72 Flavius Silva, the Roman governor, resolved to crush the fortress. He marched on Masada with his Tenth Legion, its auxiliary troops and thousands of prisoners of war carrying water and provisions. The Jews, led by Eleazar ben Yair, prepared themselves for defence. Silva's men built a ramp of earth and stones on the western slope of the rock. A battering ram was brought up the ramp, against fierce and ingenious resistance from the fortress. It eventually managed to breach the fortress wall. The 960 occupants — men, women and children — had decided to end their lives at their own hands rather than allow themselves to become slaves.

4. T. Brooks, *Precious Remedies against Satan's Devices*, (Banner of Truth, 1984), p.153.

5. *Ibid.,* p.152.

6. *Ibid.,* p.154, n.47.

7. In a healthy body the flesh clings to the bones, but in a diseased body the bones are weak and the flesh and skin appear to hold the bones together. Job's disease may now be in an advanced condition so that he appears to be the victim of some modern African famine.

8. The expression 'the skin of my teeth' is usually thought to imply that a person barely escapes alive from the situation in view. But it can also be taken to mean that Job has no skin left on him except the skin of his teeth (which he does not have!). In other words, he is alive, but he might as well be dead! (See Clines, *Job,* WBC, p.450).

9. Norman Autton, *Pain: An Exploration* (Darton, Longman & Todd, 1986), p.118.

10. W. Shakespeare, *The Winter's Tale,* Act 1, Scene 1.

11. Kline, *WBC,* p.476.

12. The NIV has omitted a word expressing antithesis which begins verse 25, which ought to read, '*But* I know that...' The idea is that whether or not God will grant him his desire that future generations be given an opportunity to read and judge his case, *even now* in heaven there is one who will defend his cause. (See Smick, *Expository Bible Commentary,* vol. 4, p.941; Clines, *Job,* WBC, p.458).

13. The word is used in this way in Job.7:21; 17:16; 20:11; 21:26; cf. Ps. 22:29; Isa. 26:19. This view would tie in well with what follows: where Job foresees the destruction of his body in the grave: 'and after my skin has been destroyed' — cf. AV 'worms destroy this body' (though the Hebrew has no word for 'worms').

14. For a similar thought, see Ps. 11:7: 'For the Lord is righteous, he loves justice; upright men will see his face.'

15. Green, *Argument of the Book of Job Unfolded*, p.208.

16. Andersen, *Job*, p.195.

17. This view is the one maintained by Clines, pp.457-63, and Hartley, pp.296-7. The interpretation above is one, of course, that fails to see in Job's words a belief in the resurrection of the body. Clines, who consistently maintains the above interpretation, claims that the first half of verse 26 is 'corrupt', yet concedes that 'It clearly indicates that Job expects his case to be resolved only after his death' (p.461). In order to maintain his interpretation he then has to insist that the second half of verse 26, 'yet in my flesh...', is in contrast to what is expressed in the first half of the verse. He *expects* to die; but he *desires* to be vindicated while he is still alive. 'God will intervene before Job's death and restore him to his former status' (Hartley, *Book of Job,* p.296).

18. 'It contradicts everything the book has said previously about the finality of death' (Clines, *Job,* WBC, p.464).

19. Andersen, *Job*, p.194.

20. This is the view of such commentators as Andersen, Kline and Smick. Andersen points us to 14:13, where Job has already anticipated the question of the possibility of life after death. He adds: 'The argument that Job does not expect personal reconstitution as a man, because this idea entered Judaism only towards the very end of the biblical period, can be dismissed in the light of much recent research that shows interest in the after-life as an ancient concern for Israelite faith' (*Job,* p.194).

To Clines' question, how Job can see in verse 26 if he has no body, when following a description of his own death, Job anticipates seeing God, the answer which immediately springs to mind is the conventional Christian one: in a resurrected body. The motive for denying this possibility lies to a large extent in a reluctance to read such an 'advanced' doctrine into what is an early Old Testament source. E. J. Young had no such reluctance, writing of 'this magnificent statement of a bodily resurrection' (*A Survey of Old Testament Introduction,* Eerdmans, 1964, p.327).

21. Calvin, *Institutes,* 2:10:19.

22. The traditional translation 'and not another', implying that Job will see God for himself, is probably mistaken.

23. R. Davis, *My Journey into Alzheimer's Disease* (Tyndale Press, USA, 1993), pp.22-3.

24. Calvin, *Sermons on Job,* Sermon 63 (on Job 16:10-17), p.295.

25. *Ibid.,* Sermon 69 (on Job 19:1-12), p.325.

Chapter 14
1. John Newton's hymn: 'Glorious things of thee are spoken...'

Chapter 15
1. In verse 19, for example, Job says that 'God stores up a man's punishment for his sons.' It is quite obvious that he does not believe this to be so. That is why the NIV has prefaced these words with 'It is said', suggesting that Job is once again quoting something which he had heard his friends say.
2. What Zophar says about wealth is, of course, true. Zophar would have agreed with Spurgeon's comment: 'The snow melts not sooner than the joy of wealth, and the smoke of the chimney is as solid as the comfort of riches!' (Cited by Anthony J. Ruspantini, in *Quoting Spurgeon*, Baker, 1994, p.155).
3. Andersen, *Job,* p.199.
4. The doctrine of delayed retribution can be found in such passages as the second commandment: 'You shall not make for yourself an idol in the form of anything in heaven above or on the earth beneath or in the waters below. You shall not bow down to them or worship them; for I, the Lord your God, am a jealous God, punishing the children for the sin of the fathers to the third and fourth generation of those who hate me' (Exod. 20:4-5; cf. Exod. 34:7; Num. 14:18; Deut. 5:9).

What do these words of threat at the close of the second commandment mean? Do they mean, as some have taken them to, that God inflicts punishment for our sins on future generations yet unborn? The words 'to the third and fourth generation' can be taken to refer to the whole family, normally consisting of three or four generations, and need not be considered as applying to future (unborn) generations. Neither is there any suggestion that the sinning father himself is not to be punished in the statement as we find it. There is every reason to believe that the generations which are punished themselves share in the sin of the father. It is not that they are being punished for something of which they themselves are not guilty; they are the generations of those who 'hate God'. Furthermore, within Israel's judicial system, the law strictly forbade the infliction of a penalty on anyone other than the offender: 'Fathers shall not be put to death for their children, nor children put to death for their fathers; each is to die for his own sin' (Deut. 24:16).

The fact that Job found the doctrine of delayed retribution unacceptable does not therefore contradict anything that we find in such passages as the ones cited above.

Readers should note that we have been arguing for a 'delayed retribution' of sorts in this book as the solution to Job's problem. Retribution — the punishment of the wicked — will be inflicted upon the evildoer, if not in this world, then in the world to come at the judgement at the end of time. The delayed retribution we have been speaking of in these paragraphs has been one whereby the evildoer is not punished at all, but rather his progeny (perhaps, as yet, still unborn) will suffer the consequences of his evil actions.

5. Verse 22 is difficult. It may be that Job is citing something that the friends had been saying to him, though many commentators and translations do not adopt this view. From what follows in 21:22-26, the friends may well have been attempting to stop Job's enquiry into God's ways with man by suggesting that he had no right to ask such questions of God at all.

6. Ruspantini, *Quoting Spurgeon*, p.31.

7. J. Calvin, *Preface to the Psalms of David and others,* p.xxxvii,

8. Theodicy is that area of theology which seeks to justify what God does.

9. J. I. Packer, *Knowing God* (Hodder & Stoughton), pp.42-3.

Chapter 16

1. Opinions differ on the nature of Eliphaz's contribution at this point. 'Eliphaz is a good man. No trace of malice appears in his words,' says Andersen (*Job,* p.202). Eliphaz is guilty of 'a sad betrayal of truth and brotherhood' (Kline, *WBC,* p.478). It is true that Eliphaz, initially at least, appears without malice and as a man who genuinely desires to want to help Job — i.e., help Job come to see his (i.e. Eliphaz's point of view!). Job, for Eliphaz, is *a slight sinner.* He begins with an assumption: the innocent never suffer permanently: 'Who, being innocent, has ever perished? Where were the upright ever destroyed?' (4:7). Job must be innocent: his sin must therefore be trivial and his suffering will be over soon. 'Is not your reverence your confidence? And the integrity of your ways your hope?' (4:6). Job is essentially a righteous man temporarily chastised by God (5:17-18) for some imperfection inevitable in any mortal (4:17). Towards the end, however, Eliphaz's composure seems to have been unsettled and he makes the accusation that Job is a 'great sinner': 'Is not your wickedness great?' (22:5).

2. Eliphaz's opening questions, 'Can a man be of benefit to God? Can even a wise man benefit him?' (22:2) are, in themselves, perfectly proper questions to ask. The problem is that Eliphaz, as Calvin remarks, 'did not well in applying [them] to Job' (*Sermons on Job,* Sermon 83, on Job 22:1-8, p.389).

3. Clines, *Job* (NBC), p.474.

4. The law prohibited keeping a man's cloak overnight as a pledge (Exod. 22:26-27; Deut. 24:12-13). It was a sin condemned by the prophets (cf. Amos 2:8). The law forbade the taking of widow's cloak under any circumstances (Deut. 24:17).

5. One is reminded here of the definition of repentance as given by the *Shorter Catechism*: 'Repentance unto life is a saving grace, whereby a sinner, out of a true sense of his sin, and apprehension of the mercy of God in Christ, doth, with grief and hatred of his sin, turn from it unto God, with full purpose of, and endeavour after, new obedience.' (Answer 87).

6. Smick, *Expository Bible Commentary,* vol. 4, p.954.

Chapter 17

1. Hartley, *Book of Job,* p.338.

2. John Murray, *Collected Writings,* vol. 3 (Banner of Truth, 1982), p.164.

3. H. Bavinck, *Doctrine of God* (Baker), p.18.

4. Calvin, *Sermons on Job,* Sermon 90 (on Job 23:13-17), p.423.

5. John White, *The Masks of Melancholy* (IVP, 1982), p.202.

6. Calvin, *Sermons on Job,* Sermon 90 (on Job 23:13-17), p.421.

7. White, *Masks of Melancholy,* p.202.

8. Murray, *Collected Writings,* p.166.

9. Richard Sibbes, *Works* (Banner of Truth, 1982), vol. 7, p.490.

10. *Ibid.*

11. John Bunyan, *Pilgrim's Progress, Works* (Banner of Truth, 1991), vol. 3, p.242.

12. Lewis, *Mere Christianity,* p.172.

Chapter 18

1. Kline, *WBC,* p.479.

Chapter 19

1. Andersen, *Job,* p.216.

2. 'Sheol' in Job can mean different things depending on the context. It can refer to the realm to which all men go at death. Everyone goes there, from the best of men to the worst. There is no mention of punishment or reward. The idea is that of a place of shadows, 'the land of gloom and deep shadow' (10:21). C. S. Lewis tried to picture it by referring to it as 'the grey town' (*The Great Divorce,* p.18). Several times in the NIV the word has been translated as 'grave' (21:13; 24:19).

3. Jonathan Edwards, in a sermon entitled 'There is such a thing as eternity', cited by John Blanchard, *Whatever Happened to Hell?* (Evangelical Press, 1993), p.160.

4. Andersen comments on this passage (26:5-14): 'This is one of the most fascinating cosmological passages in the entire Bible' (*Job*, p.216). There is more about the creative and providential work of God in Job than in any other book of the Bible.

5. (See notes on Job 3:8; cf. Isa. 27:1). I have commented on the Isaiah passage as follows: 'The fact that Isaiah mentions a mythical creature need not imply that the prophet was under an apprehension of its genuine existence. In the same way that we might refer to some dictator today as a "monster", Isaiah uses a figure of speech that would readily have meaning to his hearers' (*God Delivers*, Evangelical Press, 1991, pp.183-4). Curiously, and with no corroboration, Henry Morris thinks that 'the gliding serpent' in 26:13 is a reference to a star, along with 'the Bear, Orion, and Pleides'! (Job 9:9; 38:31-33). (See H. Morris, *The Remarkable Record of Job*, Baker, 1988, p.44).

6. Morris, *Remarkable Record of Job*, p.87.

7. Calvin, *Sermons on Job*, Sermon 96 (on Job 26:8-14), p.453.

Chapter 20

1. See, for example, Clines, *Job* (NBC), p.476. This used to be the view of critical scholars, i.e., that the text of chapters 27 and 28 has suffered disarrangement. But some evangelical scholars have now also adopted this point of view. The entire position is based on a supposition, however, and it is possible to contend for an interpretation of these chapters (especially chapter 28) based on the view that the original arrangement is correct. This is the view adopted in this book.

2. Calvin, *Sermons on Job*, Sermon 100 (on Job 27:13-19), p.468.

3. Johannes Vos, 'The Ethical Problem of the Imprecatory Psalms,' *Westminster Theological Journal*, cited by James Adams, *War Psalms of the Prince of Peace: Lessons from the Imprecatory Psalms* (Presbyterian and Reformed, 1991), p.50.

4. Calvin, *Sermons on Job*, Sermon 98 (on Job 27:5-8), p.460.

5. Cited by Foster, *Money, Sex and Power*, p.19.

6. A fuller discussion of Job's response to his ordeal is given in the comments on these passages.

Chapter 21

1. It is reminiscent of similar passages in Proverbs (3:19-20; 8:22-31) extolling wisdom and even personifying it.

2. Sinclair Ferguson, *A Heart for God* (Banner of Truth, 1987), p.71.

3. *Westminster Shorter Catechism,* Answer to Question 7.

4. Packer, *Knowing God,* pp.80-81.

5. See Calvin's comment cited from his *Institutes* in note 6.

6. This image has been radically altered by the Fall, but not obliterated. Calvin's doctrine of the effects of the Fall on the image of God in man is inconsistent. Sometimes he speaks of it as 'blotted out ... by Adam's sin' (*Sermons on Job,* Sermon 56, on Job 14:16-22, p.261). In another place, Calvin speaks of it as being 'defaced' (*Ibid.,* Sermon 120, on Job 32:4-10, p.564). Elsewhere, however, he comments: 'For in as much as we be reasonable creatures, we have the image of God printed in our natures' (*Ibid.,* Sermon 17, on Job 4:20-5:2, p.76). In the *Institutes,* however, Calvin is clearer: in the diversity of human nature we see 'some remaining traces of the image of God, which distinguish the entire human race from the other creatures' (II.2.17). Calvin also denied the fact that the image of God in man consisted in his dominion over the world (*Institutes* I.15.4). A full analysis of Calvin's view on the image of God in man can be found in A. A. Hoekema, *Created in God's Image* (Eerdmans, 1986), pp.42-9.

7. It is man as a *creation* of God that Job is thinking about in this chapter (cf. 28:25-27).

8. The fact that man ought to respect the planet, taking care to maintain its integrity — a 'green' mandate, if you like — needs also to be borne in mind, but is not, of course, the focus of Job's thought here.

9. William Shakespeare, *Hamlet,* Act II, Scene 2.

10. Job mentions 'Abaddon', the deepest hell, and 'Sheol', the land of shadows, or the realm of the dead in general.

11. Calvin, *Sermons on Job,* Sermon 103 (on Job 28:10-28), p.486.

12. Jean Brown was the mother of John Brown of Wamphray (1610-1679), the Scottish expositor and pastor who was later to suffer ejection and banishment for his principles in the Great Ejection of 1660.

13. *Letters of Samuel Rutherford,* Letter 131, p.258. The letter was written in Aberdeen and dated March 1637.

Chapter 22

1. Cities provided protection to workers who passed through the city gates to work on the land outside the city walls. When Boaz wanted to settle with Ruth's kinsman-redeemer the question of who should marry her, he met

him 'at the town gate' of Bethlehem (Ruth 4:1). Gathering some elders together (Ruth 4:2), he settled the issue there and then, calling upon some witnesses (4:9-11) to ratify the matter. Similarly, Lot is found 'sitting in the gateway of the city' of Sodom (Gen.19:1), implying that he too was a member of Sodom's ruling council. It was at the gate of Hebron that Abraham purchased the cave of Machpelah (where he buried his wife, Sarah) from Ephron, son of Zohar (Gen. 23:10). Absalom conspired against his father's throne at the gate of the city (2 Sam. 15:2), and at his death David sat at the gate to receive the sympathy of the people (2 Sam. 19:8). Rebellious sons were to be brought to the city gate for justice (Deut. 21:19). Prophets delivered many of their oracles at the gate (Jer. 17:19-20; 36:10).

2. The NIV translation of verse 18 obliterates the fanciful notion that the word 'sand', in 'My days as numerous as the grains of sand,' can refer to the 'Phoenix', the legendary bird of longevity with supposed powers to renew itself. Job has already expressed his belief in a resurrection and could hardly be suggesting reincarnation here!

3. Calvin, *Sermons on Job,* Sermon 107 (on Job 29:18-25), p.502.

4. *Ibid.*

5. Cited by Charles R. Swindoll in *Growing Strong in the Seasons of Life* (Hodder & Stoughton, 1988), p.22.

6. T. Watson, *The Ten Commandments* (Banner of Truth), p.169.

7. 'Many Christians feel uncomfortable with affirming their value before God. Fearing self-aggrandizement, they run from every positive feeling about themselves. As pious as this outlook may seem, it leads us into serious danger. Failing to acknowledge the honour God has given us leads directly to the path of rebellion. Satan is looking for ways to rob us of our sense of dignity... When he succeeds, he has us right where he wants us' (Richard L. Pratt, Jr, *Designed For Dignity* , Presbyterian and Reformed, 1993, p.44).

8. Hartley, *Book of Job,* p.402.

9. Autton, *Pain, An Exploration*, p.10.

10. Examples of these are found in the Psalms: e.g. 'Break the teeth in their mouths, O God; tear out, O Lord, the fangs of the lions!' (Ps. 58:6); 'Let death take my enemies by surprise; let them go down alive to the grave, for evil finds lodging among them' (Ps. 55:15). Other psalms where imprecations can be found include Psalms 35, 59, 69, 109 and 137.

11. Kline, *WBC,* p.482. Commentators are not wholly agreed here. Some, in an attempt to maintain the unity of the argument that Job is basically an innocent sufferer, the cause of which lies elsewhere than as a direct result

of his sin, have wanted to maintain Job's total innocence. Hartley, for example, comments that 'Job ... has sworn this oath of innocence out of a desperate need to hear from God, not out of arrogance' (*Book of Job*, p.408).

12. The word is Abaddon — the place of dead.
13. Calvin, *Sermons on Job*, Sermon 113 (on Job 31:9-15), p.533.
14. John Stott, *Issues Facing Christians Today* (IVP, 1984), p.145.
15. Cited by Richard Foster, *Money, Sex and Power*, pp.43-4.
16. 1:1, 'blameless' (NIV, NKJV) is a better translation than 'perfect' (AV).
17. Calvin, *Sermons on Job*, Sermon 117 (on Job 31:33-34), p.550.
18. J. C. Ryle, *Practical Religion*, (James Clarke & Co. Ltd, 1970), p.37.
19. *Ibid.,* p.41.
20. Calvin, *Sermons on Job*, Sermon 115 (on Job 31: 24-28), p.540.
21. e.g., Kline, *WBC*, p.482.
22. Calvin, *Sermons on Job*, Sermon 118 (on Job 31: 35-40), p.555.

Chapter 23
1. D. A. Carson, *How Long, O Lord? Reflections on Suffering and Evil* (IVP, 1990), p.168. Certainly, commentators vary widely in their assessment of Elihu's contribution. Whilst older commentators are largely sympathetic to it (Calvin, for example, is almost totally uncritical of Elihu's contribution), most modern commentators are doubtful of Elihu's overall understanding of the situation. There are exceptions: Kline and Carson interpret Elihu favourably. Kline sees Elihu as the 'forerunner' to the Lord himself (*WBC*, p.486). See note 3 of next chapter.
2. Atkinson, p.122.
3. Kline, *WBC*, p.482
4. Calvin, *Sermons on Job*, Sermon 119 (on Job 32:1-3), p.558.
5. Philip, *Lord, From the Depths I Cry*, pp.103-4.
6. D. M. Lloyd-Jones commenting on Ephesians 4:26-27 in *Darkness and Light* (Banner of Truth, 1982), pp.233-4.
7. It is possible to read this chapter so as to make Elihu appear pompous in the extreme. However, if allowance is made for a pause after verse 14, thus allowing his friends time to respond, the speech appears far less assertive. As Hartley observes, 'His attitude depends on the tone in which he offered these words... It is possible to view him as a reflective young man who had been irritated by some of the ideas and arguments floating about and who, believing that he had some insight to offer, with rising emotions awaited an occasion to speak. Taking advantage of that opportunity, he expressed

his deference to his elders in a sincere though wordy apology' (*Book of Job,* p.435).

8. *Sir.* 25:4-6 Cited by Hartley, *Book of Job,* p.433, n.22.

9. Calvin, *Sermons on Job,* Sermon 120 (on Job 32:4-10), p.564.

10. *Ibid.,* Sermon 120 (on Job 32:4-10), p.565.

11. Andersen thinks that Elihu is making a more general point here, that anyone who speaks wisdom does so by the ministry of the Spirit. Elihu is 'not claiming special revelation' (p.246). Others, for example, Atkinson think that Elihu 'claims to have inspiration from God' (Atkinson, p.123).

12. Hartley, *Book of Job,* p.438.

13. As we have already hinted, this gentler spirit soon evaporates in the heat of Elihu's wordy response.

14. Calvin, *Sermons on Job,* Sermon 122 (on Job 33:1-7), p.577.

15. Kline, *WBC,* p.483.

16. Littleton, *When God Seems Far Away,* p.98.

17. C. S. Lewis, *The Problem of Pain,* p.93.

18. Even the most evangelical of commentators are reluctant to identify this angel as Jesus Christ. Andersen refuses to concede that Elihu is speaking of a unique 'angel', commenting: 'The designation *one in a thousand* rules out the idea that there is one angel who is a specialist in such negotiations. It implies rather that God has a large team available for such a task' (*Job,* p.250). Others are prepared to see by the expression 'one in a thousand' a reference to a unique being. Kline speaks of the 'pre-eminence of his angel-mediator' (*WBC,* p.484). Hartley, though, points to the way the phrase is used in 9:3 and thinks it is better understood as having a very restrictive force: 'Therefore, this mediating angel is a very special heavenly creature. He may be identified with "the angel of Yahweh". In some OT passages (e.g., Gen. 16:7-13; Num. 22:35) there is a close identification between Yahweh and his angel' (*Job,* p.447).

19. Kline, *WBC,* p.484.

Chapter 24

1. For verse 5a see 13:18; 23:10; 27:6; for 5b see 27:2; for verse 6 see 9:20; 16:13; for verse 9 see 9:22; 10:3; 21:7-16; 24:1-12.

2. Carson, *How Long, O Lord?,* p.170.

3. Cf. Hartley: 'Elihu prepares Job for a proper response ... but unfortunately at the high price of blatantly condemning him and making him apprehensive about being smitten with worse suffering' (*Book of Job,* p.462).

4. Carson, *How Long, O Lord?,* p.168.

5. Cited by Douglas F. Kelly, *If God Already Knows, Why Pray?* (Wolgemuth & Hyatt, 1989), pp.184-5.

6. Calvin does not accept this interpretation of Elihu's words here. He thinks that Elihu is merely saying that in so far as he is speaking God's Word as it has been revealed to him he will not add to it or subtract from it (*Sermons on Job*, Sermon139, on Job 36:1-7, p.654). Calvin is generally more sympathetic to Elihu than most commentators. Kline thinks that Elihu is not speaking about himself at all, but God. Job need not be afraid because God is with him (*WBC*, p.485).

7. The Hebrew is not quite the same as the English translation makes it out to appear.

8. Andersen, *Job*, p.258.

9. 'Let us not murmur any longer,' says Calvin, 'when we see that God sends troubles into the world, neither let us be offended at it as if He had his eyes closed' (*Sermons on Job*, Sermon 140, on Job 36:6-14, p.657).

10. *Ibid.,* p.658.

11. Cited by R. Berkouwer, *The Providence of God*, p.234. The first article of the *Belgic Confession* states: 'We believe with all our hearts and confess with our mouth, that there is one single and simple spiritual essence whom we call God: eternal, incomprehensible, invisible, immutable, infinite, almighty, absolutely wise, just, good, and an overflowing fountain of all good.'

12. E. W. Hengstenberg, 'Interpreting the Book of Job,' *Classical Evangelical Essays in Old Testament Interpretation*, edited by Walter C. Kaiser, Jr (Baker, 1972), pp.94-5.

13. Calvin, *Sermons on Job,* Sermon 69 (on Job 19:1-12), p.325.

14. Paul Helm, *The Providence of God* (IVP, 1993), p.223.

15. Philip, *Lord ,From the Depths I Cry,* p.105.

16. Some commentators (Kline, for example) are more sympathetic to Elihu at this point. It is possible to interpret some of what Elihu says to mean that if you react properly to God's discipline you can expect the affliction to go away as soon as the specific purpose for it is realized. Furthermore, those who 'react to God's afflictive warnings with sullen rage ... may expect only to be early fatalities of their debaucheries' (*WBC*, p.485). This is true, but Elihu does appear to be saying more than that.

17, Andersen, *Job*, p.259.

18. Kline, *WBC,* p.486.

Chapter 25

1. Andersen, *Job*, p.268.

2. *Ibid.*, p.269.

3. 'The imagery of the divine challenge is drawn from the popular ancient sport of belt-wrestling. The figure is especially suitable in this context because belt-wrestling was used as an ordeal in court, and it is by ordeal that Job's case is being settled' (Kline, *WBC*, pp.486-7. cf. Meredith Kline, 'Trial by Ordeal,' in *Through Christ's Word: A Festschrift for Dr.Philip E. Hughes*, edited by W. R. Godfrey and Jesse L. Boyd III (Presbyterian and Reformed,1985), p.88.

4. Clines, *Job* (WBC), p.xlvi.

5. Calvin, *Sermons on Job*, Sermon 123 (on Job 33:8-14), p.582.

6. *Ibid.*, Sermon 150 (on Job 38:18-32), p.706.

7. *Ibid.*, Sermon 8 (on Job 2:1), p.33.

8. *Ibid.*, Sermon 50 (on Job 13:11-15), p.232.

9. Calvin, *Institutes*, p.52 (1:5:1).

10. *Ibid.*, 1:5:1, n.3. Preaching just two years later, on Friday, 10 April 1556, on the book of Deuteronomy, Calvin comments on Deuteronomy 29:29, 'The secret things belong to the Lord our God': 'For it is the greatest wisdom that can be in men, not to be inquisitive of further things than God has revealed to them, and simply to content themselves with that which they are able to conceive' (*Sermons on Deuteronomy*, Facsimile edition of 1583 (Banner of Truth, 1987), Sermon 168 (on Deuteronomy 29:22-29), p.1044).

11. Packer, *A Passion for Holiness*, p.120.

12. Earecksen Tada, *Secret Strength*, p.216.

13. J. Stafford Wright, 'The Interpretation of Ecclesiastes,' *Evangelical Quarterly* XVIII, 1946, pp.11-34.

14. The NIV/NKJV translation of 40:2 is debatable. Instead of 'Will the one who contends with the Almighty *correct* him?' (cf. AV, 'instruct him'), it is possible to translate it instead: 'Will the contender with the Almighty *yield*?' This allows for a continuation of the image of a wrestling contest between God and Job (See, Smick, *Expository Bible Commentary*, vol. 4, p.1044, note on 40:2).

15. The Hebrew word for 'unworthy' (40:4) means 'to be light, to be small, to be of little account' (Brown, Driver, Briggs, p.886).

Chapter 26

1. Kline, *WBC*, p.487.

2. *Ibid.*, p.488.

3. This is the interpretation accepted by Kline (*WBC*, p.488; 'Trial by Ordeal', p.90).

4. This is the view taken by Henry M. Morris in *The Remarkable Record of Job*, pp.115-19. He identifies behemoth as a dinosaur, and leviathan as a fire-breathing dragon!
5. This is an interesting idea since it would then be hinting to Job that his struggle is with a power from another world altogether, i.e. that it is satanic.
6. Calvin, *Sermons on Job,* Sermon 156 (on Job 40:20 - 41:25), p.732.
7. McKenna, *Job,* pp.304-5.
8. Calvin, *Sermons on Job,* Sermon 50 (on Job 13:11-15), p.232.
9. Not everyone accepts that Job is repentant. Some have argued that when Job lays his hand on his mouth (40:4) and 'repents' (42:6), he is in effect expressing the pointlessness of talking to a God who seems so unconcerned about his suffering. Some have even suggested that at the end, Job is 'totally disenchanted with God', finally rejecting God altogether! There are several problems with this view:

In the first place, as we have seen earlier, Job has accused God of many things, including the following:

> oppressing him while smiling on the schemes of the wicked (10:3);
> attacking him in anger and shattering him (16:9,12);
> wronging him and counting him an enemy (19:6-11);
> denying him justice (27:1);
> maltreating him ruthlessly (30:19-21).

But alongside all these are statements in which Job expresses his continued faith in God and his dealings with him (e.g. 12:13; 13:15; 14:15-17; 17:3; 19:25; 23:6-7,10-12). Job does not appear to be turning away from God.

Secondly, in the two speeches from God, three accusations are made against Job:

1. Job uses words without knowledge when he accuses God of wrongdoing (38:2). In doing so, Job had placed himself on an equal footing with God.
2. Job is wrong in asserting that God does not care; God shows his care and concern for both the world of animals and the inanimate creation. Job can do nothing but submit (40:2).
3. Job had challenged God's justice (40:7). He had condemned God in order to justify himself. He had thus set himself up as a rival god. When challenged to take on the administration of justice for the

world, Job is unable to do so. Once again Job's weakness and inadequacy are exposed.

10. The point needs to be stressed that Job's rebellion was itself sinful, and is the reason why he feels it necessary to repent. Some commentators are unhappy with the idea of repentance in Job, insisting that Job was not guilty of any sin. In answer to the question: 'What does Job repent of?', David Clines replies, 'It cannot be some sin, because we have known from the beginning that Job is no sinner; he can repent only of the extreme language he has used or of his ignorance' (*Job*, NBC, p.484). Clines is correct to underline the point that Job has not been suffering directly as a consequence of his sin, but on the other hand his suffering has drawn forth from him the latent sinful disposition of his heart. Andersen's comment, that Job 'confesses no sins here'(*Job*, p.292) seems also to be far too general a statement. David Atkinson's comment, 'Job has not been overawed by God and humiliated' *(Job,* p.157) seems also to miss the point. Job most certainly has been 'overawed' by a sight of God's greatness and lordship. If there is one thing he has learnt it is the fact that he must not question God's ways and that in having done so, he has sinned.

11. The verb 'to despise' is also capable of being rendered, 'to reject'. In the Hebrew it lacks an object, but it is clear from verse 3 what it is that Job rejects: his rash words. They have been spoken in error. In this Job has sinned and now he 'repents'.

12. Calvin, *Sermons on Job,* Sermon 33 (on Job 9:1-6), p.151.

13. Philip E. Hughes, *Hope for a Despairing World* (Baker, 1977), p.14.

14. It may be worth pointing out that the word 'repent' in verse 6 has a breadth of meaning that includes not only 'to be sorry, repent' but also 'to console oneself' or 'be comforted'. 'So it may be that Job was saying that ... he now understood that God was his friend, not his enemy. So he was consoled and comforted though still suffering' (Smick, *Expository Bible Commentary,* vol. 4, p.1056). Most commentators allow for this interpretation of the Hebrew *nhm,* though Lynne Newell insists that 'Whenever *nhm* is caused by sin or by turning or straying from the Lord, it means "repent".' ('Job: Repentant or Rebellious?', in *Westminster Theological Journal,* vol. XLVI, Fall 1984, p.314).

15. R. A. Torrey, *How to Succeed*, p.83, cited by J. M. Boice, *Foundations of the Christian Faith* (IVP, 1986), p.500.

16. I say 'can hardly be avoided', but in fact most commentators do avoid it as though to draw any typological connection between Job and Christ were completely sacrosanct!

17. Atkinson, *Job*, p.158. A similar comment is found in Kline's commentary: 'The turning point in Job's external circumstances, his deliverance from the hands of Satan, was marked by the act in which he spiritually exemplified the righteousness of God's kingdom (cf. Matt. 6:33) and ceremonially typified the Messianic sacrifice which establishes that righteousness' (*WBC*, p.489).

18. Calvin, *Sermons on Job*, Sermon 159 (on Job 42:9-17), p.749.

19. *Ibid.*, pp.750-51.

Select bibliography

Andersen, Francis, I. *Job. Tyndale Old Testament Commentaries.* IVP, 1976.

A good modern commentary, ideal for those who can afford only one small reference work. Andersen's grasp of the theological argument is consistently strong.

Calvin, John. *Sermons on Job* (Facsimile edition of the 1574 edition). Banner of Truth, 1993.

This recent facsimile reproduction of Calvin's sermons on Job is a timely and important landmark in our understanding of Job, and of God himself. No amount of praise can possibly exaggerate the help gained from reading these sermons. Calvin grasps clearly the key that unlocks the meaning of the book: Job has a good case, but argues it badly; his friends have a bad case but argue it very well. In particular, Calvin sees the book of Job as essentially one in which God's *incomprehensibility* is set forth — not that God is unknowable, but that he is infinitely beyond our grasp.

Readers should note that the facsimile is in Elizabethan English. However, perseverance will pay rich rewards, and those who seek for treasure will soon grow patient with the pain of the search.

Readers may be interested to know that I have written two articles on Calvin's understanding of Job in issues 336 and 337 of the *Banner of Truth* magazine (March and April 1994).

Carson, D. A. *How Long, O Lord? Reflections on Suffering and Evil.* Inter Varsity Press, 1990.

The book contains references to the problem of evil in general, but also contains an excellent summary of the book of Job.

Caryl, Joseph. *Exposition of Job.* Sovereign Grace Publishers, 1959. Caryl began his expositions of Job in May 1643 and finished them some twenty-four years later in 1666. The Sovereign Grace edition contains only a selection of the original twelve-volume set, published as it was by the express order of a committee of the House of Commons. Caryl was an Independent who preached frequently before the 'Long Parliament'. A member of the Westminster Assembly in 1643, he became the minister of St Magnus, London Bridge, where he continued until his ejection in 1662. He served as chaplain both to Charles I and to Cromwell. In the year of the Great Ejection (1662), Caryl gathered an independent congregation at Leadenhall Street, London. This congregation numbered 130 at the time of his death and subsequently united with John Owen's congregation.

Caryl's exposition of Job consists of over 500 lectures/sermons and is over 8,000 pages in length. Readers who can avail themselves of a set will profit from its exact and practical style.

Clines, David J. A. *Job 1-20. Word Biblical Commentary, vol. 17.* Waco, Texas: Word Books, 1989.

The style and layout of the Word Commentary series in general is appallingly off-putting. The series is meant for 'serious' students (i.e. students and ministers). Clines is far and away the best modern commentator on Job. The work is exhaustive, though it is a pity that he is so reticent to see Christological implications in some of Job's outpourings. For a discerning reader, it is to be highly recommended.

Clines, David J. A. *'Job', New Bible Commentary, 21st Century edition.* Inter Varsity Press, 1994.

An abridged version of the more difficult Word series. It is masterful and no one attempting to study Job should miss Clines' contributions. For the 'average' reader, this may well be a good place to start.

Ellison, H. L. *From Tragedy to Triumph: The message of the Book of Job* . The Paternoster Press, 1958.

Concise, and somewhat dull.

Green, J. H. *The Argument of the Book of Job Unfolded.* Klock & Klock, 1977.
This is perhaps the best summary of the book of Job available from a Reformed point of view.

Hartley, John E. *Job. The New International Commentary on the Old Testament.* Eerdmans, 1988.
Useful as a quick reference aid on the meaning of certain words in Job.

Hengstenberg, E. W. 'Interpreting the Book of Job,' in *Classical Evangelical essays in Old Testament Interpretation*, edited by Walter Kaiser. Baker, 1972.
Another useful summary of Job's message, though manifesting less insight than Green.

Kline, Meredith. *'Job', The Wycliffe Bible Commentary.* Moody Press, 1962.
The best commentary on Job available! This is a concise, consistently Reformed approach to Job with masterful insight into the theological argument.

Kline, Meredith. 'Trial by Ordeal' in *Through Christ's Word: A Festschrift for Dr Philip E. Hughes, edited by W. R. Godfrey and Jesse L. Boyd III.* Presbyterian and Reformed, 1985.
An essential overall analysis of what Job is about.

Littleton, Mark. *When God seems Far Away — Biblical Insight for Common Depression.* NavPress, 1987.
An informal approach to Job that makes for helpful reading, particularly to those who want something 'simple'.

McKenna, David L. *Job: The Communicator's Commentary.* Waco, Texas: Word Books, 1987.
Sermonic and somewhat north-American in his style, McKenna occasionally sparks with useful insights into Job's application for today. Useful as an aid to sermon preparation.

Philip, George M. *Lord, from the Depths I Cry: A study in the Book of Job.* Glasgow: Nicholas Gray Publishing, 1986.

A brief (more often than not, too brief) exposition of Job, with many helpful comments of a pastoral nature.

Smick, Elmer, B. *'Job', Expository Bible Commentary,* vol. 4. Zondervan, 1988.

An up-to-date commentary on Job, but adds little to what is currently available elsewhere.